# An Introduction to Modern Political Theory

**By the same author**

Hayek's Social and Economic Philosophy

# An Introduction to Modern Political Theory

Norman P. Barry

*First published 1981 by*
THE MACMILLAN PRESS LTD
*London and Basingstoke*
*Associated companies in Delhi Dublin*
*Hong Kong Johannesburg Lagos Melbourne*
*New York Singapore and Tokyo*

Printed in Hong Kong

---

**British Library Cataloguing in Publication Data**

---

Barry, Norman P
  An introduction to modern political theory.
  1. Political science
  I. Title
  320′.01        JA66

  ISBN 0–333–26890–3
  ISBN 0–333–26891–1 Pbk

---

# Contents

Part Two   Values

# Preface

This is a general book on contemporary social and political theory, designed to introduce the reader to the kinds of problems political theorists deal with and to some of the answers that have been suggested. There is very little in it that is original, but originality has not been the aim of this author. Rather, the intention has been to present in a coherent form a growing body of knowledge which will provide the student with a foundation on which he (or she) can build by consulting more advanced work in the specialist journals.

Yet even this modest task requires some explanation, if not justification. The writing of a general book on social and political theory is likely to be provocative for at least two reasons. First, the necessarily controversial nature of the subject matter, and secondly, the absence of any real agreement as to what the subject is about. The first of these reasons seems to me trivial. The fact that the concepts analysed in this book are used in political argument does not mean that rational, dispassionate analysis is impossible; in fact, it makes the need for such an approach all the more pressing. The second reason is a little more disturbing since it is true that political theory, when it is not just history of political thought, is taught in a great variety of ways in university social science departments. Nevertheless, I feel that the kinds of topic dealt with in this book are of primary importance to political theory courses, even though the manner of treating them will no doubt meet with some opposition.

The major justification for a book of this kind, however, is the enormous increase in the volume of literature in social and political theory that has occurred in the last ten years. Twenty years ago there was little more than a handful of books and articles of importance in a subject area which was thought to be infertile. This of course reflected the dominance of linguistic philosophy and 'empirical' political science, and both those

disciplines eschewed the substantive normative questions that had traditionally been the concern of social and political theory. Even the use of
the term 'theory' was questioned here since scientifically-minded political scientists (and philosophers) objected to an activity being described as
'theoretical' which did not concern itself with producing theories with
empirical content, and which could not generate hypotheses that could be
'tested'. However, the kind of linguistic analysis that once threatened to
banish political philosophy from the field no longer monopolises the
subject and the empirically-biased political scientists have not been
conspicuously successful in the production of general theories. Curiously
enough, the most successful theories in politics that have appeared in
recent decades have not come from the behaviouralists at all (and indeed
they can hardly be called empirical) but from economics. They also have
a clear relevance to some traditional concerns of political theory. This is
especially true of the theory of democracy (see Chapter 10).

The major contributions to contemporary political theory have come
from a number of academic disciplines – mainly law, economics and
philosophy – so that the subject retains the heterogeneous nature it has
always had. It is this that makes the subject difficult for the beginner and a
major purpose of this book is to present some important ideas that have
emerged from these disciplines in such a way as to make them relevant to
the interests of students of politics.

Nevertheless, the book is not designed for beginners in political studies
but for second-year (or third-year) students of politics who have already
done some history of political thought and introductory courses in other
social science subjects. It is for this reason that I have not filled the text
with long quotations from the 'classics' of political philosophy but
concentrated mainly on getting some contemporary and less familiar
ideas across. Although the standard topics in the subject are covered I
have included consideration of some less familiar ones and left out one or
two traditional subjects. Of the latter my omission of a sustained discussion of political obligation requires some explanation. Although some
important books and articles have appeared on this subject in recent
years, and it has assumed importance in the practical world of politics, I
say little about it because it illustrates much less well than other concepts
the special contributions law, philosophy and economics make to political studies. The question of whether one ought to obey the state seems to
give rise to the type of answer which does not involve the kind of rational
argument that is characteristic of the questions of justice, income distribution, the public interest and procedural democracy. In other words, the

problem of political obligation involves a subjective, personal judgement in a way that other topics do not.

Despite the above comments the book could be tackled by readers with very little knowledge of the subject area. No knowledge is assumed and while the complete beginner might find the first two chapters a little difficult, the going does get easier. It is important, however, that the early chapters be properly absorbed since ideas discussed there reappear throughout the book. Concepts explained in the early stages are employed in a variety of contexts.

The book is divided into two parts, one dealing with the conceptual problems involved in the explanation of social institutions such as rules, law and state, and the other with the traditional political and moral 'values', such as justice, equality, freedom and rights. This is for convenience only and the author would be the first person to insist that there is an obvious connection between, say, statements about law and statements about justice and equality. Any arbitrariness in the presentation of the topics, then, is the consequence of an attempt to find a way of introducing certain concepts to students in a manageable form.

There is one feature of the book which is perhaps more difficult to explain away. It is written from a certain point of view, which may be called 'liberal-rationalist'. This is an intellectual rather than a political standpoint and I do not use the word liberal in a party political sense at all (nor in the sense in which it is typically used in American politics). The liberal-rationalist approach assumes that many political problems, at least in reasonably stable societies, are capable of being resolved by analytical methods, so that political discord is not always the clash of irreconcilable values but often represents a failure to explore properly the relationship between principles and policies. Also, the liberal-rationalist claims some objectivity in that his main concern is to examine the consequences of holding certain principles rather than to advance party or class interests. Thus liberals find themselves 'left-wing' on some issues and 'right-wing' on others. Of course, they would reject such labels anyway as being severe hindrances to a proper analytical approach to political problems.

While I follow this approach throughout the book I have contrasted it with other approaches so that someone unsympathetic to liberal-rationalism would, I hope, still find the book of some use. In fact, the analytical problems in Part One do not involve the kind of value questions that appear in Part Two and should be of interest to all students of social philosophy, whatever their political views. A further justification for my approach is that many of the innovations in the subject in recent years have come from writers in this tradition.

As on a former occasion I am grateful to Barbara Abbott for her excellent work in typing the bulk of the manuscript; and to Margaret Sheridan for help in the final stages.

I am indebted to my colleague John Cunliffe. He read the entire typescript with great care and made many extremely helpful suggestions, most of which have been incorporated into the text. To my wife, Lynda, my gratitude extends way beyond the normal compliments one sees in a Preface. Despite having important academic work of her own she still found the time to read and correct the entire manuscript: not only did she point out grammatical errors and infelicities of style but she also made contributions to the argument at important stages. The errors that remain therefore are entirely of my own making and, regrettably, I must take the final responsibility for them.

*Birmingham, England*                                    NORMAN P. BARRY
*October 1979*

# Glossary

Below are listed the meanings of various terms used in the text. It should be made clear at the outset that no attempt is being made to give *exact* definitions of these terms. All that is being conveyed is an indication of the way the words are used in the political analysis and argument that appear in the book.

**Anthropomorphism.** The attribution of human properties to inanimate things. 'Society' is frequently treated anthropomorphically, as if it were capable of being praised or blamed in the way that humans are. A crude example is the phrase, 'it is all society's fault'.

**Behaviouralism.** A form of social explanation in which observed behaviour is stressed rather than the simple description of institutions. In behavioural political science formal political institutions are dissolved into 'systems' and 'processes'. It is distinct from *behaviourism* in that it is not a psychological theory about individual behaviour but involves sociological statements about collectivities.

**Behaviourism.** The psychological doctrine which holds that the only basis for the study of human behaviour is *observable* behaviour. Therefore all statements about mental phenomena, such as motives and intentions, are irrelevant because they depend upon introspective knowledge which cannot be verified by experimental methods.

**Collectivism.** The methodological doctrine that collective terms such as 'state', 'society' and 'class' stand for entities which have a real existence over and above that of individuals. Collectivists argue that theories of social phenomena cast solely in terms of individual action fail to capture the significance of general social factors in the determination of events.

**Deduction.** The form of reasoning in which the conclusion of an argument *necessarily* follows from the premises. The validity of a deductive argument is established if it is impossible to assert the premises and deny the conclusion without self-contradiction. In the social sciences only economic theory makes extensive use of the deductive method.

**Deontology.** The ethical theory that holds that certain moral duties are absolutely binding irrespective of consequences. Normally it emphasises the importance of strict compliance with moral rules to the exclusion of a consideration of the benefits which adherence to the rules may or may not bring about.

**Empiricism.** The epistemological doctrine that the only foundation for knowledge, apart from mathematical and logical relationships, is experience. It is contrasted with the various forms of *idealism*, all of which maintain that the mind is already equipped with the conceptual apparatus which enables us to understand the external world. In the social sciences empiricists reject *a priori* reasoning about man and society in favour of factual and statistical enquiries. See also *behaviourism* and *positivism*.

**Epistemology.** The theory of knowledge. The major questions of epistemology concern the nature of our knowledge of the external world, the source of knowledge and how claims to knowledge can be substantiated.

**Essentialism.** The doctrine that the key to the understanding of social phenomena is in discerning the true nature or essence of things which lies behind their external manifestations. In Plato's theory of the state, for example, it is argued that existing state organisations are pale reflections of an underlying essence or *form* of the state, knowledge of which is acquired by philosophical reflection.

**Historical materialism.** The Marxist doctrine that the factors determining historical development are ultimately economic. Changes in the 'superstructure' of society, that is the state organisation, law, religion and morality, are a function of changes in the substructure, that is, the economic mode of production. The doctrine is especially directed at those theories that emphasise the independent influence of ideas in the determination of historical change.

**Historicism.** The doctrine, mainly but by no means exclusively associated with Marxism, that the study of history reveals trends or patterns, of a law-like kind, from which it is possible to predict *future* economic and social structures and historical events. Historicist 'laws' are of a quasi-empirical kind in that they are based on supposedly observable regularities and are therefore different from the laws of conventional economics which are ahistorical deductions from axioms of human nature.

**Individualism.** The methodological doctrine, associated with Popper and Hayek, that collective words such as 'state' or 'society' do not stand for real entities. The behaviour of collectivities can only be understood in terms of individual motivations and volitions.

**Induction.** The method of reasoning by which general statements are derived from the observation of particular facts. Therefore inductive arguments are always *probabilistic*, in contrast to deductive arguments. Induction was thought to characterise physical science in that laws were established by the constant confirmation of observed regularities. However, since no amount of observations can establish a general law (the most firmly established regularity may be refuted in the future) the generalities established by science seemed to rest on insecure, if not irrational, foundations. Popper argued that while theories cannot logically be established by repeated confirmations they may be falsified.

**Metaphysical.** A metaphysical proposition is one which cannot be tested by normal empirical methods. Logical Positivists thought that a statement which was neither tautological nor empirically verifiable was metaphysical and hence meaningless. Metaphysical statements are not normally thought to be meaningless by contemporary philosophers.

**Nominalism.** The theory of language that accounts for the meaning of general words *not* in terms of some universal entity they represent, but as *labels* to attach to things that share a common property. Nominalism is the approach to language adopted by the empirical sciences.

**Normative.** Normative statements set standards and prescribe forms of conduct; they do not describe facts or events. While they are frequently used in connection with moral standards this is not always the case. Legal rules are technically normative in that they make certain forms of conduct obligatory, but they are not necessarily moral. Normative statements typically involve the use of words such as 'ought', 'should' and 'must'.

**Persuasive definition.** A definition of a word which is designed not to explicate its meaning but to excite favourable (or unfavourable) attitudes. Persuasive definitions of the state, for example, do not convey information about existing states but aim at provoking approval (or disapproval) of it.

**Positivism.** This has two meanings. First, a positivist believes in the clear separation of fact and value and argues that theoretical and descriptive accounts of man and society can be made which do not involve evaluative judgements. For example, in jurisprudence a positive lawyer maintains that law must be separated from morals so that a rule is assessed for legal validity not by reference to its content but to certain objective, non-moral criteria. In the second and more extreme sense, it is the theory that only phenomena which are in principle capable of being observed are of any significance for social science. See also *empiricism* and *behaviourism*.

**Sociology of knowledge.** The attempt to explain the social origins of beliefs that people hold. It is also used by some Marxists to mean that all knowledge in the social sciences is *relative* to the particular class position of those who profess it, so that there cannot be *objective* knowledge of society.

**Teleology.** A doctrine that explains the nature of things in terms of the ends or purposes they are designed to bring about. In teleological ethics, moral action is evaluated in accordance with how far it brings about a desirable state of affairs. For example, utilitarian ethics evaluates actions in terms of their contribution to the general happiness.

# Part One
# Rules, Laws and Society

# 1

# Philosophy, Social Science and Political Theory

## 1. The current state of political theory

The major difficulty in introducing the subject of political theory to the student is the fact that there is so little agreement amongst the practitioners as to what the subject is about. While it is true of all social science subjects that they involve from the outset highly contentious methodological questions, so much so that the concepts in social science have been called 'essentially contested' concepts, the difficulty seems to be greater in political theory than in, say, economic theory. While economists do engage in fierce methodological disputes, especially in macroeconomics, there is nevertheless some considerable agreement about the contents of an introductory course book for students. At least such books are not likely to handle radically different material and, within the limits of the Western world, are not likely to differ all that much from place to place.

But in political theory this state of affairs is only true of courses in the history of political thought. Books in this area consist largely of *descriptions* of particular political philosophies plus an historical account of the subject's development, usually from Plato to the present day. While such enquiries involve considerable sophistication the subject as a whole is not thought to be a genuinely theoretical discipline in the sense that other social science subjects might claim to be. It has been claimed that in the great works of political philosophy there are generalisations of a sociological kind, usually to do with the requisite conditions for political stability, but these works are more often studied for a rather different reason. This is that they contain *normative* statements about the desirability of certain types of laws and institutions and such recommendations are supported by rational argument. The 'classics' of political philosophy are thought to contain truths and insights which are of permanent relevance for anyone who thinks philosophically about man and society.

It has been suggested that there has been something of a decline in normative political theorising of the traditional kind (although, as we shall see, this supposed decline has been halted in the past decade) and this, if true, has undoubtedly stemmed from what has been called the 'revolution' in philosophy (Ayer, 1956). This revolution is, in England, associated with the Logical Positivists and dates from the 1930s. Logical Positivism is characterised by a distaste for metaphysical thinking and a belief in the importance of empirical science. Its effect on political science was to distract attention away from the traditional questions of political philosophy and encourage attempts to establish a science of politics. While there are considerable differences in the individual schools of philosophy that have emerged from this revolution, there is agreement on what they regard as the limits of the philosophical method. Philosophy is said to be a *second-order* discipline. This means that it is not a form of enquiry which yields new truths about the world in the manner of scientific and empirical subjects, but is limited to secondary questions to do with the methods of enquiry and, primarily, with questions of language – that is, the clarification of concepts used in the *first-order*, empirical subjects. Thus, in this view, political philosophy is parasitic upon a properly developed political science. An empirical science of politics would provide additional information about the world but political philosophy should properly be interested in only the methodology of political science and the clarification of the more familiar concepts used in political argument such as sovereignty, the state, rights and obligations, freedom, equality, justice and so on.

The first casualty in this assault on the traditional subject matter of politics was the ethical side of political theorising found in the history of political thought. The traditional concern with values, present in writers as diverse as Plato, Hobbes, Rousseau and the utilitarians, was attacked by the Positivists with their criterion of *meaning*. On this criterion, any proposition which is not *analytically* true, as the tautologies of mathematics and formal logic can be shown to be analytically true by inspection, or empirically verifiable, as the propositions of science are thought to be verifiable, is not meaningful. It is not that propositions which fall outside the criterion of meaning suggested by the Positivists are false; it is that, strictly speaking, they are 'non-sense'. Obviously a proposition in political philosophy such as 'an individual ought to obey the state because it embodies the General Will' would be regarded as non-sense since it is clearly not true by inspection and does not contain anything that can be remotely called 'empirical'. This led to the idea that all ethical statements are necessarily non-cognitive – that is, they do not convey any information about the world, but at the most convey only the feelings or emotions of the speaker.

The moral philosopher does undoubtedly have a professional interest in the *language* of ethics and moral philosophy did progress considerably from the crude formulations of the Logical Positivists in enquiring into the form that ethical judgements take (the relevance of these enquiries to politics will be considered in Part Two of this book) but for a very long time it was thought that the philosopher as philosopher could have very little to say on the first-order questions of the justification of moral values and the resolution of moral conflicts. In the field of normative politics it was held, for example by Weldon (1953; 1956), that principles could have no relevance to the discussion of questions of public policy. This extreme view will be shown in Part Two to be highly misleading – first, because it exaggerates the disagreement that exists between people on matters of principle, and secondly, because it completely ignores the subtle connections between principles and policies which make arguments about, say, the appropriate level of income tax turn upon the values of equality and liberty, and not merely on questions of experience or evidence as to the effect of one tax policy or another. Arguments here are not limited to clarifying the concepts of equality and liberty either.

There has developed out of the revolution in philosophy a broadly philosophical subject called political theory which is analytical in style and concerned with methodology, clarification of concepts and, in contrast with the Logical Positivists, the logic of political appraisal. Much of this book is written in this vein. Indeed, it is important to note that it is a much richer vein than existed twenty years ago, when, in the heyday of Logical Positivism, there was very little interesting work in analytical theory of this type. Only in the philosophy of law did the new techniques appear to yield interesting results for the student of society. However, in the last decade the writings of, amongst others, Rawls (1972) and Nozick (1974) (and the uses made of some fairly elementary principles of political economy) have breathed new life into the discipline so that to say that political philosophy is dead, as was once said so confidently, would be a gross exaggeration.

To establish that there is a body of knowledge called analytical political theory is not enough, however, to settle preliminary disputes about the nature of the subject. For one thing the use of the word theory in this context might well be questioned. It has always been the aim of some students of political behaviour to establish an empirical science of politics, so that ultimately political theory could break away from the intellectual tutelage of philosophy and become an independent discipline, just as the natural sciences had done in their historical development. In this view the word *theory* belongs properly to that part of political studies concerned with the making of generalisations about political phenomena, the construction of hypotheses from which predictions can be derived – predictions which can, in principle, be falsified by normal empirical methods. While the particular methodological position adopted by the Logical Positivists is inadequate (the Positivists' commitment to verification as the hallmark of science is very different from the falsification principle[1]), the aim of an empirical science of politics is common to all those who reject the traditional political theorist's concern with values and historical description.

It would be no exaggeration to say that the empiricists' programme has not been met. The problem is not simply that the political and social sciences have failed to produce any generalisations equivalent to those found in the natural sciences; it is that political and social scientists are divided as to whether their subjects can ever achieve this sort of precision. That is to say, the regularities that undoubtedly do exist in social life may be better explained by some other methods than the typical causal analysis and techniques of observation found in the purely physical sciences. The importance of the view of social life as *rule-governed* behaviour, and thus not strictly analysable in causal terms, will be considered in more detail later, but at this stage it can be said that because of the difficulties that explanation in the social sciences involves there will always be room for a political philosophy that disputes at least some parts of the empiricists' programme. Even in the most advanced social science discipline, economics, where some of the material is quantifiable and observable, there is no agreement amongst economists that the subject should only concern itself with that which is measurable and predictable.[2] Some would go further and maintain that the well established laws of economics do not help at all in the prediction of particular, discrete events but are limited to the explanation of fairly general phenomena, such as the price system itself.

From these observations it should be apparent that political theory is an eclectic subject which draws upon a variety of disciplines. There is no body of knowledge or method of analysis which can be classified as belonging exclusively to political theory. In the rest of this book we shall be concerned with exploring the connection between politics and a number of differing subject areas and methodological approaches. Hence the book is as much about philosophy, law, ethics and political economy as it is about politics.

## 2. Language

We have already noted that political theorists are now more self-conscious about language than they were in the past. But this emphasis on language can be overstated. Whatever may have been the case in formal philosophy, it was never true that the problems of political philosophy were exhausted by the clarification of concepts. This is partly because political philosophers are concerned with the rather large questions of justice, rights, liberty, the limitations on the state and so on, and clarification is only a preliminary to this; and partly because political philosophers are also concerned with genuinely explanatory theories in the social sciences. Indeed Sir Karl Popper, one of the most distinguished philosophers of science of this century, who has also written extensively on the philosophy of politics, has explicitly stated important objections to linguistic philosophy (Popper, 1976, pp. 22–4). In his view it is *theories*, and whether they are true or false, that are important, and not the *meanings* of words. Nevertheless, we shall maintain that the clarification of concepts is important in political analysis. It may not be the case that political arguments turn upon the use of words but it is certainly true that conceptual clarification is required even to know what the arguments are about. A moment's reflection on the use of the concept of liberty in contemporary arguments about national and other liberation movements should confirm this.

Furthermore, Popper has himself contributed much to the kind of analysis that is important in political philosophy. His attack on *essentialism* (Popper, 1962, ɪ, pp. 31–4), the idea that words like 'state' and 'society' stand for necessary entities which it is the duty of the philosopher to discern by the use of a special intellectual intuition, which he has detected in political philosophy from Plato through to Marx, would be applauded by all contemporary linguistic philosophers. It is largely through his work that political theorists are less likely to ask such essentialist questions as 'what is the state?' or 'what is law?' It is true, though, that Popper goes no further on language than this but adopts the methodological nominalist's position that words are no more than labels of convenience used to describe phenomena in the generation of explanatory social theories. However, we shall have to say a little more about conceptual questions in this book. For one thing, in social philosophy we cannot find explanatory theories as powerful as those found in the natural sciences. It is the case that in the economic theory of democracy we shall adopt a broadly nominalist approach precisely because that is a social theory that has some predictive power. Questions of meaning here are less important than the truth or falsehood of the theory. But this is certainly not true of the theory of law, where questions of, for example, *validity* in a legal system or the problem of whether a legal order can be satisfactorily understood in terms of primary and secondary rules, do involve crucial conceptual issues.

One reason for the lack of interest that some have felt for the purely linguistic approach to political philosophy, apart from the fact that it seems to drain the subject of its traditional significance, is that all too often the meaning of a familiar concept in politics is confused with a definition, or with a misleading idea of definition. Some political theorists seem to believe that the clarification of concepts involves the search for exact definitions.

This important point requires a little more explanation. In an exact definition a word is given a verbal equivalent such that the word in question can be replaced by its verbal equivalent and used in a sentence without a loss in meaning. A clear example of this type of definition is that of the word 'bachelor'. This can always be replaced in a proposition by the phrase 'unmarried man' with exactly the same information being conveyed.

Unfortunately, what distinguishes the words typically used in discourse about politics, society and law is that they do not have definitions of the type described. The words not only seem to have no secure and stable definition but also the perennial disputes about meaning have led to the construction of political and legal theories which seriously distort the phenomena they are designed to explain. Exact definition may be appropriate in scientific classification where there is no dispute about the nature of the phenomena but this is not true of social phenomena (Hart, 1961, pp. 14 – 15).

The main reason for the disappointing results of the search for meaning in terms of exact definition was that single words such as law, state, sovereignty and rights were taken out of the context of their typical usage and defined as separate entities. For example, it was assumed that the word 'state' represented some factual counterpart in the empirical world which could be clearly and indisputably identified. The task of analysis was therefore to reduce complicated verbal expressions to observable phenomena. In the command theory of law it was traditionally maintained that *all* law was a species of command, emanating from a determinate sovereign backed up by sanctions. But this simple and appealing theory seriously distorts the very *different* types of phenomena which expressions containing the word law typically describe.

The problem is especially difficult in social and political philosophy where so many of the words in use appear to refer to collective entities; words such as 'state', 'society' and 'class'. It is impossible to identify such collective entities in the empirical world yet it is clear that these words do have meanings and are an indispensable part of any discourse in politics. The problem is further compounded in political philosophy by the fact that many of the key words are often given 'persuasive definitions' by social theorists, that is, definitions designed to provoke some favourable or unfavourable response from the reader. In the history of political thought the concept of the state has been a frequent victim of this approach, being defined in highly favourable and highly derogatory terms.

While the Logical Positivists in the 1930s made short work of some of the pretensions of existing political philosophies, their extremely narrow and rigid theory of meaning was of little help in the analysis of the language of politics. If a proposition was to be meaningful in their view, as we have seen, it had to be either a tautological statement of mathematics or formal logic, or an empirical statement capable, in principle, of verification. All other statements were metaphysical, that is, non-sense. If statements used typically in *ordinary language* failed to meet the verifiability criterion, then they, too, were meaningless. While the Positivists had no trouble in cutting through the fictitious entities constructed by metaphysical philosophers they failed in the attempt to reduce statements about political and social phenomena into elements which could be readily observed in the empirical world.

It was a reaction to the Logical Positivists' highly restrictive account of meaning that inspired the school of 'ordinary language' philosophy. Meaningfulness is, in this school's view, to be found in the *use* to which words are put. Since common usage itself is the bench-mark of meaningfulness there is a much greater variety of meaningful statements than appears to be the case with Logical Positivism, and the meaning of words such as law and state can be found only by locating the particular uses such words have in the languages of law and politics. The emphasis moved away from the problem of defining single words to the complex task of elucidating the use that key concepts have in typical sentences. Linguistic analysis consists, then, in unravelling some of the puzzling features that characterise common utterances about politics, taking ordinary language as the canon of meaningfulness. Of course, on substantive questions such as 'what are the grounds of political obligation?' or 'what are the criteria for a just distribution of income?' the school of ordinary language was at one with Logical Positivism in protesting the irrelevance of philosophy for their resolution. However, it would at least concede that such questions are meaningful. Nevertheless, both schools distinguished between first- and second-order activities and agreed that philosophy as a second-order discipline could no more generate new truths about the world of politics (this belonged to the discipline of political science) than it could resolve moral issues.

While there is a concern for language throughout this book it must be stressed that this is not the only interest of the political philosopher and it may be a diminishing one. Of particular importance is the general discussion of *collective* words in this chapter, and that of the difference between 'emotive' and 'descriptive' meaning in Chapter 5; but these and other examples of linguistic analysis are presented as aids in the investigation of the traditional problems of political theory rather than ends in themselves. It is also important to note that the most impressive single work in analytical social philosophy, H. L. A. Hart's *The Concept of Law*, can hardly be described as merely clarificatory. In this book the reader is presented with much more than an account of the verbal perplexities associated with the word 'law'. Furthermore, in those subjects which have a claim to be scientific, such as economics and the application of economic theory to political and social phenomena, questions of meaning are of much less relevance than the truth and predictive power of the particular theories. These considerations, plus the recent appearance of important books on the substantive questions of justice, freedom, rights and democracy, suggest that the dominance of the purely linguistic approach to political philosophy is at an end.

A convenient way of approaching the substantive methodological and evaluative problems of modern political theory is through particular frameworks of analysis. In the next two sections liberal-rationalism and Marxism are distinguished as types of political theory. The point is not to give an historical or systematic account of either doctrine but to use both as devices for illustrating some of the abiding problems of man and society. The general philosophy of liberal-rationalism is considered in more detail, not only because it is the approach that underlies the bulk of analysis and argument in this book but also because it illuminates a variety of problems in the methodology of social science and in political philosophy generally.

## 3. Liberal-rationalism[3]

Liberal-rationalism embraces both *explanation* and *evaluation*. Its explanatory concern is with accounting for that order of events which we call a *social order*; and this includes economic, legal and political phenomena. Its interest in evaluation consists largely in showing how, from the standpoint of a particularly individualistic conception of liberty, existing social orders may be improved. However, liberal-rationalists maintain that these two aspects are separate and that their contributions to the scientific study of society are valuable in their own right irrespective of the individualistic bias of their evaluative and prescriptive writings. In fact, most of Part One of this book is concerned only with the liberal contribution to the scientific understanding of society.

Liberal-rationalists maintain that the regularities that undoubtedly characterise social life can be given a scientific explanation but their views on this differ considerably from others who also believe in a scientific study of society. Those who have traditionally believed in the 'unity of scientific method' based their argument on the claim that there were regularities in the social world analogous to regularities in the physical world which could in principle be given a mechanical explanation not dissimilar to those found in physics. It was thought there were *regularities* enabling *generalisations* to be made about social behaviour which could be established by direct observation and predictions of future events derived from them. In this *inductive* approach 'scientific laws' of society are *trends*, statements of probability or statistical generalisations which are based on observations of past events.

The more extreme exponents of this methodology asserted that it was the business of social science to discover certain 'historical' laws which explained social development and from which could be derived prophecies about the future course of history. The most famous example of this is Marxism which, in at least one interpretation, supposes that social structures change in accordance with changes in the mode of production so that the modern industrial world can be understood in terms of a series of 'revolutions'; bourgeois capitalism emerged necessarily from feudalism and capitalism would itself give way to socialism and ultimately Communism. The future course of events could be predicted then from the knowledge of historical laws which operated independently of man's will.

In fact, there are less spectacular examples than this of the purely observational, inductive approach and it would be true to say that most adherents of this methodology are not historicists. Nevertheless, there are many social scientists who believe that a genuine social science must be based on empirical observation. A good example, from earlier in this century, was the attempt to explain and predict booms and slumps in the capitalist market economy by extrapolating trends from extensive inductive enquiries into the course of the business cycle. In political sociology, those who try to explain power in society by repeated observations of decision-making in the political system reveal a not dissimilar commitment to empiricism. In psychology the 'behaviourist' school rejects any explanation of human action in terms of 'intentions' and 'motives' precisely because such mental phenomena cannot be observed and measured by the external enquirer. Whatever their other differences these approaches may be called 'positivist' in that they restrict knowledge in the social sciences to that which is empirically verifiable. This identification of science with the inductive bias was one of the unfortunate legacies of Logical Positivism.

Now liberal-rationalists claim that they are 'positivists' in the sense that they eliminate values from formal social science, but emphatically reject the central tenet of the positivist epistemology which claims that the purpose of social science is to discover empirical regularities in the social world (Popper, 1957, pp. 105–19). Laws are not derived inductively but are *deduced* from a small number of simple propositions about human nature. The regularities revealed by social science are not historical or social 'facts' but are properties of human nature which can be assumed to be unchanging. It is, of course, liberal economics which has produced the most systematic body of *theoretical* knowledge, and indeed a large part of economic theory consists of highly sophisticated deductions from simple axioms based on human nature. The 'laws of economics' are said to be universal because they are derived from an unchanging concept of man (Hayek, 1952, pp. 74–6).

Microeconomics provides the best examples of theoretical knowledge of this kind. If we want to understand the role of the price mechanism in the allocation of resources in a market economy we have to use certain generalisations about consumer behaviour. Decreasing marginal utility theory tells us that an individual will consume units of a good until the marginal utility of the last unit of the good equals its cost, in terms of other goods he must forego in order to consume it. From this fundamental generalisation we can predict that if the price of a good falls the demand will go up. But it is to be noted that while generalisations of this type are not historical trends based on observation, nevertheless they do generate theories with some predictive power. For example, the laws of consumer behaviour can be used to predict that if the government subsidises the rent of council housing the demand for such housing will go up and queues will develop. This, of course, is not an historical prophecy that at some date in the future queues will develop for council housing, but a theoretical inference of what must happen if certain generalisations are true and if certain initial conditions are met. While 'laws' are not derived from 'facts' most liberal-rationalists maintain that the general predictions derived from their theories can be tested empirically. In fact, it is possible to deduce the complex structure or order of the market from a small number of axioms (Hayek, 1952, ch. 4; and 1967, ch. 1).

This methodology has been applied to political systems as well as economic systems and in the final chapter of this book we shall consider the economic theory of democracy, but at this point the other features of liberal-rationalism must be sketched. A crucial point is that explanation is couched entirely in individualistic terms. Social processes are understandable only as reconstructions out of individual actions. Collective words such as 'class', 'state' or 'society' do not describe observable entities, and statements containing them only have meaning when translated into statements about individual action. For example, we do not say a 'class' or 'society' saves or invests because saving and investment are functions of individuals; and actions of the 'state' must be interpreted as the actions of individual officials operating under certain rules.

Furthermore, and this point has been consistently opposed by collectivist social theorists, the individual under consideration is *abstracted* from historical and social circumstances. The concept of man that underlies the methodological individualist's model is based on a very few simple propositions about human nature: that men act so as to put themselves in a preferred position (though this does not have to be understood in purely monetary terms), that they prefer present to future satisfactions, and that they can have only a limited knowledge of the world around them. This information about men is available to us all by what is called the method of 'introspection'. It is assumed that men are pretty much the same throughout the world and that by examining ourselves we can have knowledge of how others will act; for example, introspective knowledge of human nature will tell us that the imposition of very high marginal rates of taxation is likely to have some effect on people's work patterns and/or lead to widespread attempts at tax evasion.

A further feature of this approach is that many of the theoretical applications have a somewhat limited empirical content. The predictions are of a *negative* kind (Hayek, 1967, p. 32), telling us what cannot happen rather than saying what precisely will happen. Some economists say that we cannot reduce unemployment below the 'natural' rate by monetary methods and at the same time maintain a stable price level, or that we cannot have an efficient allocation of resources and at the same time pursue egalitarian tax policies. One possible negative conclusion that is being drawn from the economic theory of democracy is that we cannot have unrestrained party competition for votes and at the same time generate the public interest. However, as we shall show later, these negative conclusions can be of great importance to the normative political theorist concerned with evaluating public policies.

A further aspect of the liberal-rationalist explanation of social regularities is the emphasis on *rules* and *rule-following*. This is not the simple point that a market exchange system requires a *particular* set of rules, that is, those which respect personal and property rights, but the more complex argument that *all* social order, continuity and permanence is explicable only in terms of the notion of rule-following. The major rival scientific explanation of social order comes from the positivist theory of society. In the positivist explanation of social order, rules and rule-following are not considered to be adequate for a scientific explanation of that order because their effects are not susceptible to empirical observation.

The most extreme and uncompromising positivist's explanation of social order is that produced by the behaviourist psychologists, notably B. F. Skinner (1972). Behaviourists argue that social regularities can be explained in terms of the 'learning process'. This means that just as regularised animal behaviour can be explained in terms of the conditioned reflex so can human behaviour, although human beings are more complicated mechanisms. The fact that societies display an order and coherence through time is explained by the behaviourists in terms of the environment 'reinforcing' individual action. In the past an individual action was followed by a certain result and this result positively reinforces the pattern of behaviour so making its re-occurrence all the more likely. In effect each individual is conditioned to behave in a socially acceptable manner by a system of rewards and punishments rather in the way that an animal is trained. Since all human behaviour is causally determined it is argued that the way to 'improve' society is to perfect the causal mechanisms (the reinforcement agencies) and point them in some desired direction. The behaviourist's social programme, in so far as he has one, is to subject human behaviour to greater control through the learning process.

Extreme behaviourism was never regarded by social scientists as a satisfactory explanation of regularised *social* action, although less radical theories of socialisation which involve similar assumptions about the potential malleability of human beings have always been popular. Behaviourism itself suffered a damaging blow in the 1950s with the refutation of its explanation of how people master the skills of language. It was argued by Chomsky (1959) that speaking a language is such an immensely skilful and complex activity that it could never be learnt in the manner suggested by Skinner. Virtually every sentence uttered is completely new and therefore could not have been learnt via a reward and punishment technique. The capacity to construct sentences is a function of the capacity to master the rules of grammar and this capacity presupposes the notion of a mind already equipped with some essential skills. Much of our understanding of social regularities as instances of rule-following is advanced by an analogy with language as a rule-governed activity.

Liberal-rationalism completely rejects the idea that conformity and social order is a product of conditioning and maintains that such order as there is is a consequence of individuals following and internalising rules (Winch, 1958; Hart, 1961). This presupposes that individuals can understand that rules set appropriate standards of behaviour to which they ought to conform.

In the simple case of regularised behaviour on the road we say that this is a function of traffic rules setting standards of motoring rather than an example of road-users being conditioned to do the correct thing by the appropriate reinforcing agencies. All rules operate as aids which make life reasonably predictable for the participants in a social process by indicating the range of permitted actions.

Some general features of rules may now be delineated. First, all rules, whether they are legal, moral, religious or political, are normative or prescriptive. So far we have been using the word normative in a moral sense only, that is, in distinguishing moral or evaluative statements from scientific statements. But not all normative arguments are moral, and not all uses of the word 'ought' are moral uses. Thus a simple legal rule which makes driving on the left obligatory sets standards which *ought* to be followed just as much as our moral rules do. Furthermore, although general rules indicate the right thing to do this does not mean that it is right in a moral sense. Indeed, many simple, primitive societies have customary rules which would be regarded as objectionable from the point of view of a critical Western morality.

Rule-governed behaviour is often contrasted with habitual or automatic behaviour on the ground that it involves the idea of 'internalisation'. A rule is internalised when it is understood by participants in a social practice as indicating a right and wrong way of doing things (Hart, 1961, pp. 55–6). Unlike the carefully trained animal in the zoo who follows his master's instructions automatically, individuals who are guided by rules regard them as expressing *meaningful* standards of behaviour. Furthermore rules entail the idea of choice for, unlike well-trained animals, humans may disobey rules. Sanctions are, of course, needed to cope with the minority of rule-breakers but this does not mean that sanctions can replace internalisation as the guarantor of regularised behaviour. It should be obvious that a social system which relied solely on sanctions to secure conformity would be highly insecure. For one thing, it would require a very large police force to impose the sanctions. But in that event, how could obedience by the police be ensured?

Rules must be carefully distinguished from predictions. Some empirically-minded social theorists have argued that a rule is a disguised prediction that if a forbidden course of action is undertaken a court will impose a sanction; or if it is a moral rule that is broken the community will express its displeasure in some less precise manner. But this is false. That a rule has been breached constitutes a *reason* or *justification* for the infliction of the sanction. It is because the internal obligatoriness of a rule cannot be verified by external observation that some extreme empiricists have tried to translate them into predictions; in their analysis rules appear as 'ghostly entities' and the only relevant features of a social system are those that are observable.

To complete our description of the view of the understanding of social behaviour in terms of rule-following we need to say something of the *types* and *classes* of rules which are important to the social theorist. There are many different types of rules and any comprehensive classification would include constitutional rules, legal rules, customary rules, rules that govern games and rules that order family and personal relationships (Twining and Miers, 1976, ch. 2). For convenience they are often divided into legal, moral (and religious) and political rules. There are important differences between these which will emerge in detail in our consideration of the concept of law, but one or two elementary points can be made here.

Moral and legal rules are devices for regulating personal conduct while political rules govern the allocation of power and authority in a society. An example of a moral rule might be the rule that says one ought to look after one's aged parents; a legal rule one that makes driving on the left obligatory; and a political rule one that requires the Prime Minister to resign if he fails to secure a majority in the House of Commons. Although these rules are clearly distinct – for example, they emanate from different sources, and breaches are met with different sanctions – they exhibit the same logic. They are normative statements, as distinct from factual statements. The most important feature is that they put limitations on individual conduct by making the performance of some actions in some sense obligatory.

It is clear that systems of rules do not have to be 'created' or emanate from a particular source; indeed, classical liberals argued persuasively that the most reliable systems were those that had evolved spontaneously, such as the common law. While conceding that political and constitutional rules were essential they denied that all social order was a product of political will. In fact, there is much to be said for this view. The complete breakdown of a social order is much rarer than is sometimes supposed even though many countries experience frequent constitutional change and upheaval. It is because of the relative instability of political rules that contemporary liberal-rationalists wish to delimit the area of social life occupied by *public* rules, and this assumes that social order, brought about by rule-following, can survive with little political direction. What is of particular interest to the liberal-rationalist social theorist is the existence of general systems such as legal and economic orders which, although not designed or intended by any one single individual or group, serve men's purposes more effectively than deliberately contrived or planned institutions (Hayek, 1967, ch. 6).

## 4. Marxism

The difficulty in presenting Marxism as a major alternative to the kind of analysis employed in the preceding sections is that there has been a serious dispute in the past two decades as to what Marx's political philosophy and political economy is.[4] Whereas up to the Second World War the debate was about whether Marx's prognostications about the future of capitalist society were true or false, the argument now is the rather more scholastic one of what the foundations of those prognostications are. Thus a consideration of the question of whether Communist states are 'Marxist' or not begs the question of what Marxism is.

The variety of interpretations can be reduced to two broad categories. The first and more traditional view holds that Marxism is a body of social science doctrine that explains the development of all societies in terms of a number of key explanatory categories, and furthermore, makes predictions about future social change. Such a view claims to be strictly scientific, determinist and objective, and maintains that the movement of society which it describes takes place independently of man's will, even though conscious political activity may speed the process up.[5] The second, more humanistic view, which derives from Marx's early writings on alienation, is openly more subjective and less deterministic (Bottomore, 1963). Instead of the emphasis being on the inevitable collapse of capitalism through its inner contradictions, the stress is now on the dehumanising aspects of the capitalist production process itself, such as the factory system, the division of labour, the institution of money and the oppressive systems of state and law that reinforce the property system and class divisions associated with bourgeois society. Also, to the extent that these things characterise overtly socialist societies, then those societies, too, are to be condemned by this Marxist critique. And it is surely no coincidence that many of the early protagonists of this Marxist humanism came from Eastern European Communist regimes.

The newer view of Marx is probably now more dominant and has led to a more *critical*, and less rigidly determinist, social philosophy which attempts to combine theoretical analysis with practical activity. In fact the older view accords very well with our description of the extreme positivist explanation of scientific methodology in the study of society. The idea that knowledge of history revealed a definite trend and destination towards which society was moving, according to inexorable laws derived ultimately from the laws of the physical world, was associated more with Engels and Plekhanov and later Marxist writers than with Marx. It is a methodology which maintains that the business of social science is to prophesy discrete, historical events, on the basis of observation of past historical data, rather than to make conditional predictions of a general kind which we associate with the ahistorical, orthodox laws of economics. One reason, perhaps, for the relative decline of this 'mechanical Marxism' is that the most important of the prophecies have been shown to be quite false (Popper, 1972, II).

Nevertheless, the two styles still have very much in common and this is best seen in comparison with the philosophy of what we have called the 'liberal-rationalist' approach, a philosophy which underlies the first part of this chapter and on which the rest of the book will be broadly based. We can learn a lot about Marxism simply by seeing how the doctrine differs from traditional liberalism and orthodox social science.

Methodological individualism is almost completely rejected by all Marxists. It is not simply that social behaviour is analysed in terms of collective entities, such as 'class', rather than individual volitions; it is that the Marxist concept of 'man' is radically different. Individualism is specifically criticised for abstracting man from his historical and social circumstances and presenting him as an individual with given wants for whom action consists solely of satisfying those wants according to the scale in which he subjectively ranks them. The psychological postulates upon which liberal economic theory is based are said to be too simple in that they exclude from consideration all the social forces and influences that contribute to the determination of the human personality (Lukes, 1972). The concept of economic man that informs classical economics was specifically criticised by Marx as belonging only to nineteenth-century bourgeois capitalist society; it was not universal as the economists claimed. Indeed, it is orthodox Marxist doctrine that change of self coincides with change of circumstance so that the replacement of the capitalist mode of production – based on the extensive social division of labour, private property and the money economy – by a socialist and ultimately Communist economic system characterised by social ownership and the abolition of both money and the social division of labour, would entail the replacement of the egoistic man of capitalism by a co-operative, altruistic personality.

A similar point would apply to the individualist's explanation of the need for rules to make social life reasonably regular and predictable. Underlying all liberal theories of law we find a number of proposed universally true features of the human condition which are said to make rules with some specific content inevitable in society (Hart, 1961, pp. 189–95). The fact of human insecurity makes prohibitions against the use of violence necessary; the fact that human desires are infinite entails that there will always be scarcity so that rules of property (public or private) are essential; and the fact of human ignorance – that no person can know much more about the world than that which affects him personally – means that general rules setting appropriate standards of behaviour save him the task of having to work out all the consequences of other people's actions. Yet against these very general propositions Marxists would account for rules in terms of particular historical and institutional settings and present them as the means by which one class dominates another rather than as universally necessary devices of social control.

An equally persistent criticism made by Marxists concerns the role of ideology. Marxists would argue that the kind of knowledge that characterises liberal social science is 'ideological' knowledge. This means that it is impossible for there to be objective knowledge of social affairs, that is, knowledge that is not relative to the class position of the social scientist. Thus classical economics was not an objective, scientific explanation of economic relationships but the ideology of the bourgeois, property-owning class under capitalism. Marx was not saying, crudely, that the classical economists were being hypocritical in their claims of objectivity – he was making the radical philosophical plea that all knowledge in the social sciences is socially determined. Marxists have never been able to counter the obvious retort to this which is that if knowledge is determined by social factors then Marxism itself must be so determined and cannot therefore be an objective explanation of social development. But, nevertheless, the 'sociology of knowledge' is a permanent feature of their doctrines. Liberal social scientists would argue here that the origin of a particular theory is of no relevance at all to its truth or falsity and that the latter can be established by normal scientific procedures. Furthermore, they would claim that the problem of bias in social investigation has been misunderstood. Impartiality is not a property of the individual social theorist, many of whom are highly committed to their ideas in an emotional sense, but of the *public* world of knowledge where theories can be subjected to free discussion and rigorous criticism (Popper, 1957, pp. 155–6).

The differences between what may be called the 'liberal-rationalist' approach to social affairs and the Marxist approach will become apparent in succeeding chapters but two aspects of social theory are of special importance: the role of reason in social explanation and the concept of 'human nature'. Liberals in social science are 'critical rationalists'; this means that they believe that existing social institutions can be analysed with the traditional tools of logical argument and with the use of empirical evidence where appropriate. They also assume that if the basic explanation of *social order* is understood, suggestions for the improvement of institutions can be made which are capable of securing wide support. Marxists, however, maintain that social order is a product of force and that classes are in irreconcilable conflict. In such circumstances agreement over values is impossible so that progress does not come about through rational criticism but through the wholesale reconstruction of society according to *rational principles*.

It is here that the concept of human nature becomes important. Marxists believe that human nature is a product of historical forces and social conditioning; a change in social institutions will bring about a change in human nature which will make their 'utopias' more viable While liberal-rationalists are not in unanimous agreement on the details of their concept of man their ideas appear similar, at least in comparison to those of their rivals. The liberal's scepticism about the beneficial consequences of wholesale social change in the West is grounded upon what are regarded as certain enduring features of the human condition. While liberal-rationalists do not believe that man is necessarily selfish, as the classical economists implied, they do believe that human behaviour is self-interested enough to make it quite impossible for society to rely for its survival and progress on a general altruism. Therefore, they are more interested in enquiring into those institutions that best cope with the consequences of self-regarding action than with trying to change human nature.

# 2

# Law and Social Control

## 1. Law and social philosophy

We have shown in the first chapter how some aspects of regularised social phenomena can be explained in terms of rule-following, and we have outlined the ways in which rules differ from commands and predictions. In this chapter we have to consider in some detail that special form of social control which we understand as legal control. Undoubtedly a legal system is a specialised system of rules, distinct from moral rules, which at the very least provides a framework in which individual behaviour can in some sense be regulated and an element of certainty guaranteed, and which at the very most may provide a comprehensive framework of regulations covering nearly all aspects of the individual's life. Just how desirable it is for the law to enter a wide area of social life is something which will be considered later but the elementary facts of human nature seem to indicate the necessity for some rules, many of which are bound to be backed by organised sanctions.

It is true that some political philosophers have toyed with the idea of the possibility of social order without law: indeed, the first major work on the subject, Plato's *Republic*, describes a lawless utopia in which the free play of the intelligence of the philosopher-kings is allowed to proceed untrammelled by legal restraints. Also, Karl Marx's future classless society would be free from the restraints of civil and criminal law because those very factors that give rise to the need for law – the institution of money, the social division of labour and the system of private property – would have been removed. What, of course, unites all the differing 'lawless' utopias is the requirement that these desirable states of affairs can only be brought about by a fundamental change in human nature. Other political theorists, perhaps with a less elevated view of human potential, have argued that individuals have found the best form of protection in the existence of general rules of conduct binding on all. Still others, more cynical of human nature, have argued that peace and sociability are only possible if one supreme person or body in a community is given the power to command all laws, while that body or person is above the law.

Political philosophers have always been very much concerned with questions of jurisprudence, or the philosophy of law, and there has been a great variety of these questions. Dominating them all is the essentialist question of 'what is law?'. The assumption behind this question is that there is a set of necessary and sufficient conditions for the truth of statements about the word 'law'. Essentialist definitions depend upon there being a set of properties which the word law uniquely describes. The difficulty is, however, that all the proposed definitions have, in their endeavour to capture in a phrase or sentence the essential properties of law, misrepresented the familiar features of legal systems, or arbitrarily restricted the range of application of the word law. The most obvious example is the command theory of law which defined law solely in terms of the orders of a determinate sovereign and therefore excluded many familiar forms of law (such as international law, constitutional law and tribal law) from the category of 'proper' law. Another example is the attempt to assimilate the notion of legal rules to moral rules, which results in a concealment of the different features of law and morality and a misrepresentation of the different ways in which they regulate social behaviour.

While it is probably true now to say that the search for an exclusive definition of law has been called off, the familiar questions in jurisprudence remain. These centre on the problem of the necessary conditions for the existence of a legal system; criteria of validity of legal rules; the role of sanctions; and the relationship between law and morality. Is it necessary, for example, that a legal system should have courts and organised sanctions? Is it possible to locate a definitive test for the validity of a purported rule of law in a legal system? Is a sanction a necessary condition for the existence of a legal rule? And does the *content* of any particular law have to meet with supposed universal standards of morality for the law to be a genuine law?

Perhaps the most elementary distinction to be made in jurisprudence is that between natural law and positive law: for although there are many types of positive law they are all united in a fundamental opposition to natural law (Hart, 1958). The distinction turns upon questions of the meaning of law and the validity of purported claims to law. Natural law, which has a long and honourable tradition that dates back to ancient Greece, holds that not only must we evaluate law in accordance with universal moral standards, but that for a rule to be accorded the dignity and status of the word 'law' it must satisfy these standards. Questions about validity turn necessarily upon the *content* of the rules in a legal system. Thus a particular rule would not be entitled to be called valid law if in substance it breached a moral principle – even if it emanated from an authoritative source and was legitimate in a formal sense.

Positivists, however, insist upon a logical separation between law and morality and maintain that the content of a law (that is, the ends or purposes which it is designed to bring about) has no relevance to its status as a law; although, as we shall see in the next section, not all legal theorists who call themselves positivists maintain quite this indifference to the content of law. This doctrine does not in any way imply a lack of interest in moral questions on the part of positivist legal theorists – on the contrary, many legal positivists have been rigorous critics of existing legal systems – but it does mean that if intellectual clarity is to be achieved and some element of certainty in the law guaranteed, questions of validity have to be separated from questions of moral worth. One of the objections made by an eminent legal positivist to the use of natural law criteria in post-war West German courts, in consideration of the difficult question as to whether Nazi statutes were really law, turned precisely on the claim that the admission of such criteria would make for potential confusion and uncertainty in the law (Hart, 1961, pp. 205–7).

But the use of the word positivism in legal philosophy has problems of its own. This is because legal theorists use the word only to mark off a distinction between law and morals whereas we have used the word in a slightly different sense in our first chapter. There, it will be recalled, an extreme positivist in social science was one who maintained that the only meaningful propositions about social phenomena were those that, in principle at least, could be subjected to empirical tests. In this doctrine the only social theories worthy of the name science are those that explain and predict observable events. And, as we shall see, some legal positivists can be interpreted in this way, especially those who locate the essence of law in observable commands of a determinate sovereign, and those who define law solely as a set of predictions of judicial behaviour. Other positivists, while insisting on the distinction between law and morality, nevertheless emphasise the importance of the internalisation of legal rules – a phenomenon which is not strictly observable – in the understanding of a legal order. The different explanations of social regularities, from the point of view of the external observer and from the point of view of the participant in a rule-governed process, are then highly relevant for the understanding of law.

## 2. Natural law

The history of jurisprudence reveals a great variety of theories of natural law and perhaps the only common factor in the conflicting doctrines is an aversion to legal positivism. For convenience they may be divided into two categories: highly abstract and 'rationalistic' theories which rest upon the assumption that the human mind is capable of determining a set of moral principles of universal validity which should govern all social, political and personal relationships, and more modest doctrines which maintain that societies spontaneously develop systems of rules which protect personal and property rights (the English common law is an example of such a system), and that statute or 'created' law should be strictly limited to making piecemeal improvements on 'natural' systems.

As we remarked earlier in this chapter, what characterises the 'rationalistic' models of natural law is that they maintain that law must have some specific content if it is to be valid. St Thomas Aquinas's jurisprudence, which still underlies contemporary Catholic teaching on politics, law and morals, illustrates this point. From the simple proposition that 'good is to be done and pursued and evil avoided' he hoped to deduce the whole body of natural law concerning life and death, marriage, the family and economic and political relationships. Any laws at variance with natural law were not proper laws.

The difficulty with all natural law theories of the absolutist kind is that of securing agreement on the ends which men ought to pursue. Natural lawyers often write as if their prescriptions were as necessary as the laws that govern the physical world but clearly this is not so. Natural law relates to human conduct and has therefore quite a different logic from scientific law; it is normative, not predictive or descriptive, and is therefore concerned with demonstrating those rules of behaviour which *ought* to be followed. But men's needs and desires change and actions which were regarded as immoral by one generation may be acceptable to another. Even the absolutist nature of Thomist natural law is qualified by the admission that the subsidiary rules of natural law may alter. In fact, social and economic consequences have seen a number of changes in

Catholic natural law, most notably the lifting of the prohibition on usury in the Middle Ages (O'Connor, 1967, pp. 78–9). Natural lawyers do try to maintain the absolute nature of their prescriptions by making them highly general in form. This, however, makes them difficult to apply in particular cases. The natural law against the arbitrary taking of life may be superficially uncontroversial but men sincerely differ over cases in which the taking of life is or is not justified.

The non-rationalist theories of natural law are much less concerned with demonstrating the necessary content which law must have than with pointing to the advantages that evolving systems of rules have over deliberately created law. The arguments here depend much more on experience than reason, and thinkers from David Hume onwards have stressed the value of known and settled rules which have been shown to be effective. The positive law theories of the utilitarian philosopher, Jeremy Bentham, were aimed at what he thought were the highly conservative implications of the natural law interpretation of the English common law. Twentieth-century collectivist legal thinkers claim that these elaborate and complex systems of rules serve only to protect personal and property rights while their libertarian critics claim that most public or statute law is 'invalid' precisely because it abrogates those individual rights that are enshrined in 'natural' and common law.

While positivists have dominated English jurisprudence, their central tenet, that law may technically have any content, is not perhaps as persuasive as it once was. Even those lawyers who would not accept the modest version of natural law described above as being relevant to the question of validity might still say that law must relate to human needs and purposes if it is to be understood adequately. Such an eminent positivist as H. L. A. Hart maintains that it is meaningful to speak of 'natural law with minimum content'. By this he means that certain 'truisms' about the human condition necessitate that if a society is to survive at all, there will have to be some rules limiting the use of violence, rules of property (public or private), elementary rules of government and the authorisation of sanctions (Hart, 1961, pp. 189–95). However, unlike natural law proper, he claims that his 'natural law with minimum account' would not prevent many oppressive laws from being called 'law'. A legal system could survive if rules of protection were not extended to certain minorities, and almost all the rules in today's highly illiberal regimes would pass Hart's *technical* test of validity. In fact, Hart's rules are so minimal as to make this aspect of his jurisprudence unacceptable to conventional natural law theorists.

## 3. Law as command

The English command theory of law until recently dominated English jurisprudence and although it has suffered severe attacks, which have perhaps fatally exposed the weaknesses in its basic structure, an examination of its elements is still a fruitful way of approaching the study of legal systems. It is associated with English utilitarianism, in that the major command theorists were also utilitarians in ethics and political philosophy.[1] The doctrine is conventionally presented through the jurisprudence of Austin, especially his *The Province of Jurisprudence Determined* (1954), and we shall follow this pattern. However, the recently published edition of Bentham's *Of Laws in General* (1970) has shown that writer to be a more sophisticated legal theorist than Austin, and his version of the command theory is not quite so vulnerable to the traditional criticisms. As a matter of fact, the theory predates both these writers, receiving its first rigorous formulation from Thomas Hobbes. In his endeavour to refute natural lawyers and common lawyers who wanted to submit law to 'reason', Hobbes emphatically asserted that only the 'will' of the sovereign can be the source of law: 'Law is the word of him that by right hath command over others' (1968, p. 217). It was from Hobbes that command theorists derived the idea that the judge-made law in the common law system is subordinate to statute law and owes its validity ultimately to the sovereign.

The command theory is really a rather simple theory in that it hopes to encapsulate the essence of legal phenomena in a precise definition. Austin first of all distinguished law from morality. While not denying that there was an historical connection between law and morality, or that in English law one could find examples of moral principles, he nevertheless emphatically asserted that a rule which broke a moral principle was still a rule if it emanated from a determinate sovereign, and that the moral desirability of a rule was not sufficient to make it a genuine law.

Austin defined a law as: 'a rule laid down for the guidance of an intelligent being by an intelligent being having power over him' (1954, p. 14). There are four essential elements in the structure of a municipal legal system: command, sanction, duty and sovereignty. Before looking at these properties in detail it would be wise to comment briefly on the nature of this definition, for it immediately seems to exclude some familiar types of legal phenomena – notably, customary law, international law and constitutional law. Austin called these 'laws by analogy' only; in his view the rules of international law were merely rules of positive morality since there was no sovereign with sanctions to enforce obedience to them. It has often been pointed out that Austin, by concentrating exclusively on the penal statute of the municipal legal system, systematically distorted the familiar features of legal systems. If Austin's account of law is intended as a *definition* of law then, in a sense, it cannot be falsified, so that attempts to refute it by pointing to examples of legal systems without sovereigns are beside the point (the rules in such a system would not be 'laws'); but such a restricted, stipulative definition would be of little help in understanding the wide range of legal phenomena in the world. Furthermore, as we shall see later, such a definition may seriously distort the understanding of the very legal system it was designed to describe – the modern, complex system of a 'sovereign' state.

The various elements in Austin's model of law can now be described. Laws are a species of command. A command is usually couched in the form of an imperative such as 'do $x$' or 'refrain from doing $y$'. Propositions in the imperative form are not, unlike factual propositions, capable of being true or false. They are normative and indicate a course of action that *ought* to be pursued; although in the case of Austin's theory of law this is not, of course, a moral ought. Commands also presuppose an author and a specific purpose to which the command is addressed. In the law, commands or imperatives are addressed to *classes* of persons. Typical laws of a municipal legal system which fit the imperative model are 'murder is forbidden' or 'income tax must be paid'.

What distinguishes, for Austin, a command from other significations of desire is that 'the party to whom it is directed is liable to evil . . . in case he comply not with the desire'. What characterises the commands in a legal system is that they are backed by sanctions; they are orders backed by threats. Duty is defined then in terms of the fear of sanctions. A person is under a duty when a command is issued and it is backed by a sanction: any other explanation of duty, perhaps one deriving from morality, would be dismissed as metaphysical and irrelevant to the science of law.

The notion of sovereignty is vital to the understanding of Austin's jurisprudence. The sovereign, the author of law, is defined as that determinate person, or body of persons, to whom the bulk of the population owes habitual obedience, while he, the sovereign, owes obedience to no other person or body. A sovereign is said to be logically necessary for the existence of a legal system and must be illimitable (that is, he [it] cannot be restrained by any fundamental law) and indivisible (that is, sovereign power cannot be divided up into two or more bodies without destroying the unity of that sovereign power). It is to be noted that

Austin's theory of law is a combination of two distinct elements: these are command and habitual obedience to an all-powerful sovereign. The first element (command) refers to the logical form in which laws must be cast if they are to qualify as laws, the second to a certain factual or sociological requirement for a legal system to exist, which is the fact of habitual obedience to the sovereign.

While logically all laws must emanate from the sovereign to be proper laws, Austin was obviously aware of the existence of the common law, the law created by judicial interpretation of rules from case to case. In the command theory it is recognised that the sovereign cannot be in complete control of the legal system and therefore courts appear as agents of the sovereign which, although they may create new rules in discharging their duties, nevertheless owe their existence to the will of the sovereign. Furthermore, common law is emphatically subordinate to statute law and, although its content might appear to emanate from a source other than the sovereign, the command theorists argue that it is implicitly a product of the sovereign's will since it only survives with his consent. The sovereign could repeal the whole of the common law overnight.

Many critics of the command system have argued that just because the sovereign can, as a matter of fact, repeal the whole of the common law, this does not make him its author (Hayek, 1973, pp. 45–6). The content of the common law is the product of hundreds of years of judicial reasoning, and that, according to critics of the command theory, is its virtue. For many command theorists the judiciary is responsible for the needless technicalities, illogicalities and conservative elements in the law. Bentham was especially critical of what he called 'Judge and Co.' and looked forward to a legal utopia in which judges would be deprived of discretion and reduced to the role of clerks administering a comprehensive system of law based on statute.

The common criticism levelled against Austin's command theory is that it tries to reduce all law to one type – the duty-imposing type. The criminal statute does seem to some extent to resemble this type since it lays duties upon individuals to perform, or refrain from performing, certain actions under fear of penalty. Yet the legal system of a modern state is characterised not just by duty-imposing laws but by what are called power-conferring rules (Hart, 1961, pp. 27–33). Power-conferring laws are legal devices to enable people to do certain things such as marry, leave wills, convey property and so on. Obviously there is no legal duty to do any of these things, but a framework of rules is required for their performance. The whole structure of civil law, which largely consists of power-conferring rules, seems not to be explicable in the command theory's terms.

An obvious difference is that power-conferring rules do not have sanctions behind them to create a legal duty in the way that criminal statutes do. However, in the endeavour to represent all laws as if they were of one logical type, the Austinian command theorists tried to argue that 'nullity' in the civil law was the equivalent to sanction in the criminal law. This cannot possibly work since nullities, as they are not directed at motives in the way that sanctions are, cannot create legal duties in the Austinian sense. Nullities are merely legal consequences of not fulfilling the procedural requirements set out in the particular rule: they are not 'evils' designed to secure obedience to the law (Hart, 1961, pp. 33–5). No one is punished for failing to meet with all the legal conditions in a civil law, all that happens is that individuals do not succeed in realising their plans.

A further crucial error in the simple command model is its failure to account for the complex structure of legislative authority that exists in any modern state. It is perfectly possible for subordinate bodies to be granted legislative power, but the constitutional rules which regulate such grants of power cannot be understood as duty-imposing laws (Hart, 1961, pp. 30–3). These rules indicate the range of activities on which the subordinate body has power to legislate. If that body should go beyond this then its legislation merely fails to take effect, that is, it is not genuine law. Rules that determine the lawfulness of the acts of subordinate authorities do not impose duties on them in the sense defined by the command model. The Government of Ireland Act, passed by the Westminster Parliament in 1920, empowered the subordinate Parliament in Northern Ireland to make laws for the province subject to the conditions laid down in the 1920 Act: appeal to the courts was possible on the ground that the subordinate authority had acted unlawfully. It would be extremely odd to interpret such legal limitations as a species of command or instruction. The rules that govern subordinate legislative bodies are, then, power-conferring rules.

Another main attack on the command model has centred on its central tenet that in any legal system there must be a sovereign, as the author of all law, to whom the bulk of the population owe habitual obedience, and who in turn owes obedience to no one. Early critics of the doctrine were quick to point out that it failed to explain law in federal systems where there appeared to be no one illimitable and indivisible sovereign. Also, it was pointed out that primitive societies had some form of social control through law but no sovereigns or organised sanctions; and indeed the history of medieval Europe seemed to be characterised by despotic rulers who, although they might in some senses fit the Austinian model, were not regarded as authorised to make 'law'. While these empirical 'refutations' might appear to vitiate Austin's theory, they cannot really do so if the theory is regarded as *a definition*: in the federal example Austinians maintain that there is a sovereign somewhere, and in other deviant cases, such as primitive society, it might be maintained that law, properly understood, does not exist there.

A more effective attack on the necessity of sovereignty thesis than the mere reciting of numerous counter-examples is to explore the inner logic of the thesis to see whether it explains certain crucial features of a legal system in the context most favourable to the theory, that of the municipal legal system familiar to Western writers on jurisprudence.

One of the major criticisms of the command model is that it fails to explain the element of continuity in a legal system. Austin's own experience was of a political/legal order with very few artificial 'breaks' (or revolutions) and it is this that distinguishes a system of law from the casual commands of the leader of an organised gang. Can the concept of sovereignty provide that element of persistence which clearly characterises legal orders?

As long as sovereignty is defined solely in terms of *power*, which itself, according to the command theory, generates legitimacy, it is clear that it cannot do the job assigned to it. Hobbes, the originator of the command theory, was aware of the difficulty of transmitting sovereign power from one person (or body) to another. He says that, in the question of succession, the sovereign indicates or *points to* his successor and the authority of the new sovereign is a consequence of the power of the incumbent (Hobbes, 1968, pp. 247–9). But, in the sovereign power model, the obligation of the citizens is owed to the person who indicates the successor, not the successor himself. Once the sovereign dies the authority of his commands dies with him. In fact the sovereignty model which identifies authority by reference to *persons* rather than rules or procedures, entails a legal hiatus every time a sovereign dies or is replaced.

There are further problems in the sovereignty thesis, which are of relevance not only to Austin's jurisprudence but to political theory in general. There is the confusion between *de jure* sovereignty, the formalised legal claim to supreme legislative power, and *de facto* sovereignty, the actual exercise of power. As Dicey and other later theorists of sovereignty recognised, the two may not always be in the same hands; for example Parliament might be the supreme legislative power but it might be as a matter of fact, dictated to by some outside body. Austin, by defining sovereignty in terms of habitual obedience, cannot properly explain the situation in which a supreme legislative power habitually obeys some other powerful body, yet the commands of the latter are not, properly speaking, law and it is not therefore a *de jure* sovereign. Austin was not much interested in sociological questions about the factual basis of sovereignty even though his theory of validity partly turns on this. The problem is that Austin's theory of law is partly a theory of the form that laws must take – they must be commands – and partly a theory of what makes law effective. This involves the feature of habitual obedience to the sovereign. As we have said, such obedience may be owed to a different body from that entitled to make law.

The theory of illimitable sovereignty breaks down because it cannot admit constitutions into the explanation of law. According to Austin a sovereign cannot be limited by positive law since he is the author of all law, therefore constitutional law is not really law. This must follow because in Austin's theory the existence of a legal limitation implies the existence of a duty, and no sovereign can be under a duty. But even an extreme sovereignty theorist must admit some *procedural* considerations into the understanding of a legal system, since what counts as a sovereign is an important question. There must be some minimal rules to determine who the sovereign is. The question 'what is Parliament?' has turned out to be a very real one in the past thirty years in legal systems which are nominally of the sovereignty type. Also, it makes perfect sense to speak of the procedural rules that govern sovereignty while accepting that there are no formal limitations on the substantive content of the acts of the sovereign. Since Austin rejected constitutional law on *a priori* grounds there is no way of distinguishing between the *public* and *private* acts of the sovereign in his system (Raz, 1970, p. 38).

In fact, it is perfectly in order to speak of legal limitations on sovereign authority, as the existence of constitutional government has amply demonstrated: general rules may limit supreme legislatures or divide up legislative authority between a number of bodies, as in a federal system. Since Austin saw laws only as the duty-imposing type he thought there must be some *ultimate* sovereign behind all complex rule structures.

In the United States of America, for example, he thought that there must be a sovereign somehow 'behind' the Constitution and he located it in the peculiar, aggregate body that amends the Constitution – two-thirds of

Congress and three-quarters of the states' legislatures. But it is surely eccentric to attribute sovereignty to a body that exercises legislative power so rarely. Furthermore, there is, one clause in the American Constitution that cannot be amended.[2] Even the British system, which superficially resembles the Austinian model, is, as the author of the command theory had to admit, difficult to represent accurately in terms of the sovereign power model. Since the composition of Parliament is partly the product of the electoral process, Austin claimed that the real sovereign in Britain is the electorate. It is, however, extremely difficult to conceive of the electorate as a 'sovereign' in the original sense of the term (Hart, 1961, p. 76).

Austin's version of the command theory of law, however, is by no means the most sophisticated and is acknowledged to be much more simplistic than that of his master, Jeremy Bentham. Austin's jurisprudence has always been presented as the paradigm of the command theory, partly because of its very simplicity, and partly because Bentham's major contribution to jurisprudence, *Of Laws in General*, has only recently been published in an authoritative edition and critical literature on it is only now beginning to emerge (James, 1973).

In this work Bentham said some very important things about the logical structure of law which were significantly different from the crude model which was later developed by Austin. He did not define law solely in terms of statute and was able to account for 'permissive' laws more satisfactorily than Austin while still retaining the basic elements of the command/sanction model (James, 1973). However, the real interest for the political theorist in this work lies in Bentham's complex theory of sovereignty.

While Bentham said that all law is made valid by the sovereign either through his *adoption* of existing laws or his *conception* of new ones, he did not assume that sovereignty must necessarily be indivisible and illimitable (Bentham, 1970, pp. 18–19). On a number of occasions he said that sovereign power could be divided up into two or more legislative bodies and that a supreme legislative power might be limited by 'express convention'. Bentham indicated that the concept of sovereignty which by definition excludes obedience of the sovereign to another body, as Austin's concept did, could not explain federal systems and other cases of limitations on sovereignty that have occurred in history.

It was probably Bentham's view that limitations on sovereignty were dangerous rather than impossible. It does appear, however, that Bentham envisaged the possibility of constitutional law in his system. For Austin constitutional law must be incomplete law because it lacks a penal sanction, but Bentham argued that *auxiliary* sanctions, of morality and religion, may very well bind a sovereign in the way that conventional sanctions bind subjects (Bentham, 1970, pp.67–71). Bentham even thought that a sovereign might bind his successor.

In however sophisticated a form the command theory is presented it is clear that it does not accurately describe the typical elements of municipal legal systems. We have already seen that the attempt to reduce all law to one type, the duty-imposing type, blurs the important logical distinction between this kind of rule and the power-conferring, non-obligative type of rule. We have also seen that the concept of sovereignty cannot explain continuity in a legal system. However, some critical observations of a more general kind, and which derive from some distinctions made in Chapter 1, can now be made.

The problem with the command theory is that it is not only positivist in that it separates law from morality; it is also positivist in the sense that it explains the existence of a legal system in terms of observable phenomena, such as habits of obedience, determinate sovereignty and sanctions. It cannot explain legal systems in the language of rules since rules which authorise and validate claims to authority are not strictly observable in the way that commands backed up by sanctions may be said to be. The problem goes back to Hobbes, the originator of the theory, who regarded rules as ghostly or metaphysical entities that could not possibly create legal obligations in the way that the command of a sovereign with sanctions could. Yet, as we have seen, the idea of rules, the obligatory nature of which cannot be explained in terms of sanctions, is logically necessary for the explanation of the transmission of legal authority.

There are other positivist theories of law which, in their different ways, misunderstand the nature and purpose of rules in the explanation of a legal order. One of the most interesting for the political theorist is American realism. This is because the advocates of the theory not only attempted to give a 'scientific' explanation of law but were also eager to show how law could be used as a method of social control.

## 4. Legal realism

Realism, and its successor judicial behaviouralism, began at the turn of the century as a reaction against the formalism of all types of European jurisprudence which saw the judicial decision as a logical deduction from a general rule. Against this, American realism focused attention on the independent role that the courts have in law creation, the sociological factors that determine the judicial decision and the use to which the law can be put for social control if the right sort of empirical knowledge of society is available.

It was not surprising that scepticism about the binding nature of rules should emerge from the United States since that country's federal system gives a much greater opportunity for judicial legislation than does a country like Britain which is characterised by parliamentary sovereignty. Since the Supreme Court can declare that a Congressional statute, or one from a state legislature, is unconstitutional and therefore invalid, it has considerable influence in determining the shape of a government's law and policy. Because of what Hart has called the 'open texture' of law (Hart, 1961, pp. 121–7), the fact that particular legal rules are at points indeterminate so that disputes inevitably arise as to what they mean and where they should apply, the formal model of the judicial decision as an axiomatic deduction from a general rule is clearly inadequate. It was, in effect, the 'open texture' of law that provided what intellectual justification there was for Justice Holmes's (1897, p. 461) famous statement that 'the prophecies of what the courts will do in fact, and nothing more pretentious, are what I mean by the law'. Holmes also called this the 'bad man's' view of law, meaning that people are interested in the likely decision of a particular court and that this fact is a much more significant determinant of behaviour than anything else.

There are really two major aspects of American realism: an intellectual approach to the study of jurisprudence, and a sociologically-based use of law as an instrument of social control. The intellectual approach, from Holmes, was that rules were only useful as aids to the prediction of court decisions. The important point, however, is that most realists stressed that court decisions were less predictable if the observer were to rely *only* on the rules of law. The attempt was made therefore to find uniformities or regularities in actual judicial behaviour. It is this that constituted the 'brute empiricism' or positivism of some realists in that laws lost their normative character in setting standards and prescribing conduct and were treated as observable 'facts' for the purpose of scientific investigation. The schools of jurimetrics and judicial behaviouralism are the contemporary exponents of this realism and have, with their stress on the measurable factors that determine the judicial decision, been incorporated virtually into the positive social sciences (Schubert, 1959).

The other feature of realism, which is about the use of law in social engineering, also in a sense derives from Holmes. It would appear to be the realists' view that the law should be concerned with social policy, that it must be appropriate for the needs of a developing and changing society and that, to this end, the lawyer must be equipped with the relevant empirical knowledge. A classic instance of Holmes's general approach is his dissenting opinion in *Lochner* v. *New York* (1935), a case in which the Supreme Court declared a statute limiting the number of hours a person may work in a bakery unconstitutional (See Lloyd, 1972, pp. 432–3). Holmes argued that 'The Fourteenth Amendment does not enact Mr Herbert Spencer's *Social Statics*': to the suggestion that the statute violated liberty, Holmes said that the court was constantly interfering with personal liberty and would continue to do so in the light of social needs and purposes. Holmes's views represented not just a rejection of the mechanistic jurisprudence provided by a strict rules model of law, but also the *individualism* that the traditional common law embodies. Indeed many have associated the rise of legal realism in the United States with the transition from an extremely individualistic society to a more collectivist society with considerable central authority in the economy and in welfare, health and housing. In Britain, laws to do with race relations, employment and the welfare state have a similar purpose. Law is not solely a body of rules to enable individuals to conduct their lives in a reasonably predictable manner: it is an instrument to be used to bring about certain social states held to be desirable. It is this rise of 'public' law to which liberal individualists have strongly objected. In their view law functions as a method of social control by providing rules for the facilitating of *private* purposes. Public law should be limited to those things, such as defence and police protection, which cannot be generated privately.

## 5. Legal systems as systems of rules

The dominant theory of law in Western democracies has probably been that which understands a legal system as, in some sense or other, a *system of rules*. The clearest exposition of this view is in H. L. A. Hart's *The Concept of Law* (1961). Of course, it is *not* a truism to say that a legal system consists of a system of rules, since we have already seen two important theories that deny this – the command theory, which interprets all law in terms of orders backed by threats, and the realist theory, which says that rules are at most no more than disguised predictions of how courts will decide particular cases. In fact Hart's theory of law emerges from a criticism of these two theories since both were deficient in that they ignored the *internal* aspect of rules (see Chapter 1).

It would follow from this that the rules theory is not merely a doctrine of jurisprudence but an attempt to describe the general features of a legal system in the context of a general theory of society. Thus Hart is not concerned with 'real definition', the delineation of the necessary and sufficient conditions for the use of the word 'law', but with reproducing the main features of a municipal legal system. It is for this reason that Hart, although he is a legal positivist in the sense of separating law from morality, insists that law must have some purpose. Certain enduring features of man and society make some sorts of rules essential.

Arising out of the criticism of the command theory of law came a distinction between duty-imposing and power-conferring rules. As we have seen, this is the distinction between rules that prescribe certain courses of conduct as obligatory (as, for example, the criminal law does) and those that *enable* individuals, or public authorities, to pursue certain courses of action. Hart makes a further distinction between primary and secondary rules and uses this to explain the foundations of a legal system. However, certain critics have suggested that there is some inconsistency in his analysis in that it is not clear whether power-conferring rules are primary or secondary rules (Sartorius, 1971, pp. 136–8).

The 'key' to jurisprudence is described as the 'union of primary and secondary rules'. The primary rules, such as a system of criminal law, set standards and regulate behaviour and therefore provide the 'content' of a legal system, while secondary rules, such as rules that govern legislatures and courts, are concerned with the primary rules themselves (Hart, 1961, pp. 77–9). While it is true that a society could maintain itself by a system of primary rules alone, and many have done so, such a system has three major disadvantages: uncertainty, which means that there is no mechanism for determining disputed rules; the fact that in a system consisting of primary rules alone change is slow; and the fact that such a system lacks an agency for determining conclusively the case of a breach of the rules (Hart, 1961, p. 92). To remedy these deficiencies Hart says that a mature legal system will develop secondary rules of adjudication and change, and rules for the determination of transgressions of the primary rules. Thus there will be a rule of *recognition*, an ultimate constitutional rule which will determine the validity of primary rules, rules governing the operation of legislatures or other institutions empowered to introduce new primary rules, and rules authorising courts to make decisions concerning breaches of rules (Hart, 1961, pp. 92–3).

It would not be quite true, however, to say that in Hart's theory the 'union of primary and secondary rules' exhaustively describes a legal system. As we have noted earlier in this chapter, in this theory certain universally true facts about human nature mean that law must have some minimal content if it is to guarantee human survival.

The most important feature of this doctrine is the rule of recognition which in many ways functions as a replacement of the Austinian concept of a sovereign to settle the question of validity in a legal system. In a mature legal system there must be some ultimate rule by which the validity of subordinate rules can be tested. The rule of parliamentary sovereignty, where the final authority of law is located in the will of Parliament, is an example of a simple rule of recognition, the American Constitution an example of an extremely complex one. It is to be noted that the rule of recognition is not itself a rule of law, like, for example, the law of contract, but is a rule by which the validity of subordinate rules can be established.

The rule that states that what Parliament wills is law cannot itself be tested for validity because if it were there would have to be some higher rule to refer to, and so on indefinitely. One interesting consequence of Britain's entry into the European Economic Community has been a shift in the rule of recognition. In signing the Treaty of Rome Britain accepted limitations, in certain fields, on the legislative sovereignty of Parliament so that it is now theoretically possible for the European Court to strike down a parliamentary statute as being in conflict with European legislation (Scarman, 1974, pp. 21–3). The general point about the rule of recognition is that even if a constitution allows unlimited legislative sovereignty, this is itself a product of a rule which is accepted as a fact by the officials of the system and cannot logically be a product of command.

It has been suggested by Ronald Dworkin (1977), in a powerful critique of Hart, that it is not possible to analyse a legal system in terms of rules alone. This is mainly because of the problem of 'hard' cases; that is, disputed cases where the application of a rule does not give a clear answer. Of course, the realists' objection to the idea of internally binding rules derives from the fact that courts do have considerable discretion in deciding cases, and Hart (1961, p. 125) himself says that the 'penumbral' aspect of law, the fact that rules are likely to be vague in some applications so that people genuinely differ as to their meaning, entails that the dream of a mechanical jurisprudence can never be realised. In difficult cases judges will have to use extra-legal criteria when reaching a decision.

Dworkin maintains that a crucial role is played by *principles* in legal systems, and that this aspect cannot be captured by the positivists with their view of law as a structure of rules. Dworkin (1977, pp. 22–8) says that there is a clear distinction between rules and principles. Rules are precise and it is possible to enumerate the applications of a rule, while principles are necessarily imprecise and may conflict. Furthermore, principles do not dictate a particular decision but suggest reasons or justifications for a decision. Also, a legal principle, unlike a rule, may not apply in all cases. An example of a principle he gives is: 'no man may profit from his own wrongs'. Dworkin then shows that it may or may not apply in particular cases. The argument is that principles are not extra-legal criteria; they are used by judges in hard cases and are therefore part of the law. Judges are in a sense indulging in *political theory* in making their decisions, in that they will *weigh* principles and balance one against another. However, their discretion does not mean they have complete freedom, for the principles which will reflect prevailing constitutional standards do control what they do, and judges' decisions are always subject to criticism. Dworkin claims that the complexity of a legal system cannot be described by the model of rules and that the idea of a master rule, the rule of recognition, as a determinant of validity, cannot possibly be applied to principles (Dworkin, 1977, pp. 39–45). Principles do not form a hierarchy, with one superior principle determining the validity of subordinate ones. If anything, validity appears to be established from general political theory.

While he does not have the sociological bias of the realists, Dworkin (who, as an American, is naturally much influenced by controversial Supreme Court cases) nevertheless shares their scepticism concerning the importance of rules in the understanding of a legal process. In fact, Dworkin distorts the function of rules in society by suggesting that the distinction between rules and principles turns upon the fact that all the applications of a rule can be specified. But this is not so. All rules may to some extent reveal indeterminacies but the virtue of a legal system in which the judiciary, in interpreting particular rules, is nevertheless controlled by more general rules and procedures lies in the fact that this makes life more predictable for citizens. By admitting necessarily vague and imprecise principles into law, and arguing that decision-making in law can only take place by reference to a general political theory so that legal rules become a species of moral rules, Dworkin's approach comes close to destroying the distinction between politics and law. This becomes apparent when his set of principles turns out to be a radical conception of rights. Yet Dworkin insists that judges do not reach out for extra-legal criteria in hard cases but make decisions, according to principles, which can be assessed as right or wrong.

The conception of a legal system as a system of rules is the most illuminating approach and does place the study of law more firmly in the general body of social and political theory but it does not answer all the problems concerned with a legal system. Is it necessary, for example, that a legal system have courts, officials and legislatures? Can the language and concepts of Western jurisprudence be applied to primitive societies?

This latter question can be dealt with first. It is often said that modern and primitive societies are so different that social concepts cannot be applied to both cultures and that this fact makes meaningful comparison impossible. It is true that there are some obvious differences. Tribal law is characterised more by conciliation (finding a settlement between two parties in dispute) than adjudication (authoritative determination of right and wrong): tribal law consists almost entirely of custom, and some of the familiar legal phenomena, such as courts and a police system, may be absent (Gluckman, 1965, ch. 5). Yet, surely certain general features of the human condition make the control of human behaviour through rules a universal feature of social life? It is obvious that the form that property takes, for example, varies considerably from society to society, but nevertheless the concept of property has a fairly general explanatory application.

To the question of what constitutes a legal system there have been many differing answers. Hart says that while the concepts of secondary rules and the rule of recognition provide the key to jurisprudence he would not deny that the word law is correctly used to describe systems that lack these. But could we properly describe systems that had no courts, organised sanctions or legislatures as legal systems, or must there be some minimum degree of 'jural complexity' (Golding, 1975, pp. 15–17)? Of course, the existence of some rules is a logical necessity for the existence of a legal system, but this seems to be the only logically necessary institution. Primitive systems do survive without a differentiated court and sanction system.

The interesting issue for the political theorist is the way that primitive societies cope with various jural problems. For example, dispute settling in Eskimo society is by 'song-duels' between the interested parties; we would certainly not say that this procedure resembled a court, but nevertheless it is a *procedure*. Also, in addition to not having courts to make authoritative determinations of breaches of rules, a society may not have a formalised police system so that punishment and compensation for wrongs have to be secured by the aggrieved party himself. This explains the persistence of vendettas and feuds in primitive society, though this can be exaggerated. Finally, customary law is not the only form of social control in a primitive society: witchcraft and sorcery are frequently used for this purpose (Gluckman, 1965, ch. 6).

Hart (1961, p. 41) maintains that the step from a primitive, simple society governed by primary rules to a more complex system in which secondary rules provide for the determination of law, the creation of legislatures and specialised sanctions procedures is as important a step for mankind as the invention of the wheel. A more helpful analogy for the social theorist might be the invention of money. Just as the use of a common medium of exchange frees people from the inconveniences and inefficiencies of a barter economy so the discovery of secondary rules removes the uncertainties, insecurities and wasteful expenditure, in de-centralised systems of law enforcement, which characterise systems consisting only of primary rules. Furthermore, the social theorist does not have to 'observe' primitive societies of this kind because he can imagine – that is, mentally reconstruct – what a society would be like without secondary rules and without the institution of money, in order to appreciate their importance.

## 6.  Law, society and the rule of law

Despite the fact that theorists of law who stress the crucial importance of rules claim that their interpretation of law integrates legal phenomena with social phenomena in general, their accounts of law are primarily analytical rather than sociological; that is to say they are much more concerned to state the necessary conditions for the existence of legal systems in general than to account for the particular legal institutions that might arise in particular societies.

In contrast, Marxist theories of law concentrate exclusively on the relationship between law and particular historical, social and economic structures. Systems of rules, and the state itself, are seen as part of the 'superstructure' that enforces a particular set of property relationships, and their form is determined by the existing economic mode of production (Marx, 1977; Kinsey, 1978, pp. 202–7). Thus the common law system of criminal and civil law, which protects personal and property rights and guarantees a necessary element of predictability in social life, is regarded as no more than a system of coercion designed to protect bourgeois ownership of the means of production. When the bourgeois system of ownership is abolished and a classless society emerges it is assumed that 'law' will 'wither away' along with the state. It is not clear, however, whether it is suggested that *all* legal rules will disappear or just those associated with bourgeois democracy. The most elementary knowledge of human nature would make the first interpretation fantastically optimistic, even though Marx stresses that the abolition of the social division of labour associated with the bourgeois mode of production would entail a change in human nature. Can we really even conceive of a society without a general system of criminal law?

Soviet jurists in the past did proceed on the assumption that a Communist society would have no need of bourgeois law (Berman, 1963). By bourgeois law they meant *private* law, those civil and criminal rules that govern the relationships between individuals, and they argued that this would be replaced by *administration*. Administrative law of this type, which was required for extensive economic planning, was not regarded as 'law' by Western observers precisely because it granted massive discretionary power to officials and therefore did not offer individuals the protection of general rules. It was indeed a part of collectivist economic philosophy that administration would replace 'law', that socialism and 'law' were antithetical.

However, in practice Communist regimes have maintained some sort of court system and, indeed, as the dream of a stateless, coercionless society faded, the notion of 'legality' crept back into Soviet jurisprudence. In the 1936 Constitution law was revived and made consistent with socialism; and even some Western legal concepts and practices which would previously have been denounced as bourgeois reappeared in the later development of the Soviet legal system. Thus there is a legal order in the Soviet system. However, the fact that law does not apply to the political sphere, and the difficulty of differentiating 'law' from administrative fiat, mean that legality and arbitrariness exist side by side. In no sense can a socialist system of law meet the demands set by the Western concept of the 'rule of law'.

The recent interest in the rule of law is not entirely a result of the apparent collapse of legality in the Communist world, for the believers in the doctrine also say that much milder policies of welfare and planning may bring about totalitarian results not intended by the authors of the schemes. It is argued that the substantial increase in state activity in Western countries in the last thirty years has not only had economic consequences but also has subtly changed the nature of the kind of legal systems operating in these societies. Instead of a society's legal system being characterised by a set of general rules which enables individuals to pursue their private plans with reasonable security and predictability, it is said that the collectivised delivery of welfare services (health, education, pensions and so on) brings about a vast increase in *public* law, the law that authorises officials to carry out public plans. Such law invests these officials with great discretionary power over individuals (Hayek, 1960, ch. 17).

The rule of law doctrine then appears to be not unlike the natural law doctrine in that it provides for the critical evaluation of existing laws. But unlike traditional natural law doctrines it does not so much base this evaluation on a set of external moral norms, held to be objectively true, as on a consideration of the *procedural* requirements that a purported law must satisfy if it is to be law. Thus the positivist's 'rule of recognition' in the legal system could be assessed by the criteria contained in the rule of law doctrine. Implicit in the rule of law doctrine is a distinction between law and the state. The argument is that legal systems develop spontaneously those rules required for the protection of free exchanges between individuals and do not require the coercive power of the state to validate them. The common law tradition is perhaps the best example of this and it contrasts strongly with the command theory which specifically locates validity in the will of the sovereign.

The aim of the rule of law doctrine is that citizens should know how laws will affect them.[3] The main elements of the doctrine can be briefly summarised (Hayek, 1960, pp. 153–61; Lucas, 1966, pp. 106–17; Raz, 1977). Laws should be perfectly *general* in form so that no individual or group is specifically picked out for preferential treatment; they should treat people equally; they should not be retrospective in application; and all laws should bind everyone, including governments. This last point links the idea of the rule of law to the idea of *constitutionalism* and may be exemplified by systems of government that have a rigorous separation of powers, written constitutions and other devices to limit the actions of officials by general rules. It should be clear that the doctrine is, in principle, in conflict with the notion of sovereignty as traditionally understood since in a sovereignty system, although the unlimited power of Parliament is authorised by the rule of recognition, the legislative body is permitted to do things which are in conflict with the rule of law. The demands for a written constitution in Britain are essentially demands to put the legislature under the rule of law.

There are, of course, many examples of parliamentary statutes breaching the rule of law in Britain. Trade union legislation is frequently cited. The 1906 Trade Disputes Act, and subsequent legislation, which makes trade unions immune from tort actions for wrongful acts committed in the furtherance of industrial disputes, effectively puts unions above the law. The recent legislation which removed penalties on the Clay Cross councillors for offences committed under local government law is an example of retrospective law, and there are similar examples from immigration law.

It is, however, extremely difficult to formulate a set of criteria of the rule of law which would entirely eliminate arbitrary legislation. It has often been pointed out that it is possible to formulate perfectly general laws in such a way that they do pick out individuals for special treatment; in a mainly Protestantant country a law forbidding Sunday sport may be perfectly general yet it discriminates against Roman Catholics, who normally play sport on a Sunday. A more traditional natural lawyer might claim that it is not enough merely to look at the *form* in which a law is cast – one must also examine its *content* in order to adjudicate on its 'legality'.

A criticism from a more collectivist approach might be that the rule of law doctrine, since it finds its most prominent expression in the common law tradition, protects only *individual* rights and private property. Oddly enough the foremost contemporary advocate of the rule of law, F. A. von Hayek, while stressing that this ideal is more likely to be advanced by common law judges protecting individual rights than by legislatures, does concede something of the collectivist argument by admitting that in the past the 'law' has occasionally protected particular interests. He says that landlord and tenant law in Britain in the nineteenth century did, in fact, discriminate in favour of the propertied class and had to be altered by legislation (Hayek, 1973, p. 89).

The main theme of the rule of law philosophy is that the ideal of certainty in the law is better advanced by 'judge-made' law than 'legislation'. The argument is that in Western democracies today, because of the vast increase in the number of laws, most of which are addressed to public purposes rather than the protection of private rights, the individual cannot know how the law will affect him and therefore is less able to plan his life securely. It is maintained that traditional common law rules, although they are often in dispute, provide better security for the individual since judges are not likely to be persuaded by policy considerations in making their decisions.

Not all liberals, however, have such confidence in the spontaneous development of legal rules and would claim that although a market does indeed develop in this way, a legal order may not. There is, of course, much historical evidence for this view. Legal systems frequently develop in chaotic and haphazard ways which provide little security for the individual. It is for this reason, and because of their sceptical attitude towards the legal profession, that some liberal advocates of the rule of law, while being hostile to publicly-oriented law, still maintain that the individual is better protected by strict legal codes than judge-made rules.

The whole subject of the rule of law is at the heart of the issue about the state and its role, and it is to this subject that we must now turn.

# 3

# The State

## 1. The state in political philosophy

In the past decades there has been a surprising dearth of books and articles by philosophers about the concept of the state. This is curious if only because the history of political theory has been mainly concerned with the state. There has been a bewildering variety of theories of the state in traditional political philosophy and different answers to a series of recurring questions. The theories have included organic theories that present the state as a political institution embodying collective values which are held to be superior to individual ones, 'social contract' theories that treat the state as a device voluntarily agreed to by individuals to advance purely personal values, 'night-watchmen' theories which severely limit the role of the state to fulfilling the minimum of collective purposes, and coercive theories of the state which regard its function as solely oppressive. Typical questions asked about the state have been about the moral limitations on the authority of the state and about the grounds of political obligation.

One reason why political philosophers write so little about the state is that a distinction is now made between the social and legal order in general and the particular institutional device, the modern state, based on coercion. Political philosophers, at least before Hobbes, wrote about the former, which is much easier to justify. There is no logical necessity for social order to depend upon an institution possessing a monopoly of coercion, the state, and indeed the most casual empirical observation confirms this. In European history the emergence of the state with its claim to sovereignty in the creation and enforcement of law is a comparatively recent phenomenon, dating from about the sixteenth and seventeenth centuries. Anthropologists have given vivid accounts of tribal societies which do have systems of rules yet do not have states, and may not even have specialised police agencies (Krader, 1968, Ch. 2; Gluckman, 1965, Ch. 3). We have already seen that of necessity the concept of 'society' implies the presence of rules which set standards and make relationships between individuals reasonably predictable, but this does not at all justify the existence of the state as a specialised type of rule-enforcement agency.

The conceptual distinction between law and state is, moreover, crucially important in the question of the justification of the state. The sophisticated anarchist, for example, is not disputing the necessity of rules – his ideal law may very well be something like a common law system which protects individual rights. What he is objecting to is the existence of a centralised agency with a monopoly of coercion which imposes collective decisions upon individuals. The identification of law, and social order in general, with the state not only obscures the distinctive features of the state but also makes moral arguments about the place, and limits, of the state in social life needlessly confusing.

The argument about the limits of the state is one of the most important in contemporary political theory, and many of its ramifications cannot be understood without reference to evaluative political principles in general. The nature of principles will be considered in later chapters but some important issues can be analysed at this stage. However, before the role of the state can be assessed we must know what it is that we are talking about. What follows in the next section, then, is a basic philosophical analysis of the concept of the state; an analysis which is helped by the use of some elementary anthropological findings.

## 2. Analysis of the state

As with so many other concepts in social and political theory, the analyses of the state produced by philosophers have been beset by the search for the 'real essence' of the state. Philosophical speculation about the state has for the most part been taken up with delineating the necessary properties of the state: the knowledge of such properties was thought to be obtained by a special intuition, possessed exclusively by the philosophers, and very little that was said about the subject was derived from the observation of existing empirical states. There have been exceptions to this in the history of political thought. Aristotle, for example, while remaining very much an essentialist, did include in his *Politics* extensive knowledge of Greek city-states, but the approach has been, in general, to assume that the word stands for a special entity the elements of which never change. This is most obviously true of Plato's *Republic*, in which existing empirical states are regarded as merely pale reflections of an ideally ordered polity which exists in the mind of the philosopher.

The concept of the state has also been elucidated, or perhaps distorted, by some famous analogies. Most notable was the analogy made between the state and living organisms. In the *organic* theory the state was described as a special sort of 'thing' which existed over and above the individuals in a social order. These *teleological* theories of the state supposed that the state had an end or purpose which was different from, and superior to, the ends or purposes of individual citizens. Such theories exemplify the doctrine of methodological collectivism, a doctrine that presupposes that collective words like 'class' or 'society' stand for real entities.

In the organic theory the state is thought to evolve naturally. It is also thought to be entitled to some special reverence, in some cases unlimited obligation, from its citizens, normally on the ground that the institutions of the state represent a set of moral values superior to the self-regarding actions of ordinary individuals. In its most extravagant form, in the philosophy of Hegel, the state becomes the 'march of God on earth' representing order, permanence and legality and standing over and above 'civil society' which is characterised by individualism and self-regarding action (Hegel, 1942, pp. 160–223). In the absence of the neutral arbiter, the state, civil society would be chaotic. Since in Hegel's theory there can be no limits to the authority of the state, it is not surprising that in that same theory the state should find its highest expression in war.

A diluted version of the organic theory can be found in the political philosophy of the English Idealist, T. H. Green (1941). By identifying the state with the 'common good' and opposing that concept to the competitive individualism of the utilitarians (from Bentham), Green could justify a wider role for the state; for example, it could legitimately regulate factory hours and place limitations on the freedom of individuals to make contracts. While Green himself limited the state to the establishment of the conditions for the 'good life', rather than the creation of the good life itself, his teaching spawned a generation of social philosophers who were convinced that the traditional liberal doctrines of individualism and competition within the framework of general rules were destructive of social harmony and collective values.[1]

While the organic theories of the state appear to grant that institution, by definition, almost unlimited powers which, from a liberal point of view, would mean the abolition of individuality, a rival theory, by a similar verbal sleight of hand, necessarily reduces the state to a minimal role. In this, liberal theory, the state is defined exclusively in terms of coercion and therefore is restricted to the role of law enforcement through its monopoly of coercive power. The state is strongly contrasted with society on the ground of its involuntary character.

There are many versions of the liberal theory. It is often associated with some versions of the social contract theory, most notably that of Locke, which envisage, either hypothetically or actually, individuals unanimously agreeing to set up certain central institutions with limited powers of protection and law enforcement. The state has no purpose beyond the purposes of the individuals who create it; the state is bound by natural law, and citizens always retain a right of resistance against it. The most well-known version of this limited state theory is probably the 'nightwatchman' philosophy of the state found in nineteenth-century *laissez-faire* economic theories. As we shall show (see Section 3) this type of theory is undergoing something of a revival at the moment and some extremely sophisticated theories, which entail a severely limited role for the state, have been produced by economists in the last twenty years.

The common objection to those sorts of theories was that by defining the state solely in terms of coercion, and society in terms of voluntary action, they excluded two possiblities. First, that the state may not simply act coercively, that is maintain law and order, but may act in a non-coercive manner. The state's delivery of *welfare* services is given as a typical example of this. Secondly, a definition of the state solely in terms of its monopoly of coercive power ignores the fact that other institutions in society may be as coercive towards individuals. Of course, many theorists would argue that the 'welfare state' is a coercive state, because it can only finance its services by taxation, and also that many institutions in society that appear to be as involuntary as the state, such as churches and trade unions, are only so because of special privileges conferred upon them by the state.

In fact the liberal theory of the state did spotlight one key element in the account of the state – that is, its coercive aspect – but it was deficient in a number of ways. The account of the state as a purely coercive institution is peculiarly sketchy in that it does not tell us much about the relationship between law and state, the nature of the state's rules or how states emerge. It tells us very little, in fact, about existing states. Furthermore, it really was a prescriptive account of the state, which recommended that states ought to be limited to the law and order function, disguised as a definition. There may be a sound case for a limited state but this has to be established by theoretical argument; it cannot be asserted as part of the definition of the state. There is also the argument of the genuine anarchist (that the state with a monopoly of coercive power cannot be justified on any grounds), which has not been refuted by the liberal theory, and which must be considered in any account of the state.

Most of the theories of the state that are found in the history of political thought are prescriptions of what the state should do rather than descriptions of the state as an institution. It is true that all the interesting theories of the state are indeed theories of the ends of government action but before we can consider these the basic features of the state must be described in a non-ideological manner.

This analysis will not, however, presuppose that the word state stands for an unchanging entity, neither will it dispute the claim that there can be politics outside the state. It will, however, suggest that a purely *behavioural* political analysis that attempts to explain all political phenomena in terms of 'systems' and 'processes' is deficient to the extent that it fails to emphasise the special significance of the institution of the state in the modern world.

We can understand some of the properties of the state by trying to imagine what social life would be like without it. The first thing to note is that the absence of the state would not mean the absence of rules, though Hobbes thought otherwise.[2] In the absence of a state the breach of a rule would not mean that the 'public' had been harmed but only that a person had been harmed. That person would be entitled to take appropriate action under the rules to seek compensation for the harm done. In tribal societies which have not developed specialised state institutions there would not be a 'police power' to protect the public generally against rule-breakers. There may be a variety of methods by which a person may seek restitution for a wrong suffered and in a tribal society such methods are likely to be *decentralised* to individuals and kin groups. Therefore the rules that operate in stateless societies are basically private rules governing the relationships between people who are bound together by common ties of kinship. There are no *public* rules that authorise officials to enforce sanctions or permit a centralised court system to make authoritative decisions on disputed questions of the rules (Gluckman, 1965, ch. 3). While it would be wrong to overemphasise the presence of vendettas, feuds and persistent acts of vengeance in stateless societies, it is not difficult to understand that those things will occur in a society without a centralised police function.

In a modern, complex society with a state organisation, acts of robbery, violence, murder and so on are not regarded only as harms to individuals but also as acts against society or the 'public'. It is the responsibility of the state to take appropriate action against those who commit these rule-breaches, and, while that function may be delegated to subordinate bodies under public rules, it cannot be decentralised to private individuals or organisations.

Of course, the liberal theorists of limited government would restrict the role of the state to enforcing those basic rules which prohibit acts of violence and other sorts of unfair and fraudulent actions against individuals. There would be little need for the state to create new laws in this field since the liberal believes that a legal system will spontaneously develop a common framework of general rules to govern individual relationships independently of the state. While the state will enforce these basic compulsory rules, which forbid certain courses of action, it will leave the bulk of social and economic relationships to be governed by non-compulsory rules of civil law where its only role is to provide a unified court system to settle disputes.

One measure of the extent of the state's authority is indeed the volume of 'compulsory' law. It is *logically* possible, even in modern complex societies, to envisage the complete removal of the state. If, for example, two individuals were involved in a motor accident in a stateless modern society, the dispute would centre entirely on the question of liability for damage, which is a private matter between the individuals. There would be no question of the state being involved by way of prosecution for dangerous driving, etc. The same logic could apply to more obvious cases of crime such as violence and robbery, protection against which could be secured through private arrangements, with insurance companies perhaps, without the need for the state's monopoly. However, the development of the state has meant that a range of actions, which in stateless societies are purely private in character, are now thought to have a public dimension. Whether this can provide an adequate justification for the state is, however, another matter.

The first two features of the state which we can identify then are the *public* nature of its rules and the fact of the *centralisation* of its authority. The fact that the state acts publicly does not of course imply that the state acts in the public interest: it could certainly be argued that the state generally acts in the interests of particular classes or groups, but this only implies that certain sorts of action have a public aspect and therefore cannot be settled by private negotiation between individuals. Also, the fact that the state is a centralised institution does not imply that particular states do not vary considerably in the extent of their centralisation; compare East Germany with the United States of America.

There are other features of the state, the most important being the fact that the state possesses determinate geographical boundaries. This means that once a particular territory has been marked out by boundaries as a 'state' then the nature of the rules that govern social relationships changes. In a tribal society without a formal state apparatus the rules apply only to the members of the tribe or social grouping. The range of application of the rules is a function of the social ties that bind individuals together and not a function of geographical area. But the laws of a modern state apply to whoever happens to be within the boundaries of the geographical area and not merely to the indigenous population.

It is often suggested that sovereignty is a necessary feature of the state; indeed the modern history of Western Europe is often written as the history of the rise of the sovereign state. The United Nations Organisation is said to be composed of sovereign states. However, it is not easy to see the significance of the concept of sovereignty for the political theorist. States cannot be uniquely identified in terms of sovereignty, if that is defined in terms of unlimited legal authority, since this is a most misleading way of looking at legal – political systems. With regard to their relationship with individuals, states vary a great deal. In federal systems, such as the United States, sovereignty is deliberately divided between the component states and the federal organs, and the use of the word sovereignty seems to have little or no descriptive value. In all states where the actions of officials of the state are subject to established rules and bills of rights, the traditional notion of sovereignty seems to be irrelevant.

Even in the international sphere the phrase 'sovereign state' may be equally unilluminating. To call a state sovereign does not imply that it cannot incur obligations under international law. On entering the European Economic Community in 1973, the United Kingdom to some extent accepted the superiority of law which emanates from international institutions over domestic legislation. Of course the United Kingdom, by an exercise of sovereignty in a political sense, could leave that organisation, but this does not affect the fact that up to that point the state is very much bound by laws not directly of its own making.

It is logically possible that international law in Europe might develop in such a way as seriously to undermine the structure of independent 'sovereign' states. Some liberals may very well envisage Europe as a kind of utopia characterised by very general rules of conduct which guarantee all the traditional economic and civil liberties, and which would virtually end the monopoly power that individual states have over their citizens. A modern secular version of the medieval Christian commonwealth may very well emerge. However, it is just as likely that the rules that emanate from European institutions may not be general, and may be as coercive as those of present nation-states. In which case the features of existing states will have merely reappeared on a much larger scale.

It should be clear that those features of the state that we have singled out for consideration, namely, geographical integrity, public nature of the rules, centralisation and the monopoly of coercive power, do not constitute the elements of an essentialist *definition* of the state. As has often been pointed out, the claim to possess a monopoly of coercive power may not be realised in practice, as, for example, the British have found out in Northern Ireland. It is also said that other organisations in society may be as compulsory and coercive as the state itself, and trade unions are often given as an example. However, this should not lead us to say that the state does not have distinctive features, because the coercive power that trade unions have is often a result of privileges granted by the state – something that could not have happened under a developing system of private law. Perhaps the only 'necessary' conditions for the existence of a state seem to be geographical integrity and the machinery for the making of some public rules. But states can continue for long periods either with their boundaries in dispute, or with less than universal acceptance of their rules, or both.

It is most important that an analysis of the distinctive features of the state should not mislead us into thinking that it is an entity with a 'will' of its own which is superior to that of its citizens. There is indeed a tradition of state-worship in the history of political thought which we have already discussed. The acts of the state, however, are always the acts of officials authorised by the rules of the state and the ends of the state are always the ends of the individuals and groups that use its machinery. Our account of the state is 'neutral' in that it does not identify the institution with any special purpose. The state is no more than a set of rules, and while it is perfectly legitimate to criticise those rules on moral or other grounds, the danger of anthropomorphic accounts of the state must be avoided.

We normally make a distinction between state and government on the ground that the word state in certain propositions cannot be replaced by the word government without some considerable loss in meaning (Robinson, 1964, pp. 168–73). The institutions of the state are clearly not the same thing as the 'government'. However, when we speak in the economic sphere of the extent of state control we can just as well speak of the role of government since in both cases we are normally talking about the relative merits of *public* or *private* control of economic matters. In such disputes the argument must be conducted in terms of principles which are not themselves contained in the definition of the word state. Nothing, in other words, follows about what the state ought to do, from the account of the meaning of the word state.

In fact, the range of state activities has developed significantly this century in Western democracies with little contribution from political philosophers in the way of *theory* which might justify such an extension of the public sphere. There has certainly been no systematic analysis of the question as to whether the collective (state) delivery of certain goods and services is superior to their private production and even less of the question of whether the state as a collective institution can properly be said to express individual preferences. Too often in the history of political thought the state has been presented as a special kind of entity and the relationship between the ends of the state and those of individuals never fully explained.

It was certainly assumed that the actions of the state must necessarily be for the common good in contrast to private, economic transactions which were thought to be purely self-regarding. It was not realised that the state can only act through its officials and that there can be no guarantee that such officials, either elected or appointed, will not be governed by the same motives as private individuals. If they are so governed then it does not at all follow that the state will represent the 'common good'.

A less metaphysical justification for state intervention in the economic sphere appeared in the 1930s when the basic premise of liberal economics, that unhampered market economics would tend towards the full employment of all resources, seemed to be belied by the experience of mass unemployement. For the first time a theory of centralised economic decision-making appeared, Keynesian macroeconomics, which did not depend upon a special kind of definition of the state but which could be explained in terms of economic science. Furthermore, the Keynesian demand-management policies that were designed to regulate the ups and downs in economic activity after the Second World War were accompanied in many Western countries by the state delivery of health and welfare services which severely undermined the concept of individual responsibility characteristic of nineteenth-century liberalism. In fact in the United States of America especially, and to some extent in Britain, the meaning of liberalism has significantly changed. The new 'liberal' theory of the state has now come to embody collectivist notions quite alien to the liberalism of Adam Smith and his successors.

The justification for the new liberal-collectivist state has never been systematically propounded but it might take two forms. One justification would appear to be purely paternalist; that is, individuals cannot be trusted to spend their incomes on such desirable things as health, pensions and general welfare services through private insurance schemes, so the state – that is, its officials – has to do it for them through the tax system. This enables some theorists to proclaim that the state does not necessarily act coercively and that there can be a 'welfare' state. But it is often forgotten that the foundations of the welfare state rest inevitably on coercion; not only through the tax system itself but also because the uniform, collective delivery of welfare services removes consumer choice. The real question is, therefore, whether this coercion can be justified.

The second justification of increased state activity might turn upon the argument that the state ought to implement certain values. The value most often invoked is that of equality. We shall consider the concept of equality more thoroughly in Chapter 7 but its place in the analysis of the role of the state may be considered briefly here.

The argument for the collective, public delivery of welfare services is that it is required because access to those services is unequal. An egalitarian health service, for example, is said to be required because in the modern state every person is entitled to equality of service in health matters, making due allowances for unequal treatment that different cases will require.

It does not follow, however, that the equality principle itself justifies the collective delivery of the health good by the state. Two people could agree on the undesirability of inequality but differ profoundly on the question of whether the health good should be delivered publicly, that is, by the officials of the organised state using the coercive instrument of taxation. An egalitarian might very well argue that wealth ought to be redistributed to eradicate substantial inequality but that people should be free to spend their incomes as they wish so that there would be little need for collective state activity. This approach would of course involve the use of the coercive instrument of taxation to effect the required distribution but it would not involve an extension of the state's authority beyond this.

The anti-statist view implied here derives from the objection to large bureaucracies that inevitably occur with the state delivery of goods and

services, from the rejection of the assumption that public officials necessarily maximise the public interest, and from evidence that suggests that
the state spends a smaller proportion of GNP on health and welfare
services than would be spent by individuals in their private capacities
(Harris and Seldon, 1979). This is not to say that there are not good
arguments for state action in certain fields but only to suggest that the
question of the limits of state authority is not always a question about
ultimate values, as so many political philosophers have implied, but the
different problem of the comparison between advantages and disadvantages of public and private production of goods and services. It is true that
the majority of socialists have thought that the belief that equality ought to
be maximised does entail an increase in the activities of some form of
collective authority, if not that of the traditional state, but this is not
necessarily so.[3]

The gap in the political theory literature on the role of the state has been
filled in recent years by some sophisticated work by political economists.
But before considering this some attention must be paid to those traditions
of political theorising that explicitly refute the legitimacy of the state and
maintain that it is not essential for even a modern, complex society.
Anti-state theories are, and have been, either radical socialist or radical
individualist – capitalist and both will now be analysed.

## 3. Two types of anarchism

### *Marxism*

Given that all countries that call themselves Marxist exhibit a remarkable
degree of coercive state activity, in the form explained in the preceding
section, it is perhaps surprising to find a strong anarchist streak in
Marxism. It is represented in Marx's famous prophecy that the state, in
the sense of the police, the judicial and political institutions and the armed
forces, would one day 'wither away' so that individuals would freely
order their lives without the threat of coercion. The fact that existing
Communist regimes are characterised by the complete dominance of
public law over private law, so that almost every individual act may be
interpreted as in some way affecting the state and therefore requiring
public regulation, requires some explanation in the context of Marxist
theory.

There are really two Marxist explanations of the state: one sees the state
as an executive committee of the ruling class, defined in economic terms,

which exercises force in order to preserve the economic power of that class (Engels, 1968a); the other sees the state as a kind of specialised institution with the function of maintaining order and keeping the conflict between groups and classes in civil society within reasonable bounds (Marx, 1977).

The first and more familiar account of the state can be described briefly. This theory of the state as an instrument of class oppression first arose as an essential element in Marx's critique of Hegel. Hegel's conception of the modern state placed this institution above the conflict of civil society in that it embodied law, justice and impartiality. Civil society was defined in terms of the social and economic relationships between egoistic individuals while the state was a special entity above social conflict which represented the highest level of the historical development of reason and morality.

Against this abstraction of the state from society, Marx puts the state squarely into the context of class conflict. The state, along with morality, religion and so on, is part of the 'superstructure' of society and is a product of the economic base or substructure of society. As the economic base of society changes through historical development, the institutions in the superstructure change. Thus in the feudal world, characterised by an economic base with an underdeveloped form of the division of labour, the state was an absolute monarchy. The state in advanced capitalist societies is a liberal democracy. In both cases the machinery of the state is exclusively in the hands of the dominant economic class, that is, the class that owns the means of production. It uses the system of coercion to maintain the existing set of property laws. In bourgeois society the laws ensure that the non-owning class, the proletariat, has the surplus of wealth it creates through the industrial process appropriated by capitalist owners.

This theory that the state merely represents class interests and enforces class laws applies also to the socialist state which is to emerge after the collapse of bourgeois capitalism. The socialist state is to be coercive but this time its coercion is to be exercised on behalf of the majority in society and directed towards eliminating the remaining elements of the bourgeois system of law and economy. The elimination of the bourgeois class means there will be no classes, and therefore no state. The gradual withering away of the state will mark the transition from socialism to Communism. For Marx this will be a genuine type of anarchy, the details of which are not fully explained. But unlike European anarchists of his time (Tucker, 1970, ch. 3) he thought that the abolition of the bourgeois state would not lead to Communism because the economic system of private property, money and the division of labour – which threw up that state – has to be abolished first.

In this view of the state as a purely coercive institution the phrase 'welfare state' must be a contradiction in terms. Furthermore, any positive role for the state in the development of the economy is precluded since, in the theory, the elements of the superstructure are determined by changes in the economic substructure. Yet in the Soviet Union the coercive machinery of the state was used to transform the country from a feudal economic system to an industrial system and it has survived the liquidation of the bourgeoisie (Meyer, 1962, ch. 9).

It appears that Marx makes no analytical distinction between law and state since the abolition of the bourgeois state includes the abolition of the private law which governs a commercial society and which, according to Marxism, entrenches the fundamental division between those who own property and those who do not. Presumably, the change in human nature that accompanies change of circumstance will obviate the need for law. This seems to put Marx into the same category as the 'romantic' anarchists who believe that the abolition of the state entails the abolition of private property and the law that protects it. The removal of state, law and property, it is thought, will bring forth individuals who will conduct their relationships through spontaneous co-operative activities rather than the following of general rules. This distinguishes them from the libertarian anarchists (see pp. 60–3) for whom the abolition of the state means the abolition of the institution with a *monopoly* of coercive power; law and property, of course, would survive.

Marx, while stressing the coercive nature of the state, did not thereby disclaim the importance of political action through state machinery. Workers should press for improvements in living conditions brought about through politics and implemented by the state system. But such measures could be no more than palliatives; while useful in themselves they could not change the nature of the state. This could only come about through revolutionary action.

The second view of the state that appears in the Marxist literature is that of a functional agency which does not necessarily represent any particular class, although it will inevitably develop into a class interest, but which is required for the reconciliation of class antagonisms. In fact Marx does suggest that there have been historical examples of the state and its officials becoming an independent class, not defined in economic terms, and, in a sense, living off the productive activities of other classes in society. There is some similarity between this view of the state and that of the libertarian anarchists who would criticise the state not only on the ground of its monopoly of coercion but also because its bureaucracy exploits the productive private economy (Rothbard, 1970).

Modern Marxist accounts of the state are usually critiques of modern capitalist societies rather than descriptions of a future Marxist stateless society. In the discussion of the capitalist state it is no longer regarded purely as an instrument of bourgeois domination. It would be odd to do so since in the last fifty years there has been an inexorable rise in state spending, much of it on social welfare, which has been largely generated by working-class demands. Furthermore, since in most countries the law has explicitly protected organised labour from certain sorts of legal action and granted trade unions other privileges, it would be absurd to describe the whole structure of bourgeois law as an instrument of capitalist domination.

Marxists would probably not deny that the rules of the state do represent some kind of autonomy and that, while in the long run the state will reflect the interests of capitalist owners, it is possible for the instruments of the state to be used to advance working-class aims. Again, while arguing that the working class has to use *political* power against the economic power of capital, Marxists would deny that the machinery of the liberal-democratic state, free elections, universal suffrage, the free press, and so on is adequate to overcome the inequalities of power represented by the market system.

Marxists would claim that an increase in state expenditure has occurred because the capitalist class has used the state to preserve the market system which might have otherwise collapsed under its 'internal contradictions'. Keynesian demand-management policies, which are supposed to prevent depressions, may be cited as an example of this. Also modern defence policies, which are a major cause of high state spending, involve the state and big business very closely so that many large firms depend on state contracts for survival (Foley, 1978, p. 226).

However, Marxists do not see any prospect of a reduction in state power and indeed recommend the use of political and state power for the achievement of their ends. It is certainly true that the advancement of socialism throughout the world has brought with it an unparalleled growth of the state. We seem to have moved a long way from the romantic anarchist's utopia of a self-regulating society with no need for the coercive power of the state.

However, there is an anarchist tradition in political thought which is as anti-state as Marx, and perhaps more so, yet which is firmly rooted in the individualist tradition. The intellectual foundations of this anti-statism could not be more different from Marxism.

### Anarcho-capitalism

The theory of anarchism which derives from liberal individualism has received little attention in comparison with the romantic anarchism that derives from Marxism or related collectivist political philosophies. This is surprising since the connection between nineteenth-century *laissez-faire* economics (from which contemporary libertarianism derives) and genuine anarchism would appear to be closer than any other social doctrine. The doctrine of *laissez-faire* holds that free exchanges between individuals and the untrammeled operation of market forces will produce a more efficient economic order than collectivist intervention. It maintains that there are no social or collective ends over and above individual ends (and is therefore thoroughly in the tradition of methodological individualism) and that the state should be strictly limited to those activities – normally defence, law and order and the minimum of public works – which are not automatically produced by individual action (Friedman, 1962). The state has no income of its own and therefore to finance collective activities it must use the coercive power of taxation, which is not only a threat to economic efficiency but also a great danger to individual liberty. In the words of Frederic Bastiat, the state is 'the great fictitious entity by which everyone seeks to live at the expense of everyone else' (1964, p. 144).

Anarcho-capitalists go even further than this. So great is the threat to liberty, in their view, that even the minimal state, because it has a *monopoly* of coercive power, is morally unacceptable (Rothbard, 1973). While each individual is under a moral obligation to follow moral law – that is, he must not abrogate the personal and property rights of other individuals through force or fraud – there is no moral obligation to obey the state, whose officials, through their monopoly of coercive power, will abrogate his personal and property rights. The claim that the state is justified because it provides the collective good of protection is rejected on the ground that private firms would provide protection, on insurance system principles, and generate a court or arbitration system to settle disputes.

The argument of anarcho-capitalism is especially directed against those theories that claim that the state either develops spontaneously without being specifically intended, as for example the institution of money is often said to have developed, or is the product of a voluntary agreement amongst individuals. In all cases the state, because it has a monopoly of coercive power, is illegitimate and arises only from violence. There is a tradition in political theory that the creation of states is a product of either external or internal aggression: the history of the emergence of European states would seem to confirm this.

The argument that individuals construct the state to protect their rights because of the excessive costs of the private defence of those rights is rejected by anarcho-capitalists. First, they maintain that there is nothing about the protection good that makes it a 'natural monopoly': it could be delivered competitively. Secondly, they say that if a monopoly is granted to the state there can be no limits to the accretion of state power.

One recent justification of the minimal state is that contained in Robert Nozick's *Anarchy, State and Utopia* (1974). While most critics have discussed its *minimal* nature, that is, it is simply a protection agency with no legitimate authority to regulate the economy or promote social justice, anarcho-capitalists have heavily criticised Nozick's defence of the state itself.

Nozick claims that one can imagine the emergence of the state by a kind of 'invisible hand' process from a Lockean state of nature, in which each individual has fundamental rights. An 'invisible hand' process is one which produces a beneficial outcome for individuals in society, such as the efficient allocation of resources in a market economy, even though it is not the specific intention of any individual (Nozick, 1974, pp. 18–22). In Nozick's scheme the state, with a monopoly of coercive power, emerges from the state of nature through stages. In the first instance a number of agencies compete in the delivery of the protection good, but because of the nature of the good – a kind of natural monopoly – one dominant protection agency will emerge. The *ultraminimal* state emerges when the dominant protective agency excludes other defence agencies from operating within its area. However, it provides protection at this stage only to those who have paid for it and becomes a *minimal* state when it provides protection for those who would not pay for the service themselves (Nozick, 1974, pp. 26–8). This process takes place, it is maintained, without the violation of anybody's rights. The minimal state is justified in prohibiting 'risky' activities, that is, the actions of rival defence agencies, because it *compensates* those who would undertake risky activities by providing protection free (Nozick, 1974, ch. 4).

The anarchist would deny that the Nozickean state is the product of an invisible hand that violates no one's rights. It can only exist through the forceful imposition of its will on individuals. Since in Nozick's scheme the essential feature is the *monopoly* of coercion possessed by the state, anarcho-capitalists claim that there is no limit on the transition from a minimal to a maximal state. It is true that Nozick's state contains none of the traditional apparatus of limited government, separation of powers and so on, and while Nozick claims that it is *illegitimate* for the state to go beyond protection, anarcho-capitalists would argue that his system cannot prevent this (Rothbard, 1977).

The libertarian anarchist's description of a stateless society may be very remote from political reality but it is interesting for the light it sheds on our understanding of the state. In a stateless society there would be a code of law, based on the fundamental premise that personal and property rights are inviolate. Firms would provide protection on the market, and it is claimed that, as in any other market, competition would reduce risk. In fact, the anarcho-capitalist claims that risks are increased enormously when the individual is at the mercy of a monopolistic state. The crucial feature of the stateless society is that it is entirely individualistic; there are no collective (state) goods or services. Those who could not purchase hospital care privately, for example, would have to rely upon charity. It is a central plank in the libertarian argument, for which there is some evidence, that the absence of coercive taxation would call forth a significant level of charitable donations.

One striking feature of the private government of a stateless society is the proposed solution to crime, or breaches of personal or property rights. There are no crimes against society or the public, since from the strict individualist's point of view there is no such thing as 'society'; therefore punishment would take the form of compensation paid to the victim of the crime. In some cases this might necessitate forced labour in order to secure compensation. The deterrence, or utilitarian, theory of punishment is obviously rejected by libertarian anarchists because it eliminates the individualistic nature of crime and varies punishment according to the supposed threat to 'society' that crimes bring.

While the ideal of a stateless society seems highly impracticable such theories are not merely idle speculations. In fact, they are more realistic than romantic anarchist utopias that depict a society without law, state or property, and do not require any change in the properties of human nature assumed by orthodox economics. There is nothing romantic about a theory with such a harsh retributive theory of punishment. But libertarian anarchists have never fully answered the charge that their system would generate private armies which could be as big a threat to the individual as the state. Anarcho-capitalism also depends upon people's agreement to a libertarian code of law.

However, it is important to note the historical examples of stateless societies existing under law and it is also crucial to stress the argument of the libertarian that non-collective methods of resource allocation maximise both efficiency and freedom. The libertarian would reject the state because of its threat to liberty irrespective of the question of efficiency, but there is a liberal-economic theory of the state which does consider the possibility that, under certain circumstances, the collective delivery of goods and services might be more efficient than a private one, and it is to this that we now turn.

## 4. The liberal-economic theory of the state

We have noticed that the political theory of the state is rather unsatisfactory in that when it comes to the question of the proper ambit of state authority, or the right mix of private and public activities, no coherent set of principles has been produced. Most theories have been metaphysical in that the state is celebrated as a special 'thing' that represents the 'common good' or some other value which is qualitatively superior to those individual values which are expressed through private choices. The economic theory of the state, however, is in principle individualist in a methodological sense. This means that it deals only with individual values and ends and denies that a collective entity can have a purpose apart from individual purposes. The economic theory presupposes that the state is a device for the production of goods which is to be used only when market transactions fail to deliver what individuals want. Of course, the tradition of liberal economics contains a number of different theories of state activity but they would all claim to be based on this individualistic premise (Baumol, 1965).

The liberal theory assumes that in a free market exchanges between individuals will lead to an efficient or optimal allocation of resources. The decentralised market system which enables individuals to maximise their utilities is the method by which that which is produced reflects that which is desired by consumers. In a free market, utility-maximising individuals will make gains from trade so that a market is efficient to the extent that all possibilities of exchange are exhausted. Political interference with the process causes inefficiency to the extent that it directs production away from that pattern of goods and services which would occur from the exchanges of individuals. Stark examples of this can be seen in state-directed economies where queues, shortages and of course black markets occur when production is directed towards the ends of the state managers rather than those of individuals.

The efficiency criterion of a market economy is called the Pareto-optimality criterion, after the Italian economist and sociologist, Vilfredo Pareto.[4] A situation is Pareto-optimal if no improvement can be made in the positions of individuals without making someone worse off. If further improvements would not make anyone worse off, then the position is sub-optimal and further gains from trade are possible. The Pareto criterion assumes only that an efficient allocation will occur through free exchange between individuals: it says nothing about the *initial* distribution of wealth amongst individuals. Since a Pareto-optimal outcome is possible from any given distribution of wealth, it has nothing logically to do with ethical principles of equality or social justice. A socialist could recommend that, on some moral ground, the state should equalise wealth and still adhere to the Pareto criterion from that point onwards. The argument of the liberal economist is that, given a particular distribution, and free individual choice, the state, as a matter of scientific demonstration, can only improve on the market in special circumstances. And it is here that the liberal theory of the state emerges.

Economists, following A. Pigou (1920), said there are special cases where the market may be inefficient in that it may not adequately reflect what people want: state action may therefore produce a Pareto-efficient outcome. This is in the fields of externalities and public goods. Actually both of these concepts are logically similar but it is convenient to separate them. An externality occurs when there is a difference between marginal private costs and marginal social costs in some activity. Thus, in the familiar example, a producer using the least-cost method of production may impose costs on the community at large by polluting the air and these costs do not appear in his profit-maximising calculus. But not all externalities are 'bads': some external effects of individual activity are positive, that is, they benefit the community at large without the producer of them being fully rewarded.

Public goods are really extreme cases of externality. A public good is normally defined as a good the consumption of which by one person does not reduce the amount available for others – it is non-rival in consumption. Obvious examples are defence, clean air and a system of law. A second property is non-excludability. The point is that once such goods are made available for one person they are made available for all. This means that it is impossible to prohibit someone from consuming the good who has not paid for it. In these circumstances individuals have no incentive to reveal their preferences so that in a market system it can never be known what the true demand is for a public good. This is what is known as the 'free rider' problem, and its existence means that in a free market public goods will be underproduced.

Notice here that education and health are not public goods, although they are provided at zero prices in welfare states, since they are not non-rival in consumption and it would be easy to eliminate free riders. However, some welfare economists have suggested that because they give positive externalities to the community at large, in addition to the benefits they give to individuals, they would be underproduced in a free market and this justifies state intervention. In fact, in this case the evidence is nearly all the other way, that is, underproduction tends to characterise the collective delivery of some welfare services (Buchanan, 1965).

The presence of externalities and public goods, then, provided the justification for state intervention for welfare economists of the 'Pigovian' school – a form of intervention which was justified not because of some external moral principle but because it was required to 'correct' and improve upon the market so as to approach more closely a Pareto-optimal allocation. The state, precisely because of the universality of its rules and its monopoly of coercion, could produce things which, although generally desired would not be produced privately. The kinds of intervention favoured by this school are subsidies (to prevent under production), taxes (to prevent external bads) and perhaps outright nationalisation. A further impetus to the justification of a greater role for the state comes from the recent concern that free markets will exhaust certain natural resources at a quicker rate than would be desired by individuals.

There has, however, been a recent important re-working of the liberal theory of the state and much of the above analysis is regarded by some liberal economists as highly dubious (Cheung, 1978). One major objection is that almost any piece of collective intervention can be smuggled in under the externality rubric. Since almost any individual action, even one's choice of clothes and hair-style, will have some positive or negative external effect, there are no limits to political intervention in personal choice.

What has come to be known as the 'Public Choice – Property Rights School' has challenged the foundations of the Pigovian tradition and in doing so it has re-written the liberal economic theory of the state.

First of all it has reconsidered the distinction between private and social cost. It is maintained that externalities such as pollution could be 'internalised' if there was an appropriate legal-political framework in which the parties could continue to transact until all gains from trade were realised. That is to say, questions of smoky chimneys could be settled by legal claims in which persons whose property was damaged would receive compensation. The need for state action in the form of taxes and subsidies to produce an optimal outcome would therefore be removed if individuals were able to conduct voluntary negotiations within the context of a known legal framework. The trouble with government action is that it is likely itself to be inefficient – since government officials do not have the same incentive to be as informed as private individuals – and it is also likely to 'attenuate' property rights, that is, through restrictive laws to reduce the opportunities for individuals to trade in property rights.[5]

The objection to using the coercive method of taxation to deal with external diseconomies is that such action invades the property rights of the person taxed. In the familiar case of pollution, for example, to impose a tax on the polluter is to harm him. The question then concerns who has the right to harm. In fact Ronald Coase (1960), one of the pioneers in this field, argued that if transaction costs are zero and income effects are not relevant (that is, if different income levels do not affect the pattern of demand), then an efficient allocation of resources is possible whatever the distribution of property rights. Thus under these conditions, which allow individuals through negotiation to make gains from trade in the presence of externalities, most externalities can be internalised without state intervention.

It is true, however, that transaction costs are unlikely to be zero, especially when large numbers are involved. It is very difficult for people who are affected by pollution of the atmosphere to combine to take the appropriate action against factory owners. Furthermore, the distribution of property rights may be said to have an effect on the outcome of an economic process in that the wealth (and perhaps social power) of minorities may enable them to persist in imposing externalities on others which may only be removable by political action. Some members of the Public Choice – Property Rights School do seem to regard the present distribution of property rights as inviolable (Furniss, 1978, pp. 402–3).

The essentials of the type of state action recommended by this brand of economic liberalism are worth elaborating. The point is that it is not the role of the state to establish some equilibrium by the appropriate taxes and subsidies but to specify a set of rules which govern property rights so that individuals can freely exchange with each other without imposing external costs. Since property is not just the possession of tangible goods but the right to use them in a certain way, the question as to what counts as property is an exceedingly complicated one. Does the house-owner near an airport own property in the quiet atmosphere which the noise of aircraft disturbs, and therefore should the aircraft companies have to buy up these rights?

According to the economic theory of the Public Choice – Property Rights School the state should be limited in its actions to improving upon the rules within which individual exchange takes place. A most important feature of the argument is that the actions of state officials are analysed by the utility-maximising apparatus used normally to explain the behaviour of entrepreneurs. Since public officials do not necessarily promote the public interest, and often act on behalf of private group interests, some devices are required in order to limit their actions to the production of genuine public goods (Buchanan, 1975, ch. 5 and 6). The favourite device of economic liberals is the *unanimity* rule by which everybody must agree to a proposal before it can be implemented. Since unanimity makes nobody worse off, it is regarded as the political equivalent of the Pareto criterion. There are, however, difficulties with this rule (see below, Chapter 10) and most economic liberals recommend modified versions of it.

The most important difference between the economist's theory of the extent of state activity and that of the political theorist should now be clear. The political theorist, when he is not a Marxist or an anarchist, regards the state as a special entity uniquely equipped to provide some particular social advantage sanctioned by an external moral principle. We have said very little about this approach in this chapter because we shall be concerned with it in later chapters, particularly Chapters 6 and 7. The economist, however, regards the state as no more than a device for transmitting the preferences of its individual members – an approach consistent with methodological individualism. This does not preclude the economist from arguing that the present distribution of wealth is morally wrong but it would tend to make him sceptical of the claim that an increase in state activity in the delivery of goods and services is the best way of solving this problem. Experience of the predatory modern state, and the sophistication of the economic approach, suggest that a theory of state activity based on individualistic premises is likely to be the most fruitful in the future.

# 4

# Authority and Power

## 1. Authority, power and coercion

A major difficulty with the analysis of authority and power is that while they appear to describe different phenomena, and social theorists have been at pains to stress that they indeed do, they can often be used interchangeably in ways that mask the differences. Normally people want to describe authority relationships in terms of 'legitimacy' and 'rightfulness', and power relationships in terms of the causal factors that enable one person, or group of persons, to determine the actions of others. But also we speak of, say, police or governmental authority when 'power' would do just as well. When social scientists research into 'community power structures', they are engaged in trying to determine power in the causal sense, but they are clearly not studying the kind of power exercised by the Mafia. It is, perhaps, this permissive aspect of ordinary language which has led to the frequent identification of power with authority so that they both appear as types of causal influence, albeit operating rather differently, and seem to be a threat to rationality and liberty.

It is important, though, to keep the distinction clearly in mind not only for analytical rigour but also in order to appreciate the differing explanatory concepts in social science. To elucidate the distinction between authority and power it might be helpful to suggest that the former is a philosophical concept while the latter is sociological. To ask questions about somebody in authority is, in essence, to ask a normative question about the right of that person to give orders, or to make pronouncements or decisions under a set of rules, although it may be possible to speak of instances of authority not grounded upon specific rules. Notice that the language used to describe authority is entirely prescriptive. As J. R. Lucas (1966, p. 16) says, 'a man has authority if it follows from his saying "let $x$ happen"', that $x$ ought to happen'. It is true that if authority is to be effective, and if authoritative laws are to be obeyed, then certain sociological conditions will have to be met, but to establish a claim to authority is to meet certain criteria of legitimacy, not to satisfy criteria of efficacy. Whether someone is in authority or not cannot be established by mere observation of his success in getting his way. But we shall see that authority is not always used philosophically and that some theorists treat it in a more sociological way so that it differs from power only in degree.

However, questions about power in society are more clearly sociological questions in which observation is, of course, highly relevant. To speak of a power relationship is implicitly to give a prediction of future behaviour derived from a purported causal explanation. Therefore the validity of a statement about power turns not upon the question of rules but on the adequacy of the causal theory which attempts to predict what person, or group, will prevail in social decision-making. It is the purpose of social scientists who are engaged in empirical studies of political decision-making to find out who wields power in society. The phrases used in these empirical studies bring home the full force of this distinctive feature of power, even though there has been little agreement amongst the investigators on what a correct theory of power would be like. When sociologists talk of a 'power elite' in a political community they must mean, at least implicitly, that over a given range of issues a particular group – which can be identified by some set of observable, empirical characteristics – will dominate. The question of whether the group's decisions are right or 'authoritative' is not relevant to the question of whether the group is able to get its way.

To distinguish the notion of power by reference to causation and prediction, and contrast this with the prescriptive use of the word authority, is not to deny that the exercise of power may be perfectly legitimate. While the ordinary citizen is likely to respond to the authority of the policeman, a criminal may very well only be restrained by the policeman's power. When we speak of the 'power' of the Prime Minister, the Cabinet or Parliament, we may say that it is too great, perhaps in the sense that the actions of political leaders and public officials limit too severely the private choices of individuals, but such power, although it is causal, is certainly legitimate in the way that the power of a bank-robber is not. But it is true that the political official and the bank-robber are able to cause people to act in desired ways because they have coercion at their disposal. It is because of this that despite the differences between power and authority, which can be seen by analysis, the two concepts do seem to occupy the same ground in some familiar social and political situations.

As we shall see below, an *authoritarian* state is one in which the free choices of individuals are severely limited by the commands of the authorities – commands which affect the individual in an almost entirely causal way.

There are, nevertheless, pejorative overtones which can be detected in the use of the word power. It is presented as the currency of politics and in political studies the focus of attention on power relationships is thought to indicate a suitably 'realistic' approach. The idea that the behaviour of political actors cannot be limited by rules derives, in modern times, from Machiavelli's *The Prince*, which is perhaps the most famous essay on the mechanics of power. It can be read as a specific refutation of the medieval notion that the Christian Commonwealth is ordered by a body of natural law which underlies the authority of the rulers, and which prescribes moral limitations on the actions of everybody. The modern realists who see politics as the pursuit of power and social order entirely as a product of threats may be considered, not inaccurately, as the heirs of the Machiavellian tradition.[1]

However, it is fairly easy to show the importance of authority for the understanding of social affairs without appealing to a metaphysical conception of natural law. It is quite clear that the explanation of the continuity and cohesion of society cannot be explained entirely, if indeed it can be properly explained at all, by reference to power alone. What characterises continuity in social relations is surely some agreement about social values so that there are 'right ways of doing things' and authoritative procedures. It is true, of course, that the need for someone in authority to make binding decisions arises because men cannot agree on all things, but nevertheless, the acceptance of this presupposes some minimal agreement on social procedures, if not social ends. In revolutionary situations, the power or *ability* to bring about desired actions in others may properly describe the behaviour of the ruler, but this can only be temporary. If the social order is to survive then power must become authority, if only to economise on the resources that have to be expended on the army, police and so on. But even when order does depend upon threats there must be some semblance of legitimacy, if only to guarantee the loyalty of the army. This is what Hume meant when he said that governors depend upon *opinion* since force is always on the side of the masses.

The soldan of Egypt or the Emperor of Rome might drive his harmless subjects like brute beasts against their sentiments and inclination. But he must, at least, have led his mamelukes or praetorian bands, like men, by their opinion. (Aiken, 1948, p. 307)

Indeed, one of the indications that authority has broken down in society is evidence of an increase in the use of power that has to be made in order to get people to obey. It is part of the 'philosophical' conception of a social science to show that a greater understanding of social regularities can be derived from the explanation of authority, which describes the internal aspects of behaviour, than from the study of power, which merely reveals the *external*, observable aspects of society, such as decision-making in political and economic affairs.

Another way of bringing out the particular significance of power is to contrast it with exchange. By exchange we simply mean a voluntary act between two or more people that, because it is free and uncoerced, puts them in a preferred position to not making the exchange. The economist in explaining how resources are allocated in a free exchange economy has no use for the concept of power precisely because in his model actions are a product of choices not of threats of sanctions. When he explains the effect of a price change on the pattern of demand he is deducing what will happen, given certain elementary assumptions about human nature, and not making observations in the manner of a political sociologist. Theories of exchange are therefore highly general, and their truth does not depend upon observations in particular societies, while theories of power are particular, and rooted in specific, historical and social circumstances. This is only another way of saying that theories of power belong to the extreme positivist – empiricist branch of social science, even though they do not have to be, and in most cases are not, historicist.

There is, however, a possible objection to this distinction between exchange and power. This treats the power relationship itself as explicable in exchange terms (Barry, 1976, pp. 67–101). Thus, if *A* has power over *B* in the sense of being able to determine his actions by threats, it might still be maintained that the relationship is one of exchange since *B* could, technically, have acted otherwise. Since somebody who obeys through fear of sanctions is making a choice it is logically possible to treat these types of power relationships with the same 'logic of choice' apparatus that is used in formal economics. But from the political theorist's point of view this masks some important distinctions. Somebody whose freedom of choice is limited by the threat of sanctions has to that extent had his will determined by another, whereas someone who exchanges with another without such threats exercises his will autonomously. It is of the essence of power relationships that they involve the diminution of liberty, but this is not normally a characteristic of exchange. To the extent that exchange takes place within a context of authoritative rules, freedom and authority may not be incompatible. However, while this form of authority may be compatible with liberty it is quite likely that other types of authority relationships are not. As we shall see below, we have the notion of the 'authoritarian' state to describe that situation where legitimately-constituted authorities make severe inroads into individual liberty.

We have not considered the relationship between power and coercion (or force), but clearly these are analytically distinct concepts even though they are frequently used together. Authority and power are different ways of securing obedience, getting things done and so on, and while it is true that the *threat* of coercion is one of the most important bases of power, coercion itself is not the same as power. Coercion, or the exercise of superior force, signifies the absence of power and the failure of threats to put *B* in the power of *A*. While in most cases the threat of force will be sufficient to secure obedience this is not necessarily so, as can be seen in the cases of people with strong religious or moral beliefs refusing to submit to overwhelming force.

Thomas Hobbes, the seventeenth-century English philosopher, was acutely aware of this even though his major work in political theory, *Leviathan*, is often taken, erroneously, to be a justification of a 'might is right' doctrine. Hobbes distinguished between political power and physical power (or power over things). The former indicates a genuine social relationship, such that *A* is able to secure obedience from *B*: even though such obedience may be obtained because of the threat of overwhelming sanctions, it nevertheless rests upon a form of consent. It is not therefore the mere existence of coercion that creates power but the fact that people are sufficiently motivated, albeit through fear, to obey 'voluntarily'. For this reason, Hobbes is able to say that 'sovereignty by acquisition' – that is, by conquest – has exactly the same consequences as sovereignty by contract – that is, by agreement between individuals. Hobbes put the point thus:

> It is not therefore the victory, that giveth the right of dominion over the vanquished, but his own covenant. Nor is he obliged because he is conquered . . . but because he cometh in and submitteth to the victor. (1968, pp. 255–6)

Political power is a circular, or relational, concept and its existence presupposes some interaction between the parties in conflict.

In contrast, physical power – or as we might say, force – is the exercise of coercion when there is no submission. A person who shoots another does not have power over that person, although the fact that he does this may be sufficient to give him power over *others*. Of course, the exercise of coercion may enable the coercer to get what he wants. The highwayman may kill his victim and make off with the money but it would be extremely odd to say that this has anything to do with power. It is for this reason that Hobbes had little interest in 'physical power' for, unlike political power, this concept has little explanatory value.

It follows from this analysis that it is false to say that power increases positively with an increase in the amount of coercion. The Americans in Vietnam were able to deliver massive coercion but this obviously did not give them power. In fact, the United States of America's involvement in Vietnam was characterised by the absence of power despite their possession of the instruments of coercion.

A modern analysis, however, would depart significantly from that of Hobbes on one crucial point. Hobbes is saying that since all power rests ultimately on consent it must be the same as authority. If a person through fear consents to obey then he is the *author* of all the acts of the sovereign (Hobbes, 1968, p. 232), and consent through fear is for Hobbes just as voluntary as an uncoerced promise or agreement. All the acts of a sovereign are authorised by his subjects. The phrase 'abuse of power' is therefore meaningless since all power is legitimate. Hobbes of course had good reasons for saying this. He thought that continuity and social cohesion were products of political power and could not conceive of the 'natural' evolution of laws and institutions providing stability without there being an observable sovereign.

Modern political theory distinguishes between power and authority by reference to the way obedience is secured. The existence of a person, or body of persons, in authority suggests that obedience is secured by other means than threats and implies that the exercise of authority is a product of rules. Furthermore, it is maintained that continuity and stability cannot be guaranteed by power alone, although this will characterise temporary moments in a society's development such as revolutions and *coups d' état*. In fact Hobbes himself had great difficulty in explaining the transmission of political power without reference to rules which exist independently of the sovereign.

## 2. The nature of authority

While political theorists may agree that there are important differences between authority and power, there is very little agreement as to the nature of authority itself. Some interpret all cases of authority as in some sense dependent upon rules and on the notion of 'rightfulness'. This is to say that authority relationships cannot simply be matters of command and obedience but must involve ideas of rationality and criticism. Others, however, suggest that authority must involve the suspension of rationality, and indeed freedom, such that obedience to authority cannot be consistent with rational criticism.

The modern discussion of authority begins with the German sociologist Max Weber's classification of the types of authority (1947, pp. 324–9). Weber distinguished between rational – legal authority, traditional authority and charismatic authority. Rational – legal authority is characteristic of the modern, industrial, bureaucratic state in which those entitled to make orders and pronouncements do so because of impersonal rules, the existence of which can be justified on more or less rational grounds. In traditional authority, unwritten but internally binding rules, the explanation of which is historical rather than rational, entitle individuals to obedience. The authority of the tribal chief is an instance of this. Charismatic authority, however, appears to be unrelated to rules, but is explained in terms of some *personal* quality that an individual may have which entitles him to obedience. The standard examples of charismatic authority are Jesus and Napoleon; more recent examples might be Hitler or de Gaulle.

Weber presented these types of authority as 'ideal' types essential for social analysis rather than exact descriptions of reality. Most societies will in fact exhibit elements of all three types although one is likely to be predominant. Modern Britain, for example, which might be thought to be characterised by a rational – legal structure of authority, certainly contains elements of traditional authority.

It may be the case that all of Weber's types of authority are reducible to a variety of rule-governed notions of authority. This of course would entail the elimination of charismatic authority as a special type of authority. Some writers have indeed maintained that the idea of charisma is meaningless outside a set of rules that in some sense authorises an individual, and as a necessary consequence limits what he can do in the way of making orders. Such rules would then provide grounds for the rational criticism of his actions. It would indeed be difficult to maintain that an individual could exercise authority solely because of some kind of personal magnetism. It has been pointed out that all the suggested examples of charismatic authority were successful in so far as their actions were in some way related to an ongoing set of traditional rules – even if their actions may have in some sense involved departures from the rules (Winch, 1967, pp. 107–8). It may be possible to explain cases of charismatic authority by the application of 'tests' and these tests will reflect standards of appropriate behaviour which are independent of the suggested charismatic leader.

Weber was more interested in sociological investigations into types of authority than in a philosophical analysis of the concept. Much of this analysis of *authority* itself turns upon a proposed distinction between *de facto* and *de jure* authority. Authority *de jure* means that someone is entitled to obedience because of a rule – although it is to be noted that *de jure* authority may not always be effective. Authority *de facto* exists where someone is able to get his way without either a ground or entitlement and yet without recourse to threats. While it is true that authority can be exercised in this way, the notion of *de facto* authority is difficult to grasp without the notion of a ground or entitlement creeping in, though this does not have to be a legal ground or entitlement. Peters's example (1967, p. 84) of *de facto* authority, the man in the cinema fire who directs people out of the building without having any right to do so, hardly seems good enough.

If the *de facto* concept of authority is to be any use in social theory it must surely describe situations of a more or less permanent kind rather than temporary crises. A more likely candidate would be the position of the gang-leader who is able to exercise continuing authority over his followers and whose survival largely depends upon their agreement. Yet this seems to be at some remove from pure *de facto* authority in that the more successful the gang-leader is the more he will become entitled to be obeyed by his followers. It would not be too inaccurate to describe the kind of authority exercised in this instance as quasi-legal. While it is suggested that there is a use for the concept of authority outside the framework of rules, that concept seems peculiarly difficult to pin down and seems to contribute little to our understanding of the role that authority plays in explaining the unity and cohesion of a society.

Difficult though it is to find any real agreement amongst social and political theorists as to the meaning of authority, it is clear that the concept has a variety of uses. We speak of parental authority, military authority, political authority and 'moral' authority. Melancholy books on political philosophy proclaim the 'collapse of authority' in the modern world. A familiar and important distinction is made between someone 'in authority' and 'an authority' (Peters, 1967, pp. 86–7). We say that someone is in authority when he is authorised to give orders and has a right to be obeyed. Here it is not what someone does or says that entitles him to obedience but the fact of his authoritative position in a social practice. Apart from obvious legal examples, parents and teachers may be said to be clear cases of people in authority. Someone who is *an* authority, however, is entitled to obedience not because of who he is but because of some special skill or knowledge of a particular matter, and it is therefore the content of what he says that determines his authority.

The easiest cases of people being in authority are provided by the rules of a legal system which authorise certain individuals to make decisions. The kind of authority here is that exercised by policemen, officials of the legal system, ministers and so on. Such individuals are in authority by rules but it is, of course, legitimate to ask what makes these rules authoritative. As we have seen in the theory of law, in any legal system, beyond the very simple type, there will be secondary rules that authorise people to adjudicate on and alter rules, amongst other things. The authority to make new laws even in a system of parliamentary sovereignty depends ultimately on a secondary rule which cannot logically be a product of Parliament itself. We cannot, in legal contexts, make sense of someone being in authority without the concept of secondary rules. But cases of being in authority are not exhausted by the legal system and it is quite permissible to speak of someone being in authority where the authority is not a product of legal rules but is a product of moral or religious rules, for example, in the case of a parent or a priest.

Many writers would maintain that while it is true that men need authorities because of the inevitability of conflict over interests and values, the acceptance of authority involves an abandonment of individual rational judgement. Peters (1967, pp. 94–5) argues that authority relationships are unlike scientific and moral relationships because they specifically do not depend upon reason and argument. The orders of someone entitled to make decisions do not depend upon rational justification in the way that moral and scientific theories do. Similarly, the greater the area of an individual's life that is covered by authority the less freedom he has; freedom and authority are then antithetical. It is curious that the word authority has both favourable and unfavourable connotations. In contrast with power, authority suggests rightfulness and legitimacy while at the same time its exercise implies a loss of liberty.

Other writers deny that the existence of authority implies a loss of reason and maintain that authority is never simply a matter of issuing commands but always involves an action for which reasons can be given. C. J. Friedrich argues that authority involves reasoning and says that this is not the reasoning of mathematics and logic but 'the reasoning which relates actions to opinions and beliefs, and opinions and beliefs to values, however defined' (1973, p. 172). He argues that any social system involves the communication of values and beliefs, and these values and beliefs constitute the basis of authority. Thus the actions of authority can be said to be subject to rational appraisal although, of course, this rationality will not be of an absolute kind. He says that those who sever the link between authority and reason confuse authority with totalitarianism.

However, it probably is the case that those who tie authority and rationality closely together are confusing political authority with authority in general. It seems to be in the nature of the modern state that its actions, although they may be supportable in principle by rational argument, affect people rather differently from other sorts of authority. It is the case that the state, or rather its officials, have the *right*, at least in the positive sense of right, to tax, conscript and coerce in other ways, but this is a very different sense of right action from that suggested by Friedrich. The distinguishing feature of the state's authority is, of course, its use of sanctions and this is very different from the authority of, say, a priest.

It might be said that those who respond to the state's actions through fear of sanctions are responding to power rather than authority, in the way that a criminal who is arrested by a policeman is moved by power rather than authority. But if this is so then critics of the state would say that it *typically* acts in this manner, thereby denying it legitimacy. Those who maintain that the state still acts by authority seem then committed to linking authority with coercion. This of course opens up the whole question of political obligation. It surely cannot be maintained that merely living within a state's borders, and therefore under its rules, implies an acceptance of its authority. By the same token many of the state's actions necessarily imply a loss of individual liberty. It is true that because men cannot agree upon the ends which a society should pursue they need authorities to make decisions when individual ends conflict: this explains the existence of political authority. A question about political authority is not the same thing as a question about political power (it would not be about measurement and prediction), but this type of authority is clearly different from others in that its exercise seems necessarily to limit individual liberty.

It is undoubtedly the strength of the modern state, and its mode of operation, that has given rise to a view amongst some political theorists that there has been a 'loss' of authority in the modern world. It is not always clear what this means but it might be exemplified by the decline of the moral authority that used to be exercised by churches, parents and others, so that individuals are in a sense thrown back on their own resources without the guidance of traditional standards. More importantly, the fact that on many occasions in the twentieth century political rulers have acted tyrannically, and have in many cases done so with mass approval, supports the view that societies are no longer held together by authority. Hannah Arendt (1961) was of the opinion that this was indeed so and that the collapse of authority in the modern world preceded totalitarianism. In her view genuine authority cannot conflict with liberty and liberals are therefore wrong in thinking that a loss of authority leads to a gain in liberty. 'Authoritarianism' ought not to have the pejorative overtones that it undoubtedly has and many governments classified as authoritarian she would call totalitarian. In fact, traditional liberals would say only that a fall in *political* authority increases liberty; they would not deny the dependence of liberty on general, authoritative rules of conduct.

There is a good reason for making a different distinction between authoritarianism and totalitarianism – one that does not depend upon a rarefied account of authority. Some political theorists would argue that an increase in political authority does entail diminution of individual liberty but does so in a significantly different way from totalitarianism. They would not, of course, approve of either.

In this view authoritarian government severely limits the range of choices open to the individual without at the same time postulating any ends for society at large. Thus in this 'law and order' model, characteristic of military regimes, an individual may have to conform only outwardly to certain dictates; he is not required to display any ideological support for the authorities. In fact, regimes of this type may have no grand design or overall purpose for society beyond the maintenance of stability. Such authoritarian regimes may be compatible with a considerable degree of individual liberty in certain specified areas provided that such free action does not pose a threat to what the authorities regard as law, order and social stability.[2]

By contrast, totalitarian regimes do not merely demand observance of the dictates of authority but require also a positive commitment to the ends and purposes of society. The difference between authoritarianism and totalitarianism then is not one of degree, in that the latter limits personal freedom more than the former, but rather that the two sorts of social order have different ends in view. A totalitarian regime is not simply concerned with stability but with the realisation of an ideology and with the inculcation of a new personality. Such a social order may, in theory at least, be compatible with a significant degree of participation, and certainly with positive displays of enthusiasm for its purposes.

These two sorts of social order may be contrasted by reference to the way that dissidents are treated in each. In an authoritarian society a dissident will be simply locked up, and the penalty, although it is likely to be harsh, may be fixed and known in advance. Under totalitarianism, however, a political law-breaker is often regarded as in some way mentally deranged in not appreciating the true purposes of society. He therefore requires 'treatment' rather than formal punishment. The consequences of dissidence may in fact be less harsh than in authoritarian societies and may be limited, in some cases, to public degradation and humiliation.

In practice, however, this theoretical distinction may not amount to much. Totalitarian democracies notoriously fail in their aims of creating a new 'man' and often are reduced to maintaining stability by harsh, repressive measures so that the ultimate ideological purposes of creating a new society are neglected. The histories of Marxist 'totalitarian democracies' seem to confirm this in that early ideological fervour eventually gives way to routinised *authoritarian* practice. Nevertheless, the distinction is worth retaining because it does point to some differences between the various forms of non-liberal rule and does indicate the logical possibility of the maintenance of a limited freedom of choice in purely authoritarian regimes.

## 3. The concept of power

Modern, empirically-minded political scientists have been interested in power precisely because it appears, in principle, that statements about power are eminently suited to observation and quantification – unlike statements about authority. Some theorists of power go even further and suggest that societies are somehow held together by the exercise of power, as if there has to be in every society some unique and determinate source of power. It would not be too inaccurate to interpret those theories as modern versions of that traditional doctrine in jurisprudence which holds that in every legal system 'sovereign power', or the ability to determine other men's actions, must reside somewhere. Contemporary 'power élite' theories are saying that whatever the formal structure of authority, the constitution and the system of rules, there is always a group of people who can actually get their way on a given range of issues. It is assumed to be the business of the social scientist to unravel the complexities of power in modern society.[3]

On the normative side of political theory power has been, in the main, interpreted either 'neutrally' or considered to be in principle undesirable. A neutral interpretation of power maintains that power in itself cannot be evaluated as good or evil but that such evaluation applies only to the uses to which it is put. The exercise of power to achieve desirable goals in society is not thought to be of itself reprehensible. Of course, the persuasiveness of this view depends upon a considerable amount of agreement on the proposed ends of society.

It is at this point that the normative critic of power would object. He would say that if there is this agreement about ends then power would not be needed at all to implement them, they would come about non-coercively. In other words, power can never be 'neutral'; every exercise of power involves the imposition of someone's values upon another. Hence 'liberal' critics of power recommend strict limits on the exercise of power whatever its source, including the 'uncorrupted people'. Doctrines such as the 'separation of powers' and constitutionalism in general are precisely concerned with the problem of curbing power. This is regarded as an impossibility by the 'sovereign power' theorists whether they are old-fashioned legal positivists or modern, quantitatively-minded sociologists.

We have already noticed the major differences between authority and power in the first part of this chapter and the problems associated with power can be explored further. We know that power relationships are a type of causal relationship in which one person, or a group of persons, can bring about certain actions in others and that, unlike in authority relationships, the determinants of these actions are such things as threats, sanctions, propaganda and psychological pressure. But it may be difficult to distinguish this phenomenon from, say, 'influence'. In fact, influence may be legitimately regarded as a type of power in that a person who is influenced to act in a certain way may be said to be caused so to act, even though an overt threat of sanctions will not be the motivating force.

In a famous definition Bertrand Russell said that power was the 'production of intended effects' (1938, p. 25) and while this clearly indicates an important aspect of power it misses a crucial feature of the concept. This is that the exercise of power in society always reduces the area of choice left open to individuals while not all cases of power as the production of intended effects involve this. Sometimes we do speak of someone having the power to produce certain effects which may not involve the loss of freedom to others (Partridge, 1963, p. 111). The peculiarly *social* significance of the exercise of power is that it limits the range of choices open to individuals. Power may also be intimately linked to the production of unintended effects. Some people may be said to have power over others, in the sense of determining their actions, without deliberately intending to do so, as perhaps a pop star may determine the dress and life-styles of his followers without specifically meaning to: although, it could be said that this is an example of influence rather than power. Some sociological theories of political power have, however, suggested that a group may exercise political power, perhaps because it has a *reputation* of power, without this being visible in a direct, intended way.

A more fruitful approach to the conceptual problem of power than the search for a watertight definition would be to consider some of the proposed explanations of the phenomenon. We know that it is not misleading to consider the exercise of power as being, in some sense, about the capacity of someone to determine another's actions and so to reduce the other's range of choice that his behaviour conforms to the will of the person who exercises the power, but the interesting question concerns just those factors that produce this. In other words, what are the social bases of power? In the final section of this chapter we shall consider some sociological *theories* of power but at this stage some general comments must be made on the kinds of social phenomena that generate power. There have been many suggested bases of power but three – the coercive, the psychological and the economic – are particularly important.

We have already considered some aspects of coercion when discussing Hobbes on power and undeniably this is the most important source of power. When we talk of military power we mean precisely that the ability to dispose of sanctions enables some to move others in desired directions. The power of the state similarly consists of the fact that it can induce obedience by threats, even though it may be denied that the state always acts in this way. As we said earlier, the important point to remember about coercion is that the power that emanates from this is still dependent ultimately on a kind of choice: since not all people choose to obey threats backed by sanctions, the possession of coercion does not automatically guarantee power. Power relationships that arise out of coercion are circular; there is no such thing as a 'lump' of power in the form of weaponry. Power which does emanate from coercion may either be legitimate, when it is the organised force of the state, or illegitimate, as for example, the power of the armed criminal is.

When we come to psychological power the circular aspects of power seem to diminish. We can undoubtedly speak of power in the sense of a person being psychologically caused to act in certain ways without having the very limited choice that exists in power by coercion. The clear cases of such psychological persuasion are brainwashing and other forms of indoctrination. Here one person is made the tool of another without there being overt sanctions. It would not be correct to use the word 'influence' here as it is not strong enough to bring out the crucial element of overwhelming pressure.

The difficulty with the psychological concept of power is that it can so easily be used to describe situations which fall well short of the clear case of brainwashing. It has been suggested that the 'persuasive powers' exercised by advertisers are significant enough to eliminate, or severely reduce, the freedom of consumers. Newspaper editors and proprietors are said to exercise power over their readers in a not dissimilar way, in that they can manipulate opinions and use propaganda so as to influence significantly the course of political and economic events. We speak frequently of the 'power of the press' in exactly this sense.

It is quite likely that the powers of these 'persuaders' have been greatly exaggerated. It would be extremely odd to liken advertising to brainwashing, because in the latter literally no freedom of choice is involved. Some advertising campaigns have been notoriously unsuccessful. In fact, the technique of the advertiser is to find out what people want and then to advertise the appropriate product rather than attempt to manipulate wants. It is, of course, extremely difficult to get convincing evidence of the ability of advertisers to exercise power in the manner that has been suggested. This applies equally to the power of the press. It could be said that newspaper 'propaganda' is simply an aspect of the continual process of persuasion that characterises an open society. All political leaders are involved in exactly the same activity, this being an essential part of liberal-democratic politics. Arguments about the power of the press to mould opinion are more convincing the nearer a *monopoly* is approached. The only genuine cases of a press monopoly are in totalitarian societies where the state completely controls access to information. In these cases press power should be at its peak but even here the evidence is that the state monopolies are by no means completely successful in moulding opinion.

A further area of social life where power may be said to be exercised without the explicit threat of sanctions is in the economy. The philosophical defenders of the free market economy maintain that this system is characterised by exchange, which is assumed to be voluntary; each party to an exchange puts himself in a preferred position by making the transaction. The particular virtues of an exchange process are that it allocates goods and services efficiently, in the sense of satisfying the desires of individuals as expressed by their preferences, and produces a social order that minimises power and maximises liberty. In fact, political power in the exchange model of society should only be used to produce those goods and services which, although generally desired, are not produced automatically by free markets. It is just this exchange philosophy that collectivists reject.

The collectivist argument – that the exchange process does not reduce power – is difficult to formulate precisely. It could mean that the *conditions* under which exchange takes place, that is, the prevailing system of property rights, are so unequal that they generate a system of *market power* which enables owners virtually to enslave non-owners. Or it could mean that there is something about exchange itself, under whatever conditions it takes place, that creates social and economic power.

The former argument is more plausible; it is possible to conceive of, and indeed demonstrate empirically, conditions under which market power exists. Inequality of wealth through inheritance, the concentration of industry and the exploitation of workers by monopoly may well give them little genuine choice in employment, especially in times of economic recession. Whether an employer who is able to dictate onerous terms to an employee can exercise power over him, and whether an employee suffers a loss of liberty when he has little alternative but to accept those terms, are difficult questions. While there are cases when this is so, and someone who is able to withhold a vital service from another constitutes a similar example of economic power, their incidence has probably been much exaggerated. The Marxist claim that the worker has only his 'labour power' to exchange, the surplus product of which is exploited by the employer, is a highly inaccurate description of the modern Western capitalist world in which labour organisations have used political power to alter significantly the terms under which exchange takes place. Furthermore, the existence of monopoly is quite often the product of government-sponsored privilege rather than the natural outcome of an exchange process. Finally, at the analytical level, the concept of power loses much of its descriptive force if it is applied indiscriminately to economic relationships.

The objection that exchange itself is a source, or type, of power is even more elusive. Perhaps its proponents mean to convey the idea that individual wants are not necessarily expressions of true desires but are exogenously determined by other factors. In this interpretation the psychological aspect of power is probably being drawn upon: it is claimed that individual wants can be manipulated by external pressures. If such theories are meant to be explanatory theories, they are extremely difficult to refute. Any want, however voluntarily expressed, can be said to be generated by external agents. At the heart of the objection to the exchange model is the metaphysical contention that its vision of man as a purely self-interested maximiser is a deficient concept of human nature. It is held that man does not realise his true powers through exchange since the process is entirely self-regarding. Instead of man realising his true potential as a social being, in that what he creates through co-operative activity becomes peculiarly his own, he becomes, under a market system, the prisoner of his ephemeral desires. This is what Marx probably meant by 'alienation'.

However undesirable certain aspects of the exchange process may be, and whatever the distribution of economic power is, it is not fully appreciated that to change this necessarily entails the use of another sort of power, political power. Therefore any consideration of the phenomenon of economic power must always take into account the costs that are inevitably incurred in the removal of that power. It is also true that to consider only the economic aspect of power is to ignore the point that power is a 'relational' concept. The possession of economic resources alone cannot generate power any more than the possession of the instruments of coercion can. There are far too many cases of the possession of wealth being insufficient to generate the obedience that we associate with power for the theory to be true.

## 4. Social theories of power

We suggested at the beginning of this chapter that power is essentially a sociological concept: statements about power are, in principle, statements that are testable. The definitions used by political scientists and sociologists in their studies of power are thought to be operationally significant in that they point to phenomena which are observable, and which can be explained by the traditional methods of empirical social science. It is to be noted that, in this respect, such studies of power as have been produced are of the extreme positivist kind. This means that the science of power consists almost entirely of empirical work based on particular case studies. There are no general theories of power or universally true generalisations about the phenomenon which have the logical coherence and explanatory significance of the theorems of economics. Of course, in the history of political and social thought it is possible to find a number of purported general theories of power but none of these has achieved any real scientific respectability.[4]

Theories of power are often divided into those that emanate from the political science discipline and those that come from sociology. This is a convenient distinction since, although both approaches might claim to be in the empiricist tradition, they have produced significantly different conclusions as to the nature of power. The sociological approach tends to stress the *centralisation* of power thesis, namely the theory that in every society there will be a small group that can dictate all major decisions. Political science has been associated with *pluralism*, the view that in society there is a number of influential political groups, not one of which can determine *all* decisions.

One of the most famous of the sociological models of power was C. Wright Mills's *The Power Elite* (1959). Mills claimed that the picture of the United States of America as a democratic pluralist society, characterised by decentralised decision-making and the separation of powers, was false. Beneath the veneer of constitutionality there was in reality a unified class or power élite which could always get its way on important decisions. The personnel of this élite were drawn from three interlocking elements in American society – business, politics and the military. The élite displayed group consciousness, coherence and implicit conspiracy. Mills claimed that his was a work of empirical sociology in that he thought he had identified certain key sociological factors underlying the cohesiveness of the group, such as identical family and class backgrounds and the fact that the members of the group were educated in similar schools and colleges. Mills presented a picture of élite group domination which belied the openness, pluralism and individualism traditionally descriptive of American society.

The pluralist reply to this turns mainly on methodological considerations. A sociological *description* of the properties that may unite a collection of people does not constitute a *theory* that predicts that the group will get its way on a given range of disputed decisions, where interests conflict. Political scientists of the pluralist school maintain that whenever power élite theories have been cast in a scientific form they have been easily refuted (Dahl, 1958; Polsby, 1963).

More sophisticated power élite theories have indeed accepted criticisms of the type of theory propounded by C. Wright Mills but they nevertheless maintain that the pluralist thesis itself is unsatisfactory and they insist that simple observations of political decision-making do not necessarily demonstrate the absence of a power élite. P. Bachrach and M. Baratz (1962) argued that there are 'two faces' of power: power is not only exercised in observable conflict situations but is also used to 'organise out' certain issues so that they are never part of the phenomena studied by the political scientist. The attention of the social scientist should be directed therefore as much to those areas of conflict which are suppressed by the operation of normal liberal-democratic politics as to those areas of decision-making where there are observable conflicts of interest.

Steven Lukes, in *Power: A Radical View* (1974), takes the latter analysis even further and suggests that power is also exercised in the manipulation of interests so that the absence of a conflict of interests does not necessarily mean that there is consensus. Powerful social forces, which are not revealed by the methodological individualist's analysis, determine people's interests and shape their wants. This, as Lukes readily admits, entails evaluative notions of 'power' and 'interests', and involves a 'contradiction between the interests of those exercising power and the *real interests* of those they exclude'. In other words the *subjective* interests which groups reveal in the political process are not the same as their objective or real interests because of the power and influence of dominant groups. Lukes maintains that this theory is, nevertheless, empirical and capable of refutation and indeed gives one example of how it illuminates a particular decision-making process (Lukes, 1974, pp. 42–5). However, it is difficult to see how a theory that rests upon a distinction between real and apparent interests could ever be falsified; almost anything could count as an 'objective' interest which is repressed by those who exercise power. It also depends on it being true that, for example, advertisers and the media are capable of moulding and determining wants, a proposition we have questioned earlier in this chapter.

# Part Two
# Values

# 5

# Political Principles

## 1. Political principles and political philosophy

In Part One we examined some of the major concepts used in the description of social and political phenomena. While we have touched upon some of the normative questions central to social and political philosophy, especially those to do with the nature and role of the state, we have done so without any explicit consideration of the principles that must underlie such questions.

Values and principles are the traditional concerns of the political philosopher. This is true if the activity of philosophising about politics is regarded as a purely second-order activity concerned with the clarification of the concepts used in political discourse or if, as is more often the case today, its major role lies in the evaluation of policies, law and institutions. In the latter case clarification is still an important exercise which must precede the (doubtless) more interesting task of justification.

Principles are peculiarly important in relation to the role of the state. In Chapter 3 we were mainly concerned with the task of elucidating some important differences between the notions of the *public* sphere and the *private* sphere and trying to see what specific institutional facts about the state made it peculiarly well equipped for the delivery of certain kinds of goods and services. But when we talk of the state in relation to principles we are asking a slightly different, although related, question. This is the question of the justification for the use of the state's authority to promote such things as equality and social justice or to protect human rights. Since principles are always likely to be in conflict, the philosophical arguments about politics will turn on the justification of the use of the state's coercive power to implement policies derived from these principles. Of course, not all questions of principle depend on the justification of the use of coercion: a person desiring a more liberal society, in the older sense of the word 'liberal' which is linked with free market economics, demands that the state use less of its coercive power. But this is itself a philosophical argument about the *illegitimacy* of the use of coercion; it is not necessarily an argument about the irrelevance of principles to political and social affairs.

If principles are intimately connected to justification then it should be immediately apparent that the logic of statements containing normative political principles is very different from the logic of other kinds of statements in the social sciences. In positive social science, especially that of the extreme empiricist kind, the emphasis is on those statements which can be established as true or false by the method of observation. Even in those aspects of social science that are less empirical, such as the theory of law and certain parts of economic theory, the investigator would deny that his explanations entail any particular normative viewpoint or policy prescription (although there is always some connection between science and policy in fully worked out social philosophies).

In arguing about politics, however, we are not proving and disproving, or verifying and falsifying: we are justifying a policy by reference to principles. While people often appear to disagree strongly about particular laws or policies, such disagreement may be resolved if the particular policy prescriptions prove, under analysis, to be inconsistent with sincerely held principles. It is said, however, that some political disputes may be genuinely irresolvable if there is dispute at the level of ultimate principles, because there is nothing beyond this to which the dispute can be referred. Not all political theorists would entirely agree with this last point and some of the most interesting recent work in the subject is at the level of ultimate principles.

## 2. Logical positivism and emotivism

We must now briefly examine the philosophical attack on the idea that principles have any relevance for political evaluation and justification. This stems from the revolution in philosophy which we have discussed earlier (see above, Chapter 1). As we saw there the Logical Positivists' simple criterion of meaning seemed to make rational argument in politics impossible. In fact most of the Logical Positivists' fire was directed at moral rather than political philosophy, but since the two disciplines in many respects share a common language – they are both concerned with such things as rights and duties, rules, principles and rational justification – a refutation of the one implies a refutation of the other.

The early Logical Positivists did not enquire much into the meaning of ethical or normative statements beyond the application of their criterion of meaning. If, as is clearly the case, normative statements are neither descriptive nor analytic, what are they? One school of thought known as 'emotivism', which followed on from the Logical Positivists and was highly influential for a brief period, offered an answer to this question. One or two aspects of this doctrine are important to political philosophy.

Emotivists distinguished between 'descriptive' and 'emotive' meaning. A word has descriptive meaning when it tells us something about the empirical world which can be verified. 'Emotive' meaning is that aspect of the word which excites favourable (or unfavourable) attitudes in the listener. Clearly many words in the political vocabulary are highly emotive in this sense. To describe a country as 'democratic' is not likely to convey much descriptive information about its form of government, since almost all countries these days call themselves democratic, yet it would indicate that the speaker approved of the country and hoped to persuade others to approve of it as well. Words in our political vocabulary have both descriptive and emotive elements.

The emotivists were non-cognitivists in that they argued that moral statements did not convey information about the world but were designed to alter attitudes and change behaviour. It is crucial to note that in this theory behaviour is not changed by *rational argument*, in which principles play a justificatory role, but by what amounts to pyschological pressure. To call an action 'obligatory', a policy 'good', or a distribution of income and wealth 'unjust' is not to say anything rational – since the normal rules of entailment which obtain between descriptive statements do not apply to statements designed to influence attitudes – but to engage in a propaganda exercise. If this theory is true then, in politics, the justification of a policy by reference to a principle is an irrational enterprise since principles are used only to act on people's feelings.

Contemporary political philosophers deny that normative arguments are as non-rational as the above views imply. While it is true that the desirability of principles cannot be proved empirically or demonstrated by *a priori* reasoning, it does not follow that policies and institutions cannot be appraised in terms of principles, or that the implications of holding principles cannot be explored. Furthermore, it has been shown that logical argument is possible *about* principles, even if people do disagree on the relative significance they attach to them. Principles are not necessarily propaganda devices, even though politicians may use them as such. There will of course always be some tension between political philosophy and politics in that the advocacy, and rational justification, of a policy in terms of a principle may be thought to be 'politically impossible' but this does not make the recommendation non-rational. One of the unfortunate consequences of the political realist's approach is precisely that it undermines the possibility of rational argument. One of the interesting tasks for the political theorist is to formulate appropriate institutional devices for the implementation of policy on the assumption that there is *some* agreement on principles. This will be a major concern of later chapters. At this point we must examine some of the familiar statements of the possibility of rational argument in politics. In the next section we discuss two different logical demonstrations of the nature of normative theorising and in the final three sections we consider some of the more substantive approaches to policy matters which occur frequently in philosophical arguments about politics.

## 3. Universalisability and ethical pluralism

The doctrine that the essential characteristic of principles is that they are universalisable is associated with the *prescriptivist* school in ethics but it is equally applicable to political principles. Recent important work in political philosophy relies implicitly (and in some cases explicitly) on this doctrine. Universalisability as a doctrine about the foundations of ethics is associated with the work of R. M. Hare (1963).

The basic elements of the theory can be briefly summarised. The main function of ethical statements is that they are recommendatory; they are, in other words, guides to action. Unlike propaganda and psychological persuasion, however, there are logical relationships between ethical statements. A genuine ethical statement must be universalisable. This means that if one calls $x$ good then all other similar cases of $x$ must be called good, unless they differ in some relevant respect. Universalisability, then, means that like cases must be treated alike. An example of universalisation appears in one version of the rules of justice, which states that 'people ought to be treated equally unless a morally relevant ground is produced for different treatment'. A person who commits himself to a moral principle commits himself, as a matter of logic, to the universal application of that rule in all similar cases. This, of course, means that you must apply the principle to yourself if, on some hypothetical occasion, your actions fall under it. Therefore moral rules and principles are abstract guides to conduct to apply to future unknown situations. This means that a principle would not be a moral principle if it contained proper names since then it would not be universalisable. Here is an important element of 'impartiality', in that one cannot exempt oneself from the application of a principle if the principle is to be universalisable. Rawls, in his famous derivation of the principles of justice (see Chapter 6, below) adopts a similar strategy when he tries to determine what principles would be adopted by rational moral agents to apply to future unknown situations under conditions of ignorance.

Hare, however, insists that universalisability is a logical feature of moral argument. It is not a substantive statement of impartiality, or fair treatment of individuals, because it is, as he says, logically possible to adopt any principles, as long as they can be universalised. Therefore moral argument for him is not deciding on principles because of their *content* but exploring the implications of holding whatever principles it is that we hold. Such explorations will take account of facts, since it is an empirical question as to what are similar cases, but moral argument itself is *deductive* in form (Hare, 1963, p. 30). An obligation to keep a promise, for example, cannot be derived from the fact of a promise alone but is deduced from this and the further premise that promises *ought* to be kept. Hare is therefore opposed to any kind of ethical naturalism, that is, the doctrine that words like 'good' stand for natural properties such as 'pleasure', since this undercuts the prescriptive, recommendatory force of moral argument.

The decision to adopt a moral principle is a personal decision for which no rational justification can be given, and there is no limit, in logic, on the kinds of moral principle which may be adopted. Since consistency is the main feature of moral argument, quite appalling principles may be adopted, but Hare thinks that people are unlikely to adopt principles which when universalised harm their own *interests* (1963, pp. 86–111). Thus, in his famous example, a Nazi who believed that Jews should be exterminated would have to accept (logically) that he, or his family, should be exterminated if it turned out that they had Jewish characteristics. We eliminate appalling moral principles by seeing what happens when they are universalised. Hare thinks that 'fanatics' – who would consistently support an appalling principle even if, when universalised, it would act against their own interests – are extremely rare (1963, p. 172).

It has been suggested that the universalisability thesis is trivial in that it is almost always possible to point to a difference in a situation which makes a principle inapplicable. To put it another way, the rule of justice which states that 'like cases be treated alike' may be consistent with a great variety of treatment, depending upon what are counted as similar cases.

However, the demand that moral argument be consistent is not trivial and may go a long way towards eliminating principles based purely on ignorance and prejudice. The universalisability thesis, since it asks us to adopt principles to apply to future unknown occasions, puts severe *practical* limits on the kind of principles that may be adopted. In Rawls's *A Theory of Justice*, rationally self-interested individuals, in an hypothetical state of ignorance, have to agree upon a set of principles to govern their future relationships. These principles are fully universalisable. In this procedure we have to imagine how a principle would affect us should we find ourselves in certain situations and the results of this enquiry have been shown to be far from trivial. Of course, Rawls's thesis is much stronger than the conventional universalisability thesis since he tries to show what principles would be adopted.

However, it would be quite wrong to suggest that universalisability has secured a victory over other types of normative theorising. Of its many rivals, one may be singled out for special treatment. This is the doctrine of ethical pluralism.

In describing this approach we must first distinguish the use of the word pluralism here from its use in a sociological sense to describe political activity as a process of adjustment between competing groups. In relation to principles, pluralism means that for the purpose of evaluating policy a *variety* of principles may be held: it is not possible to order or rank them under one supreme principle. Whether a particular policy is justified or not depends on how a person weights these competing principles. A person may value both freedom and equality and therefore, in considering the question of progressive income tax, for example, justification will depend on how he weights the value of the more egalitarian structure of earnings it brings about in comparison with the value of the freedom of the individual to retain earned income.

A clear statement of the ultimate plurality of values, and their irreducibility to one single principle, can be found in Sir Isaiah Berlin's *Two Concepts of Liberty*: 'Everything is what it is: liberty is liberty, not equality or fairness or justice or culture, or human happiness or a quiet conscience'. A loss of liberty may be compensated for by an increase in equality but it must be remembered that it is equality that has been increased, not another version of freedom, or even 'social utility' (Berlin, 1969, p. 125).

The most fully worked-out version of this approach is to be found in

Brian Barry's *Political Argument* (1965). In this important work Barry explained the rational basis of the pluralist approach to principles by an analogy with indifference curve theory in microeconomics. A person can show, by his preference map, that he is indifferent between various combinations of, say, liberty and equality, in exactly the same way as a housewife can be said to be indifferent between amounts of grapes and potatoes. The map will simply show how much liberty he is prepared to give up for increases in equality (it being assumed that principles are substitutable at the margin) and still remain equally satisfied. All that is required for rationality is that people be consistent in their choices.

Barry regards this pluralism as a reasonably accurate account of most people's attitudes towards principles. They are not normally *monists*, that is, they do not subordinate principles under one supreme principle but are prepared to make trade-offs at the margin. Perhaps the most controversial trade-off in political argument in the contemporary world is that between efficiency and equality. It is accepted that the aim of increasing equality in the distribution of income can only be secured by a loss in efficiency.

It is to be noted that in Barry's approach policies are related to people's wants. His most frequent examples are concerned with the conflict between policies that maximise total want-satisfaction in a community (aggregative principles) and those that distribute want-satisfaction in a certain way (by promoting more equality, for example). This is very different from the varieties of universalisation which ask us to adopt a set of principles to apply to future unknown occasions – when we are ignorant of *specific* wants and needs.

While pluralism has secured some considerable support amongst political theorists, and while it may also be a good *description* of the way people approach policy problems, it has serious drawbacks as an evaluative procedure. The problem is that individuals' weightings for various principles are likely to be dissimilar – that is, their indifference curves will be of different shapes – and there is no way of choosing between them. The rationality of individual consumers is easily demonstrated by this method, but the *justification* of government policy is quite another thing. The government must inevitably select one particular set of weightings when making policy and Barry offers no reason why any particular set should be preferred. It is no coincidence that advocates of both 'left' and 'right' economic policies can claim rationality for their programmes by the pluralist technique.

It is also the case that the rejection of this approach does not necessarily imply monism, as Barry (1973, p. 6) has conceded. Rawls offers a *set* of principles in his *A Theory of Justice* and by the use of a *priority rule* tries to demonstrate how the individual component principles will be ranked (see Chapter 6, below). Barry himself is curiously silent about the nature of ultimate principles and implies that they cannot really be argued about; rationality consists of making choices consistently from a given set with subjectively assigned weightings. Yet political theorists do maintain that some things can be said about them. Someone may weight equality very strongly and would therefore be prepared to sacrifice large amounts of liberty for small increases in equality, and here surely a question could be asked about the normally unintended *consequences* of adopting such a policy. Some notion of universalisability may very well be needed if arbitrariness is to be avoided in normative political theorising.

The above considerations have been about the 'meta-ethical' aspects of normative theorising. Meta-ethical questions are about the ultimate foundations, or logical status, of value judgements and answers to them do not entail any particular set of moral or political principles. To establish principles, additional arguments have to be advanced. Hare and Rawls's meta-ethical theories are not dissimilar, but while the former opts for a version of utilitarianism as his substantive moral theory, one of the latter's major concerns is to refute utilitarianism. In the analysis of some of the more important political concepts in succeeding chapters we shall consider both 'meta' and substantive questions. To conclude this chapter we must briefly summarise three important substantive political doctrines: utilitarianism, economic liberalism and collectivism.

## 4. Utilitarianism

This is superficially the most appealing of moral and political doctrines. Since it has always been concerned with the maximising of human happiness it seems free from the dogmatism of those alternative doctrines which stress the importance of following rules, even when the following of such rules might result in human misery. It is also a forward-looking doctrine concerned with bringing about future desirable states of affairs and is not concerned with putting right past wrongs. It has for this reason always attracted social reformers and progressive thinkers who often bring scientific techniques to the process of policy formulation. To this extent it is a 'rationalist' doctrine; its advocates believe that social problems are capable of scientific resolution and that social harmony can be engineered. But it would claim to be free from the narrow dogmatism of other ideologies, which are often designed to advance class interests, in that utilitarian judgements are made from the standpoint of the 'ideal' or impartial observer and are designed to advance the *general* interest. Utilitarianism is also said to be derived from individualistic premises.

In the past utilitarianism was a meta-ethical doctrine and a body of substantive principles. Utilitarians identified the 'good' with pleasure, and hence committed the 'naturalistic fallacy' (Moore, 1903). The most famous of them, John Stuart Mill, tried to demonstrate some sort of 'proof' of the utility principle. However, their significant achievements lay not in the foundations of ethical judgements but in the practical applications of those values in which they believed. Nowadays utilitarians are almost purely concerned with a kind of practical ethics and politics.

There is an important distinction between the utilitarian ethical doctrine, that a person ought to act so as to produce the general happiness (in the sense of beneficial consequences) on every possible occasion, and the economic, social and political doctrine which justifies government action, and therefore coercion, on the benevolence principle. Our main concern will be the economic and political doctrine since this was the primary interest of the classical utilitarians and the doctrine persists today mainly in this form. It is also important to note that the significance of utilitarianism does not lie merely in the fact that it evaluates human action, and political and social policy in general, in terms of its generally beneficial consequences (any ethical or political doctrine that did not pay very close attention to consequences would be severely deficient) but also in the very special way in which it interprets the notion of consequences. It assumes that society at large has a 'utility function', which is observable and measurable, and which consists of a sum of individual utility functions. To understand what this means we must go back to the founders of the doctrine.

Bentham provides us with the first systematic theory of utilitarianism: his basic ideas are formulated in *A Fragment on Government* (1948) and *An Introduction to the Principles of Morals and Legislation* (1970). Bentham's first aim was to found a 'science of ethics' based on some observable property in human action which could be maximised so that evaluation of action and policy did not depend on abstract, metaphysical principles which were purely subjective. An action was not right because it was in conformity with a rule of natural law: it was right only if it produced happiness. Pleasure, or happiness, was for Bentham the only good, and therefore actions and policies could only be evaluated by their *consequences*, in terms of the production of happiness.

Bentham is said to have attempted to combine two contradictory ideas in his ethical and political theory – utilitarianism and psychological egoism. He said that 'man is under the governance of two sovereign masters, *pain* and *pleasure*, it is for them alone to point out what we ought to do, as well as determine what we shall do'; this implies both that men ought to seek happiness (in fact, the *general* happiness) and that each person can do no other than seek his own happiness. It may be possible to say that under certain circumstances maximising the general interest by the individual also maximises his personal interest, but it has always been thought that there is considerable tension between utilitarianism and egoism. In fact Bentham did resolve the tension by providing each person with a motive to promote the general happiness through the sanctions of the law.

Bentham assumed that there was an objective property of pleasure attached to every action, so that the effectiveness of a policy could be measured by reference to how much pleasure (or pain) it produced for each individual. Pleasures varied only in quantity, and Bentham produced a 'felicific calculus' to show how pleasure could be measured in seven dimensions (1970, ch. iv). There was no *qualitative* distinction between different people's desires: no individual's desire had a prior claim to satisfaction on grounds of its supposed superior quality.

Furthermore, Bentham was a methodological individualist. Words like 'state' and 'society' were fictitious entities and statements containing them had to be broken down into statements about individual behaviour if they were to have any meaning. Thus the community's interest could only be an arithmetical sum of the interests of the individual members. An ideally informed legislator could, with the objective yardstick of pleasure, compute the effect of, say, policies $A$ and $B$ by assessing, with the aid of a felicific calculus, the net balance of pleasure over pain that each produced and implement that policy which yielded the highest amount of net pleasure. Pleasure was thought to be an objective measuring rod which tells how much better policy $A$ is compared to policy $B$ in exactly the same way that feet and inches, for example, enable us to compare the lengths of physical objects. In determining the policy for punishing criminals the legislator must fix penalties (pains) just sufficient to prevent future outbreaks of crime so that the community is thereby better off. Punishment must not, for example, be too excessive since this would inflict more pain on the offender than it would generate pleasures for the community. In this process questions of 'desert' and moral guilt are inadmissable since they are entirely subjective concepts.

The importance of *statute* law should now be apparent. While a legislator could derive a social utility function for the whole community from individual preferences, there was no guarantee that this would come about automatically since each individual could do no other than pursue his own pleasure. Therefore the sovereign, by the use of sanctions, had to generate artificially the coincidence between private and public interest. It is true that in economic matters Bentham believed that private actions would naturally lead to an optimal allocation of resources, and he was therefore an advocate of *laissez-faire*; but even here the logic seems to be that if the legislator could make an improvement on the private market there would be nothing in principle to prevent the use of command/statute law to bring this about. It is certainly the case that abstract concepts of individual liberty or rights, since they are not capable of being put on the utility scale, would not be allowed to stand in the way of the production of *social* utility.

It is not difficult to demonstrate some major deficiencies in this attempt to formulate a science of policy. Pleasure is not an objective property which can be summed up and put on a scale, so that policy $A$ can be said to yield so many more units of happiness than policy $B$. It is a *subjective* property inhering in each individual. The whole idea of a felicific calculus, by which pleasures can be measured on a unitary scale, is now regarded as being little short of absurd. But perhaps an even more decisive objection is the fact that the construction of the Benthamite 'social welfare' function requires that the ideal, fully-informed legislator be able to make interpersonal comparisons of utility. This means that to say that state of affairs $x$ is preferable (yields more utility) than state of affairs $y$ requires that there be some way of comparing the gains and losses to individuals that accrue through the implementation of the policy. To say that, for example, a tax policy is justified on utilitarian grounds requires that the pleasures of those who gain outweigh the pains of those who lose, in terms of utility – but there is no *scientific* way of making such a comparison.

An interesting attempt was made by later utilitarians, notably Edgeworth (1897), to justify scientifically progressive income tax. It was assumed that each individual's taste for money was the same and that if the law of diminishing marginal utility was true (that people experience decreasing marginal increases in satisfaction as the supply of a good is increased) then, by progressively transferring income from rich to poor, a legislator would be able to increase social utility. Thus an egalitarian tax policy could be justified scientifically without an appeal to the *moral* principle of equality. This was, however, a misapplication of the marginal utility principle. This principle is indispensable in explaining individual consumer behaviour in a market economy but it cannot be used as a basis for social policy because, without making an interpersonal comparison between the utilities of the rich and the poor man, we do not know whether the proposed income transfer will yield greater social utility. There can be no *scientific* basis for utilitarianism, even though utility comparisons may be made on other grounds. An egalitarian would presumably justify progressive income tax in terms of the political principle of social justice, ignoring the problem of the scientific adding and comparing of utilities.

It has often been pointed out that there is something almost totalitarian in classical utilitarianism. Despite its supposedly individualistic premises it does entail the imposition of a collective value judgement on society as a whole. If that cannot be derived from individual choices then it must emanate from the subjective will of the legislator. But if Bentham's psychological axiom is true, that every individual maximises his own utility, then the legislator will maximise his interests rather than social utility. In fact, Bentham was constantly aware of this problem. His first proposed solution was that a benevolent despot might implement the utilitarian utopia but later he was to argue that only a version of representative democracy would promote the general interest. This proposal will be considered in Chapter 10.

The Benthamite formula has also been severely criticised because in its original version it is easy to show that it is internally *incoherent*. We are told that the standard of value for a community is utility, or the Greatest Happiness of the Greatest Number, but as has frequently been observed, this is capable of at least two interpretations. Are we to maximise the greatest possible amount of happiness or distribute happiness in such a way that it is enjoyed by the greatest possible number of people? The following example illustrates the way in which the two aims of utilitarianism can be in conflict. Consider two utilitarian policies, *A* and *B*:

|  | *Policy A* | *Policy B* |
|---|---|---|
| *Person one* | 60 units of happiness | 30 units of happiness |
| *Person two* | 50 units of happiness | 30 units of happiness |
| *Person three* | 0 units of happiness | 40 units of happiness |
|  | 110 | 100 |

Under policy *A* more happiness is produced than under policy *B*, but in the latter more people enjoy happiness. The point is that utilitarianism does not give a *determinate* solution to policy problems and therefore loses its claim to superiority over its rivals. In fact, it is probably the case that Bentham himself interpreted the Greatest Happiness principle in an *aggregative* sense (that is, policy ought to be aimed at producing the greatest total happiness), and abandoned his own quasi-distributive criterion (the greatest number principle). This is how utilitarianism is normally interpreted today, and it is certainly a more consistent view, but it is still open to the very serious objection that, because it is solely concerned with consequences in terms of the production of beneficence, it obliterates some important elements in our moral and political vocabulary, namely equality, justice and rights.

Critics of the purely aggregative aspects of utilitarianism often point to some rather disturbing implications of the doctrine. Does not its deterrence theory of punishment sanction 'punishing' an innocent person, if that is the only way that others can be effectively deterred from committing crimes? On the assumption that interpersonal comparisons of utility can be made, does not utilitarianism allow slavery if the satisfactions of the slave-holders outweigh the pains of the slaves? In a popular example we are asked to imagine a healthy person going into a hospital ward where there are three patients, one requiring a heart transplant and the others kidney transplants. Does not utilitarianism require that the healthy person be made to give up his organs, as this would clearly bring about the Greatest Happiness of the Greatest Number? While utilitarians might justifiably claim that these are rather fanciful examples, they do indicate the clear deficiencies of a doctrine that is concerned solely with maximising future, collective want-satisfaction.

The most famous utilitarian, John Stuart Mill, was deeply disturbed by Bentham's concern with *mere* want-satisfaction as the sole criterion of political and moral value. In *On Liberty* he appeared to suggest that freedom of action was a value in itself irrespective of its contribution to utility in a simple quantitative sense. Indeed, in *Utilitarianism*, he undermined the foundations of the doctrine by drawing his notorious distinction between 'higher' and 'lower' pleasures. By this Mill meant that certain activities were of a higher quality than others even if they appeared to yield lesser units of happiness in a quantitative sense. Desires for intellectual contemplation, scientific and artistic enquiry and so on, therefore have a claim to satisfaction in a utilitarian society, and their value cannot be assessed by the crude hedonistic calculus. Mill insisted that the satisfaction of such elevated desires was consistent with utility, but it was a 'broadened' utility 'grounded upon the interests of man as a progressive being' (1974, p. 70). The pursuit of higher pleasures would yield more satisfactions in the long run.

We can see considerations not unlike those of Mill at work in some areas of public policy, notably in tax-funded aid for the arts. If a local authority subsidises the prices of theatre or opera seats it is in effect selecting particular wants, out of the whole range of individual wants, for preferential treatment, since without such aid the intensity of wants felt by opera and theatre-goers would not be sufficient to keep the activities going. Such subsidies would be quite inconsistent with pure Benthamism.

Mill's ideas certainly represent a more 'civilised' version of utilitarianism and his commitment to personal freedom (see below, Chapter 8) qualifies him for admission to the broader liberal tradition. But he failed to solve the problem of the conflict between utility and justice. Although he claimed that a properly articulated conception of utility would include considerations of justice and distribution, such a conception is in fact so broad as to be vacuous and can offer little or no guidance for the problems of policy.

Some contemporary utilitarians have developed the doctrine of *rule-utilitarianism* to counter some of the traditional objections to their views, and have contrasted it with *act-utilitarianism* (see Mabbott, 1956; Lyons, 1965; Smart and Williams, 1973). Act-utilitarianism means that morality requires the individual to act, on every occasion, so as to maximise the sum of human happiness. This means that moral rules, such as the rules of justice and promise-keeping, are provisional only and may be breached if the strict adherence to them would diminish the sum of human happiness. Act-utilitarianism is normally addressed to those *deontological* ethical theories that define morality as the strict following of moral rules for their own sake. Often such theories prescribe the following of moral rules which may cause great suffering. An act-utilitarian like Bentham would say that there was no rational foundation for the principles of deontological ethics; they depend on intuition.

It is easy to think of examples which lend a superficial plausibility to act-utilitarianism. There are many occasions when to tell a lie (for example, to a Hitler or a Stalin) would actually increase human happiness, and when to enforce rigidly the rules of justice, in some types of criminal cases, would be quite gratuitous. It is also true that a morality, the rules of which bore no close relationship to human needs and wants, would have little to recommend it. But these rather trivial observations do not save act-utilitarianism from the main charges levelled against it.

As a moral doctrine it licenses individuals to determine for themselves the likely consequences of actions, yet no individual can ever know these consequences (Hayek, 1976, pp. 17–23). It is because of this ignorance that men develop rules to guide their conduct so that they do not have to estimate the probable consequences of various courses of action on every occasion.

In a political and economic sense, which is after all the sense that interested the traditional utilitarians, the consequences of a thorough going act-utilitarianism are likely to be even more suspect. It seems to grant governments the discretion to act on behalf of what they think is the general interest. Since a Benthamite demonstration of the general interest requires the summing up and interpersonal comparison of individual utilities, its implementation involves considerable arbitrariness. Yet act-utilitarianism would seem to exclude binding constitutional rules which limit arbitrariness. The Benthamite system, characterised by sovereignty and statute law, does grant the legislator great discretion. But the two great problems here are first, the impossibility of the legislator calculating and comparing the consequences of alternative policies, and secondly, the design of procedures to ensure that the legislator will promote the general interest rather than his own.

Rule-utilitarianism evaluates not the consequences of particular acts but the consequences of following rules. General rules, such as promise-keeping, telling the truth and the rules of justice, are justified on utilitarian grounds. Thus the breach of a rule, which might produce an increase in happiness, would not be tolerated because it is the following of rules themselves that contributes to human welfare.

This is the kind of utilitarianism that Hume had in mind. While stressing the importance of rules it does not found them upon 'intuition' or an abstract metaphysic that is not related to human wants and social survival. In the Humean model rules are not so much planned and designed but develop almost spontaneously, and men adopt and retain those rules that prove to be useful. The rules of justice were not rationally demonstrated from an abstract notion of a 'social contract' but emerged as devices by which individuals could make their relationships predictable

(Aiken, 1948, pp. 42–69). Thus rules acquire a validity which is independent of immediate consequences but is linked with utility and welfare in the long run.

Though this is more plausible, it is difficult to see what it has to do with orthodox utilitarianism. First, there is no attempt to define some utility function or collective welfare statement for the whole community; the rules, although they are justified by reference to consequences, do not embody any collective end at all. Secondly, and following on from the first point, there is no attempt to measure utility at all. Thirdly, rule-utilitarians are sceptical of discretion, either at the personal or the political level. This has provoked the charge that rule-utilitarians are 'rule-worshippers'.

## 5. Economic liberalism

Many of the main features of the economic liberal's approach to problems of evaluation stand in some contrast with the utilitarians, especially those of the Benthamite type. Yet the odd thing is that utilitarians and economic liberals are almost invariably bracketed together. This is because both schools are associated with free market economics. However, this is about all they have in common and even this common feature requires careful explanation.

The first thing to note is that economic liberals are genuine individualists and they explicitly deny that collective judgements about the welfare of society can be derived from individual preferences. If this is the case then there is no such thing as social utility and economic liberals would accuse Benthamites of a certain kind of collectivism in their attempt to implement social utility by statute law. While there is such a thing as the public interest, in the sense of there being laws and institutions which are to the advantage of every person, there is no such thing as a collective interest which is a summation of individual interests. It is for this reason that economic liberals prefer the common law, which protects private interests, rather than statute law, which is often used to advance public purposes.

In a very important sense economic liberals deny the relevance of some principles for evaluation, because they wish to limit the area of social life subject to politicial coercion to an absolute minimum. Other political philosophers often justify the use of such coercion precisely by reference to political values. Economic liberals maintain that where men do disagree on ultimate values there is no rational way of resolving the dispute but they claim that such occurrences are rare and that most economic and social disputes can be settled by simple economic reasoning without reference to political or moral principles.

For example, two people might agree on the need to reduce poverty but one might advocate minimum wage laws and the other some sort of redistributive tax. According to Milton Friedman (1967, p. 87), this is not an argument about principles because it can easily be shown by economic reasoning that the former policy is deficient. By fixing the price of labour above the market-clearing price, a minimum wage law renders unemployed those workers whose value is less than the politically-determined minimum wage. Again, if someone seriously believed in *equality* it can be shown to be more efficient to implement this by redistribution in cash rather than the collectivised delivery of goods and services, since the former preserves free choice in consumption while the latter entails uniformity and generates wasteful bureaucracy.

Economic liberals also accept the Pareto principle (see above, Chapter 3) in their explanation of the efficient allocation of resources in an economy. In the absence of externalities a market will produce an efficient allocation (in the sense of it being impossible for a change to be made without making at least one person worse off), since it allows individuals to exchange up to the point at which there can be no further gains from trade. While economic liberals eschew moral judgements as much as possible they would obviously not deny that there is a special virtue in an economic system which gives people what they want. They are also reluctant to make interpersonal comparisons of utility and therefore would argue that increases in well-being to the worst off, which a policy of social justice might bring, cannot compensate for the losses suffered by others.

They do, however, modify the Pareto principle. Since an efficient allocation can come from any distribution of property rights, some economic liberals argue that a reallocation of property rights (which would make some worse off) would be acceptable as long as free exchange determines the allocation of resources once this has been done. Also, almost all economic liberals would argue that extra-market payments should be paid to those who fail to earn an adequate income in the market. This, of course, has nothing to do with the principles of equality or social justice.

The whole question of the argument between economic liberals and egalitarians will be discussed in detail in later chapters, but an important point can be mentioned here. It is obvious that for an economic liberal there is no trade-off between liberty and (substantive) equality. If egalitarian policies are imposed they will not only disturb the spontaneous operation of the market in an efficiency sense but also threaten the fundamental value of liberty.

Those principles of liberty, individualism, the rule of law and efficiency, which constitute the doctrine of economic liberalism, provide its adherents with a powerful critical apparatus in the evaluation of policies, laws and institutions. In political theory perhaps their most significant achievement has been to extend the technique of economic reasoning to the rather unfamiliar fields of social policy, democracy and the behaviour of officials and elected politicians (Tullock, 1976). Some of the conclusions of this research indeed reinforce their distrust of the state. Furthermore, while they often suggest that ultimate principles cannot be rationally argued about, they themselves have produced strong refutations of egalitarianism and social justice. There is also the suggestion that the principles of economic liberalism are fully universalisable, that is, they are suitable for adoption by rational agents to apply to future unknown occasions. All this puts economic liberalism in a different category from Logical Positivism.

## 6. Collectivist values

Collectivism is only a convenient label to cover a variety of positions in political philosophy. But however different Marxists, for example, might be from social democrats they are united in their hostility to pure individualism, at least of the economic type, and in their belief that collective action is justified in order to realise certain values, notably equality and social justice, which would not be generated by a decentralised exchange process. However, collectivists have not in general contributed much to the analytical questions that have characterised so much of contemporary work in ethics and social philosophy, or enquired into the logical foundations of values and principles. A concern with purely theoretical questions would be regarded primarily as an instance of bourgeois conservative morality.

Marxist ethics is itself a curious mixture of a purportedly scientific analysis of the sociology of morals and a passionate normative critique of the economic and social conditions associated with the capitalist mode of production (Kamenka, 1969). In fact, at one time the dominant view was that Marx's analysis of capitalism did not depend upon moral judgements about its supposed iniquities but was an historical prediction of its demise. Indeed the advocates of 'scientific socialism' claimed that their critique of capitalism did not turn upon such psuedo-universal notions of social justice in the way that other socialist doctrines did (Engels, 1968 b, pp. 394–428). No moral blame was attached to the capitalist since his behaviour was determined by the laws of economic development and even the 'exploitation' of labour, the process by which the 'surplus' product of labour was appropriated by the owner of the means of production, was not regarded as technically unjust. It is true that upholders of this view might be said, implicitly, to acknowledge a kind of law of evolution of morality, in which the higher stages of social development represent a superior morality and the emergence of a stateless, property-less and moneyless Communist society permits the development of a truly 'moral man' uninfluenced by the competitive instinct, but this interpretation, apart from its implausibility as a moral doctrine, hardly captures the unique features of Marx's ethics.

Marx's sociology of morals can be understood only by reference to his materialist explanation of society. Society's 'base', which consists of the 'forces' of production (the current state of technology) and the 'relations of production' (in essence the class system, defined in terms of ownership of the means of production) determines the 'superstructure' of the state, religion, law and morality. From this it follows that ethical systems are historically determined, and are relative to the prevailing mode of production and class system. Thus, from the point of view of historical materialism, no ethical system has any genuine claim to universality; the so-called rules of justice, for example, simply protect and legitimate the forms of property ownership which obtain at a particular point in time. Marx was especially critical of utilitarianism and maintained that its supposedly universally true psychological axioms merely constituted the ideology of nineteenth-century English capitalism.

This extreme materialist view is really a version of positivism and theoretically disqualifies its holder from making any kind of 'welfare' judgements. Its usefulness as a social theory depends entirely upon its success as a piece of social science. Yet Marxists are constantly making moral judgements which presumably have some rational foundation. Indeed, because of the demonstrated lack of success of Marx's scientific predictions, the moral critique of capitalism has become the predominant feature of the Marxist ideology.

Nowadays the core of Marx's ethics are to be found in his early, more philosophical writings (Bottomore, 1963). In these metaphysical specu-lations Marx postulates an 'essence' of man, as a free and self-determined moral agent, and this 'true nature' of man is said to be perverted by capitalism. Man under capitalism is 'alienated' from his true essence because of the division of labour, the institution of money, the system of private property and the state as the instrument of oppression which enforces these things. Instead of labour freely creating objects that satisfy man's true needs, it creates objects which, because they are generated by the competitive and acquisitive capitalist process, are alien to the essence of productive labour. The free market system of capitalism is not a genuinely free system since its competitive properties put economics outside man's control and enslave him. In short capitalism is *morally* condemned because it is a dehumanising process.

Apart from this doctrine's connection with certain contemporary themes such as the critique of a consumption-oriented society and the protest against regimented factory organisation, it has little to offer a philosophical enquiry into moral and political principles. Its metaphysical, abstract, and indeed redemptionist concept of man cannot really serve as a normative standard or principle nor can it illuminate the most pressing policy problems. It is most effective when taken in conjunction with more conventional political principles such as justice and equality. As we shall see, collectivism is primarily concerned with distributive questions.

Marxism is not, however, the only form of collectivist ethics and politics. Others will become apparent in the consideration of principles in succeeding chapters, but one distinctive feature of collectivism may be mentioned here. Collectivists usually have a 'picture' or 'ideal' of how a society should look: the political evaluation of policies turns upon how far such policies go towards realising the ultimate ideal. This ideal may not be the stateless, moneyless and propertyless Marxist utopia but merely the 'just society' or the 'planned economy' of rationalistic social democrats, but whatever form it takes it is analytically distinct from the liberal-individualist's approach. In this approach, the business of the political theorist is not to impose his conception of the good society but to explore those connections between principles, policies and institutions which explain how individuals may pursue a great variety of ends. State coercion is not to be used to impose values but to prevent coercion being used by private individuals.

Collectivists would deny that coercion is as essential to their doctrines as their individualist critics maintain. They would also claim that the inequalities of the market society make for a worse coercion than that entailed by political processes. Furthermore, they would insist that purely individualistic values are destructive of the principles of social co-operation.

An interesting debate along these lines took place between liberal economists and R. M. Titmuss over the question of the supply of blood for the health service (Cooper and Culyer, 1968; Titmuss, 1970). The economists maintained that the method of supplying blood by the donor system produced a short-fall and that, in order to bring forth a greater supply, blood should be priced, that is, donors paid the market rate for their product. Apart from raising certain technical objections to this, Titmuss stressed important ethical points. He argued that to allow trade in so valuable, and symbolic, a commodity as blood would dissolve social and communal bonds into pure cash relationships, to the ultimate loss of communal values. He saw the voluntary giving of blood as exemplifying the 'gift relationship' in which essential services are 'given' from individuals to the community rather than traded. However, such noble sentiments have rarely prevailed in collectivist societies where coercion has undoubtedly been the more familiar mode of operation. The disdain which Titmuss had for market relationships took no account of the very real freedoms that those relationships embody. And this, of course, would be conceded by market socialists.[1]

# 6

# Justice

## 1. The problem of justice[1]

No systematic account of political ideas can omit a discussion of justice whether the interests of the author are in the field of value-free conceptual analysis or in that of the appraisal and recommendation of laws, policies and institutions. Moreover, it has been the practice in traditional political theorising to combine both activities. The earliest and most famous systematic treatise on political philosophy, Plato's *Republic*, was significantly both an enquiry into the 'true nature' of justice and a construction of an ideally 'just' state against which existing empirical states could be evaluated.

Yet despite more than 2000 years of subsequent political theorising the concept still has no settled meaning. It is not simply that there are fundamental disputes at the normative level (it is only to be expected that individuals will disagree as to the justice or injustice of particular laws, policies and institutions), it is the fact that there is so little agreement as to what the concept *means* that causes such serious problems.

The difficulty with the meaning of the concept has been exacerbated in recent years by the dominance of *social justice* as a moral and political value. Since the last war progressive social thinkers, alienated from Marxism both by the practical examples of tyrannical Communist regimes and by more fruitful intellectual advances in the social sciences, have justified radical social and economic policies by an appeal to social justice within the general framework of Western liberal democratic value systems. As a consequence the concept of justice has been perhaps irredeemably associated with problems of the appropriate distribution of wealth and income. The protagonists of social justice have therefore been concerned to demonstrate the criteria by which social justice sanctions certain distributive policies. The criteria are usually desert, merit and need, or sometimes merely more equality for its own sake. The emphasis placed on these different, and often conflicting, criteria may vary but the members of the school of social justice are united in their belief that the concept authorises a positive role for the state. That this view is more than just a declaration of policy or the justification of a substantive set of values but involves the *appropriation* of the *meaning* of justice to the radical view can be seen in a comment by one of its leading proponents, Brian Barry. In criticising the views of David Hume, who defended a conservative, rule-based explanation of justice, Barry said: 'although Hume uses the expression "rules of justice" to cover such things as property rules, "justice" is now analytically tied to "desert" and "need", so that one could quite properly say that some of what Hume calls "rules of justice" were unjust' (Barry, 1967a, p. 193).

However, traditionally most users of the word justice were not necessarily radical, and nor is the contemporary usage necessarily tied to a reformist moral and political outlook. Those who are sceptical of social justice do not regard themselves as antithetical to what they would regard as a properly articulated conception of justice. In ordinary speech generally we talk of justice and injustice, where the words do not refer to the desirability or otherwise of states of affairs or particular income and wealth distributions but to the rules and procedures that characterise social practices and which are applied to the actions of individuals who participate in those practices. In this narrower conception justice is normally seen to be a property of individuals. When in the context of the common law we speak of a breach of the rules of 'natural justice' we are referring to an arbitrariness suffered by an individual in a rule-governed process. This latter concept has undoubtedly legalistic overtones but it should be sharply distinguished from a purely legalistic concept of justice. Justice is not merely conformity to law and it is certainly permissible to consider a law to be unjust without committing ourselves to the radical view.

The word is part of a family of concepts which are intricately related. The concept most often used in the same context as justice is that of equality and the connection between the two ideas is a complex one. While there are clearly uses of justice which do imply equality – we speak of equality before the law and often regard certain forms of inequality as arbitrary and unjust – more often than not there is tension between the concepts. Justice, for example, would not sanction equality of reward to individuals who render widely different services. Traditional liberals have been associated with the view that the attempt to impose *material* equality on unequal people is destructive of the rule of law and necessitates totalitarianism and consequent injustice towards individuals. It is impossible to separate entirely the concepts of justice and equality but for the sake of convenience some of the particular problems to do with equality will be considered in the next chapter.

The contemporary interest in substantive theories of justice is not accidental and there are good philosophical and political reasons which explain it. We can deal briefly with the political reasons first. It is significant that the most important book on political philosophy since the Second World War, John Rawls's *A Theory of Justice*, should appear in the United States of America when it did (1971).[2] Its publication coincided with the culmination of the movement for equal rights for minorities (of whom blacks were the most important example), and with the heyday of other forms of political dissent. Also, however much people might agree that capitalist and mixed economies deliver goods and services that people want more efficiently than other systems of production and exchange, there has been a persistent complaint that they do so at the cost of unacceptable inequalities of income, wealth and possibly power. There seems no reason *in justice* why some of the bizarre distributions of income and wealth in the West should be regarded as legitimate. Those political radicals who demanded political action over the questions of minority and individual *rights* and the distribution of income and wealth were explicitly appealing to the concept of justice. The publication of Rawls's book provided, for perhaps the first time this century, a direct link between a fairly abstract, philosophical theory and particular policy recommendations in both the areas of rights and distribution.

The philosophical interest in justice is related to the special significance of the concept itself in social and political theory. As Rawls himself says, 'justice is the first virtue of society' (1972, p. 3) and most people would agree that, although a society may exhibit other moral values than justice, a society characterised by injustice would be especially blameworthy. The rules of justice, whatever they are, are thought to·have a special obligatory force which other moral virtues do not have. Not only is it right to act justly, it is also specifically wrong to act unjustly. Other moral actions, such as giving a large proportion of one's income to charity, would certainly be regarded as good or morally praiseworthy but they would not be regarded as obligatory and it would not be wrong not to perform them. There seems to be a strong connection between rightness and justice and Rawls has persuasively argued that in moral and social philosophy the right is prior to the good. It could also be argued that some recent radical, egalitarian concepts of justice have so inflated the notion that there is a danger of the once strong connection between justice and rightful obligatory action being seriously weakened. It is possible that when conservatives in social philsophy today suggest that there are things that a society ought to promote other than justice they have the radical concept in mind.

It is for this reason that moral and political theorists distinguish justice from morality in general so as to elucidate its peculiar characteristics. Justice is a distributive concept. This means that it is primarily concerned with the way rewards and punishments and so on are distributed to individuals in a rule-governed practice and its intimate connection with *fairness* indicates this. For example, we may criticise certain social practices such as child marriage, polygamy and so on as immoral but we would be unlikely to say they are unjust. We describe a particular rule or policy as unjust when it arbitrarily discriminates against a named group, such as blacks or women, or when it imposes unequal burdens on individuals and groups for which no relevant reason can be given. A society's laws and economic policies may produce general benevolence but at the same time allow gross disparities of income and wealth, and even an unfair allocation of civil rights. This, of course, is the traditional objection to utilitarianism.

But it would be misleading to suggest that justice refers solely to the fair application of a rule. Some rules, although fairly applied, may produce results which are repugnant to our intuitive conceptions of justice. And, of course, there are rules which, although they do not discriminate, we would hesitate to describe as just. One can think of less fanciful examples than this suggestion, from William K. Frankena; 'if a ruler were to boil his subjects in oil, jumping in afterwards himself, it would be an injustice, but there would be no inequality of treatment' (1962, p. 17). J. R. Lucas claims that laws of strict liability, while being perfectly general and non-discriminatory, may be unjust in some familiar senses of justice as they clearly do not 'give every man his due' (1972, pp. 230–1). Rules of justice can be given some content, however, which does not tie the concept to morality in general and which does preserve its connection with the distribution of rewards and punishment, rights and duties, and liberties.

## 2. The meaning of justice

We have already indicated some aspects of the meaning of the concept of justice and we must now fill out the basic features. The conventional accounts of justice normally begin by stating a fundamental rule that derives from Aristotle. The theory is that justice means treating equals equally and unequals unequally, and that unequal treatment should be in proportion to the inequality. This is no more than a version of the idea implied in the universalisability criterion of ethics – that like cases be treated alike. This has been correctly described as a formal rule, or the principle of rationality, which holds that some reason must always be given for different treatment. It does not in itself contain any elements of what might be termed intuitive or common-sense notions of justice because it does not indicate in what ways people may be treated differently. It does not, of course, assume some fundamental equality of man because it is a purely formal rule.

This formal rule is not, however, completely useless since consistency is a necessary feature of moral and political argument. There is quite likely to be substantial agreement in some cases on what counts as relevant differences in justifying differential treatment. Differences in race, religion and sex are *not* thought to be relevant to the granting of civil and political rights, the assessment of written work in academic institutions, the selection of sports teams or in the appointment of personnel in commercial and other enterprises. However, it is not difficult to devise rules which do make such properties relevant and which are universalisable. A South African sports selector would presumably regard racial differences as highly relevant to the selection of a cricket team since he would relate sport to the whole South African way of life.

The formal principle which tells us to treat like cases alike should not be confused with the substantive egalitarian principle of justice which assumes that all departures from equality have to be morally justified. This *presumption* in favour of equality is found in Rawls's claim: 'All social values – liberty, opportunity, income and wealth and the bases of self-respect – are to be distributed equally unless an unequal distribution of any, or all, of these values is to everyone's advantage' (1972, p. 62). This latter view is a value judgement and, in Rawls's case, implies a distinction between production and distribution so that what is produced in society is regarded as a common asset to be distributed unequally only when good grounds are produced. In Rawls's case, as we shall see, inequalities in distribution are justifiable only when they are to the benefit of the worst off. This presumption in favour of equality can easily be countered by the equally valid moral principle that an individual is *entitled* to what he produces.[3] In this latter view the inequalities that emerge from a market society, however bizarre they appear to the egalitarian, do not have to be justified by some relevant difference.

The formal principle assigns individuals to categories and requires merely that the rules which apply to the categories shall be adhered to consistently; it is therefore compatible with any substantive morality. The prohibitions on discrimination mentioned above are compelling only to the extent that the principles which underpin them are themselves acceptable. At most the formal principle may be described as a principle of equity and particular rules and laws can be assessed *internally* to see if the principle that 'like cases be treated alike' is rigorously maintained. Indeed many provisions of the tax laws in Western countries can be shown to be inconsistent with the principles that underlie them.

If the theory of justice is to be more than a purely formal principle that rules must be consistently applied, there has to be some underlying concept of human equality. However, the relationship between justice and equality is a hotly disputed matter. Some social theorists would agree that justice requires that people should in some respects be treated as equals but they would reject the idea that a substantive social equality is itself desirable and also the dominant contemporary view that justice requires the justification on rational grounds of all existing inequalities. It is important to distinguish therefore between a strong and a weak sense of equality in normative discourse about justice. The more 'conservative' theorists of justice admit only a weak sense because they maintain that any other sense involves a threat to liberty, rules and social stability. These theorists would probably maintain that this idea is best expressed by the proposition that people have property rights which would be violated by an application of equality in the strong sense.

The weak sense of equality contained in the concept of justice implies that for certain purposes individuals ought to be treated as if they were equal, although this prescriptive statement does not depend on the truth of some factual proposition asserting men's equality. It simply means that for the purposes of law no person is entitled to preferential treatment by virtue of some irrelevant property, such as wealth, birth, sex, race or religion. It would require public authorities not to discriminate on such grounds when making appointments (although some libertarians would object to the legal enforcement of non-discriminatory employment practices in the private sector). In the political sphere it would guarantee equal constitutional rights so that no one would have a prior claim to office over anyone else. However, this point should be qualified by the fact that justice does not entail a commitment to (democratic) political equality. Fair rules may be impartially enforced in regimes which allow little political participation and majority rule democracies may generate arbitrary treatment of individuals and minorities.

Perhaps the minimal sense of equality described above is best captured in the principle which states that all men are entitled to 'equality of respect'. This means that whatever differences individuals display in their natural aptitudes, law and government should for certain purposes ignore these differences. To what extent governments should acknowledge this equality of respect in the area of welfare, for example, is of course a controversial subject which requires consideration of other principles. A not dissimilar idea is expressed in Kant's famous injunction to treat men always as ends in themselves and not as means only. It is for this reason that slavery is always unjust. On similar grounds the injustice of punishing an innocent man can never be compensated for by an increase in the well-being of society at large. It must be stressed that this argument alone cannot be used to justify any egalitarian social policy; rather, it puts a prohibition on state action that abrogates individual rights.

The concept of justice in much contemporary social philosophy has more to do with the justification of inequalities than it has to do with any notion of equality. The familiar concepts that belong to the family of justice are desert and need. It would clearly be *unjust* to treat people equally who differed in deserts and needs. While desert obviously provides a ground for differential treatment this is a little more complicated in the case of need. Some political theorists take need to be an aspect of the principle of equality and maintain that men are *equal* in having certain basic needs which call for government action, while others maintain that since men *differ* in these needs this justifies unequal treatment. We shall then have to consider need both as a part of justice and of general egalitarianism.

It is important, however, to make an analytical distinction between desert and need. The concept of desert refers to those properties of a man's actions that are worthy of special treatment (Barry, 1965, p. 106). To say that a man deserves reward or punishment is to say that actions, efforts and results are the things that are relevant to the way that he is treated. However, to say that a man needs something means that he lacks certain things – money, an adequate diet, clothing and so on – which are thought to be essential to the realisation of a certain standard of well-being, however defined. But need cannot be a basis for desert because it does not relate specifically to a man's actions or efforts. Thus a person may still need certain things even though he has not deserved them by his actions, efforts or results. It would not be inaccurate to say that the concept of need has virtually replaced desert in recent egalitarian welfare social philosophies. The delivery of 'welfare goods', housing aid, health care and so on, is entirely justified in terms of need.

These features of desert-based justice make it a 'backward-looking' concept because, in proposing answers to questions about the distribution of punishment and reward, it directs us to look for those qualities in an individual's past actions which are relevant to the way he is treated. This is obviously so in the retributivist theory of punishment which rests entirely on the notion of desert and contrasts strongly with the 'forward-looking' doctrine of utilitarianism. A utilitarian has no interest in the past actions of an individual, or his moral guilt, for the assessment of punishment: he justifies punishment, or more strictly, any form of penal measure, solely by reference to its deterrent effect.

When it comes to justifying differential reward the concept is a little more complicated. We have already said that desert refers to past actions, efforts and results but this requires some elaboration. Clearly, we would not relate desert to efforts alone because however praiseworthy a person's efforts might be they cannot be rewarded in isolation from what he produces. Desert must in some sense be related to the value of the product, but how a product is valued will depend upon a whole network of social principles and practices. It may be the case that because of some rare talent an individual may be able to produce something that is highly valued with very little in the way of effort. Yet we would not say that he did not deserve the differential reward that his talents enabled him to earn. Nevertheless, there is a problem here in that some social philosophers might say that some high rewards, although legitimately acquired, are not deserved because they are the result of no *merit* on the part of the fortunate individual. The earnings of popular entertainers, property speculators and financiers might fall into this category. By the same reasoning, inherited wealth would be regarded as undeserved.

The traditional liberal conception of desert solves the problem by detaching the notion of desert from *moral* desert (although as we shall see, some extreme *laissez-faire* liberals clarify the issue by eliminating completely the use of the word desert in the economic sphere). In a liberal market society a man's desert is entirely a function of the value of what he produces and this value is determined by the preferences of individuals in exchange relationships. This has nothing to do with the moral quality of his efforts, which is regarded as a purely subjective matter. This rigorous idea of desert, associated with social philosophers such as Herbert Spencer, precludes the state from meeting people's needs.[4] It follows from this, of course, that the state has few justifiable claims against the individual.

Those who interpret desert in a moral sense, however, insist that it is the business of the state to correct the outcomes of a market society when they are the result of luck or ingenuity rather than the cultivation of special skills and virtues. In fact, even in a competitive market economy, recourse may have to be made to a subjective evaluation of a person's pay and prospects since in large-scale enterprises it may be difficult to determine objectively the value of a person's contribution. A more important point, perhaps, is that this view of desert underlies some justifications (although not all) of the confiscatory taxation of inherited wealth and steeply progressive income tax. Those who advocate permanent incomes policies presumably have a notion of moral desert in mind which they feel should be decisive in the determination of rewards for different occupations.

The concept of desert features strongly in the traditional version of the liberal creed, although it requires careful clarification when applied to the economic sphere. To the extent that it stresses personal *responsibility* for actions and favours rewards for efforts and results rather than need, it typifies a rather tough-minded social philosophy. It is individualistic in that it evaluates a person's actions as products of an autonomous will rather than as the outcomes of a form of social causation. In the question of punishment the notion of desert precludes the view that crime is a kind of disease which can be 'treated' since this view abrogates individual responsibility. Indeed, not to punish a criminal according to his deserts is to degrade him as an individual and make him a mere object of social policy.

For political theorists, the important questions about justice turn upon its connection with social and economic policy. Questions of justice in social affairs crop up in circumstances of 'scarcity', which we can take to be a more or less permanent feature of the human condition. In situations of abundance the question of who should get what, and why, would not arise. We are, however, all too familiar with vexing questions as to how the supply of kidney machines should be allocated, or what the appropriate distribution of income should be. In these questions the members of the family of justice – equality, desert and need – play their most important roles.

Theorists of justice have produced many answers to these questions and to simplify the issue we can make an important distinction, which is now commonplace in social and political theory, between *procedural* justice and *social* justice. Although there are many variants of both approaches the main features of each can be briefly summarised. In procedural theories the demands of justice are satisfied if certain rules are satisfied. Therefore no comment, in terms of justice, may be made about the outcomes of such procedures. Justice is only a property of individual behaviour within rules and cannot be a feature of 'society' or 'states of affairs'. In theories of social justice, however, justice is precisely a property of some social state of affairs. A society is just, for example, if the distribution of income satisfies a certain criterion, and the state is morally entitled to use the apparatus of coercive law to bring this about. David Miller, in a recent influential book, expressed this view nicely when he said: 'it is impossible to assess the justice of actions without a prior identification of *just states of affairs*' (1976, pp. 17–18, italics added).

## 3. Procedural justice

In its rejection of social justice the school of procedural justice is firmly within the tradition of methodological individualism. Only the actions of individuals can be morally evaluated in terms of justice and fairness and it is absurd to praise or blame social processes or patterns of income distribution. However, procedural theorists of justice are most definitely not Logical Positivists; propositions about justice are meaningful and are not merely expressions of emotion. They have meaning, however, only in the context of systems of general rules such as the traditional common law. Actions are just if they are consistent with those general rules which protect property rights and prohibit the use of fraud or force in the making of contracts. Procedural justice is exemplified in competitions, such as races. A fair race is not one in which the person who wins morally deserves to win but one in which there is no cheating, nobody jumps the gun or has an unfair advantage through the use of drugs (Barry, 1965, p. 103).

Procedural theorists are hostile to the distinction between production and distribution which is made by collectivists. There is no 'social pie' which can be divided up according to abstract distributive principles, there are only individual entitlements which it would be *unjust* to interfere with by coercive laws. There is clearly a connection between procedural justice and the market economy. The market functions as a signalling mechanism to attract the factors of production to their most efficient uses: any attempt to disturb this process, by way of an incomes policy, for example, will lead to an inefficient use of resources which ultimately makes everyone worse off. Also, it is argued that the pursuit of social justice must eventuate in totalitarianism (Hayek, 1944) since it requires an ever-increasing use of coercion in economic and social life.

Procedural theorists maintain (Hayek, 1960 and 1976) that all non-market criteria of income, such as those based on 'desert' or 'need', are necessarily subjective and can only work in a regimented, oppressive and illiberal society. While most procedural theorists are concerned about 'welfare' and accept that the state has some responsibility for those who cannot earn an adequate income in the market (Hayek, for example, believes that payments outside the market should be made to the poor), they deny that this has anything to do with justice.

Nevertheless, this should not be interpreted as an entirely conservative doctrine. The doctrine of equality before the law and the demand that rules be perfectly general would be highly radical in many countries whose laws discriminate between races and groups. Its individualism also runs counter to those conservative philosophies of social justice, based on religion or natural law, which propose 'ends' or purposes for society which are as collectivist as those of socialists. Indeed, the most extreme version of procedural justice is to be found in the decidedly *unconservative* philosophy of Robert Nozick.

In *Anarchy, State and Utopia* Nozick makes two important distinctions. He distinguishes between historical principles of justice and end-state principles. Historical principles hold that 'past circumstances or actions of people can create differential entitlements or differential deserts to things' (Nozick, 1974, p. 155). In contrast, end-state theories suggest particular goals to which a distribution should conform. Utilitarianism and theories of social justice are end-state doctrines. Nozick also distinguishes between patterned and unpatterned principles of justice. A patterned principle evaluates a distribution in accordance with some 'natural dimension' (1974, p. 156). A principle of justice which states that people are to be rewarded according to their needs would be a patterned principle. Not all patterned principles are end-state: for example, the patterned principle which states that individuals should be rewarded according to their deserts is historical because it directs attention towards their past actions.

Nozick's own theory of justice is an *historical, unpatterned* theory. It is an entitlement theory in which the distribution of individual property holdings is just if it is a consequence of fair *acquisition* (without the use of fraud or force) or *transfer*. The only other aspect of justice is *rectification*, the principle which allows past injustices, that is, unfair acquisitions, to be corrected. The main point of the theory is to show that individuals have rights to their property holdings and there is no moral justification for a rearrangement of the spread of wealth in 'society'. Nozick, therefore, is a rigorous critic of the distinction between production and distribution; goods do not come into the world out of nothing but must be understood in terms of individual property holdings. The distribution of property holdings is therefore a product of people trading in their holdings. The *minimal* state protects individuals from invasions of their rights and if it goes beyond this to bring about a state of affairs which is *not* the result of free exchange it is in breach of their rights. This immediately makes all welfare programmes illegitimate

According to Nozick the attempt to establish any patterned or end-state conception of justice must eventually lead to the destruction of liberty. If, for example, the proposed pattern is that incomes shall be equal then if a government is to maintain that pattern it will have to interfere constantly with liberty. People will automatically exchange with one another and this will tend to shift the distribution of holdings away from the prescribed pattern. To maintain that pattern, governments will have to use ever-increasing amounts of coercion which will destory liberty. This is not unlike Hayek's thesis that any attempt to control people's natural inclinations to exchange must lead to totalitarianism; for example, restraints on the free movement of capital must eventually lead to restraints on the movement of people. It is a very strong thesis and has been criticised precisely because the evidence suggests that interferences with liberty do not necessarily lead to such dire consequences.

The only restriction that Nozick puts on fair acquisitions and voluntary exchanges is that these must not violate the 'Lockean proviso' (1974, pp. 175–82); this means that they must not worsen the positions of others. But the proviso is interpreted very narrowly. For someone's position to be worsened someone else must appropriate the total supply of something which is *essential to life*; for example, 'a person may not appropriate the only water hole in the desert and charge what he will' (1974, p. 179). But the proviso would not, in Nozick's theory, prevent someone who discovered a cure for a fatal disease charging whatever price he liked for it since, unlike the monopolist who appropriates the total supply of something essential for life, he does not put others in a worse position to that which they are already in. This would only be so if he physically prevented others from trying to make the discovery themselves.

There are some aspects of the theories of justice as fair rules which require highlighting. Their stress on the importance of liberty is timely in that almost all theorists of social justice in the West have been remiss in not considering the implications that their theories have for freedom. This is true even if the extreme proposition that social justice must lead to totalitarianism is less than convincing. Also, the refusal to separate production from distribution re-directs attention to the conditions that make for an efficient allocation of resources and indicates some of the likely consequences of disturbing those conditions. Of course, many of the implications of the arguments of Hayek and Nozick seem to offend against some of our fundamental moral notions and, before we consider the main rivals of procedural and historical theories, the doctrines of social justice, some general comments are in order.

Many critics of the purely rule-based view of justice would say that it concentrates on only one aspect of justice and that it is always possible to say of a situation that, although the rules were followed, the outcome was nevertheless unjust. It is said that ordinary language and 'common-sense' morality contain words like 'desert' and 'need' precisely to do this job of appraising outcomes. J. R. Lucas, who is himself a rigorous critic of social justice, nevertheless cannot accept the full implications of the minimal view of justice contained in free market economics. He says that 'free exchange is not necessarily fair exchange', and describes the economic theory of *laissez-faire* as unethical (1972, p. 245). Of course, Hayek would maintain that it is simply illegitimate to describe the process and outcome of the market in ethical terms at all.

A social theorist who believed in free exchange between individuals within general rules could still maintain, however, that social justice requires some rearrangement of the initial distribution of property holdings (which is largely a product of chance). From this point on people could exchange in the Nozickean manner: the resulting inequalities would then be acceptable and efficiency and freedom would be preserved. This action would clearly infringe the right of bequest and would therefore breach *laissez-faire* liberal principles (and it is indeed difficult to accept a right to property and deny the right of bequest), but it is certainly more acceptable than trying to impose a pattern of income distribution on an exchange process.

A pluralist would challenge the priority of liberty implied in the theory and argue that the loss of liberty consequent on the increase in social justice is perfectly justifiable. Nozick's claim that no one has a right to a minimum of welfare, because to grant it would necessitate unjustified taxation of the rich, does depend upon the inviolability of rights to liberty and property. The favoured trade-off between liberty and social justice would, of course, be unacceptable to the theorist of procedural justice even if it were the outcome of a democratic decision-making procedure, because coercive action to bring about 'desirable' states of affairs is in principle illegitimate. The believer in social justice might well concede that his decision-procedure is technically coercive in that it harms some for the benefit of others (and democratic procedures are coercive). But he would also say that market relationships, limited only by basic rules, are equally coercive, if not more so, since they put individuals at the mercy of those who have economic power. The dispute may then turn upon the nature of coercion.

An important advantage claimed by the rule-based theories of justice is that there is more likely to be agreement over rules than outcomes and that to divide up the social product according to the principles of social justice, even if they could be agreed upon, would be an impossibly complex task which if attempted would lead to great divisiveness. The problem here is that it may be equally difficult to secure agreement about rules, especially if the following of certain sorts of rules leads to distributions of income and wealth which seem repugnant to some firmly held notions of justice.

There is a related problem in that the rules of justice themselves may be capable of a variety of interpretations. The rules of justice in the making of exchanges prevent fraud, but deciding what counts as fraud is itself problematical. Could it not justify a wide range of legislation to protect the consumer or is it limited merely to preventing deliberate deception? Nozick concedes that his rectification rule is also likely to cause great problems. If every past wrong is to be put right, then there really is no limit to the number of disputed entitlements. Furthermore, despite Nozick's great stress on property rights, he pays little attention to those generated by the existence of externalities. In some cases, especially pollution and noise, we just do not know who has the property rights.

## 4. Social justice

All theories of social justice are end-state or patterned theories since they propose that the process of exchange between individuals should be controlled and checked in accordance with abstract, external moral principles. Social justice requires that society as a whole, rather than just the actions of individuals, be evaluated for its justice and injustice. While most theories of social justice are egalitarian and socialist, there are exceptions. Some versions of conservatism, and social philosophies based on religion, may make use of the concept in their descriptions of an ideal harmonious society based on unity, order and hierarchy. Such views on justice may belong in the same logical box as those of the socialists in that they are end-state and collectivist, in contrast to individualist conceptions. Nevertheless, the rest of this section is concerned with the radical arguments. There is also a problem in that most discussions of the question of social justice are bound up with a strong sense of equality and therefore there is some overlap with the next chapter. However, it is important to keep an analytical distinction between social justice and equality because, in some areas at least, proponents of the former wish to justify some inequalities. What is characteristic of radical theories of social justice is the presumption in favour of equality, departures from which are justified with reluctance.

An important feature of the approach of social justice requires special emphasis. The various theories do not propose sets of rules, or even principles, by which men can live *irrespective of their needs and wants* but instead take needs and wants, and their satisfaction, as the data by which a society can be assessed for justice. A society is just if it distributes want-satisfaction in a certain way. Social justice theories try to go behind the structure of rules to determine *who* is in need, say, of health care, educational opportunity, housing and so on. Hence in empirical studies of social injustice great use is made of 'social indicators' of various forms of deprivation. These are measures which go beyond the distribution of income and wealth to show how general social conditions, such as bad housing, areas of high unemployment, and regional imbalance, can generate social injustice.

Almost all theories of social justice require the making of interpersonal comparisons of well-being, something which the procedural theories of justice try to avoid. But as soon as it is said that a state of affairs is more just because a redistributive policy takes account of need, a judgement of this kind is being made. While such judgements are not illegitimate in a moral sense, and presumably they can be supported by rational argument, it is extremely difficult to secure agreement as to what form the policies that embody them should take. To say exactly who deserves what or needs what is an immensely complicated task even if there is agreement that the state should maximise social justice.

Some economic and social theorists suggest that these problems might be overcome by a welfare policy which guarantees the payment of 'negative income' tax to those whose earnings fall below a certain level (Friedman, 1962, ch. xii). A cash payment of this kind could be spent by the individual as he wished. The school of social justice argues that this cannot take account of special circumstances, such as large families or physical and mental handicap, which generate special needs. These cannot be dealt with by simple cash transfers. It could be said, for example, that social justice does not require that a handicapped person needs a minimum income to attain a certain level of welfare. Instead he should receive special provision to bring him up to the level he would have reached but for his handicap. For these reasons, it is said that social justice dictates the collective delivery of health and welfare services in order to ensure a minimum level of welfare for all, regardless of individuals' cash resources.

It is further argued that a purely individualistic approach to social welfare, even if it is accompanied by cash transfers to the poor, undermines those collaborative and co-operative aspects of life which are essential to social justice. It is argued that production is not an individual activity but a social activity and that therefore wealth is 'socially created'. As some wealth is available to a person because he is a social being, then a distinction can be made between production and distribution; and at least a part of society's wealth should be distributed according to the principles of social justice. Furthermore, this surplus should be distributed in the form of collective goods rather than made available for private consumption.

The inequalities that are permissible under the rubric of social justice are acceptable if they are consistent with socially-oriented principles. This is in stark contrast to the rules theorists of justice who maintain that the inequalities that result from free exchange do not have to be justified. The circumstances that lead to inequality in the market, such as chance, a certain lack of scruple perhaps, or general good fortune, lead to income differentials which are quite undeserved, in a moral sense, by the tenets of social justice. A purely market allocation of income will always lead, it is said, to certain services, which are essential to the community and therefore deserving of high reward, being underpaid.

While it is true that radical theorists of social justice are as sceptical of the concept of moral desert as are economic liberals and tend to argue for equality for its own sake (see below, Chapter 7), nevertheless, the concept is still used in the critique of income distribution in market economies. For example, some concept of desert must underlie the arguments behind centralised institutions like pay boards and relativities commissions, which try to find the 'true worth' of different occupations. The objections against these, which theorists of social justice have never answered, is that not only are their verdicts purely subjective (if they are not subjective but reflect what the market price for a certain occupation is, then such institutions are redundant) but that they are likely to be politicised. Although people may object on moral grounds to some of the outcomes of the market at least these are determined by *impersonal* forces. Resentment over pay is likely to be much greater if it is determined by politicians or officials. Against this it is often pointed out that social surveys in Britain seem to indicate that people think desert ought to be the main ground for income distribution. It would be interesting, however, to see what the results of a survey would be if it were taken in a situation where the market had been removed and incomes were determined *solely* by 'rational' principles of social justice.

It is from Marxism, of course, that the most extreme views on social justice emanate. Marx devotes considerable discussion to the concept of justice in his *Critique of the Gotha Programme*. Two types of justice are described, one appropriate for socialist society and the other for Communist society. It is an interesting question as to whether these concepts can be used in a *moral* critique of capitalism or whether Marx's sociology of morals forbids this.

The theory of justice that applies to a socialist society in which bourgeois ownership and exploitation has been abolished, holds that a distribution is just when each receives that which is in accord with his labour contribution to the social product. When deductions are made for investment to reproduce the same output, the worker receives back for consumption (in the form of public and private goods) that which he has contributed. In a socialist society there will be clear improvements over capitalism; public ownership will have been established and the worker will not have been exploited. Nevertheless, some inequality will persist, since people's labour contributions will vary according to their talents, and many of the objectionable features of a money economy will remain.

This last point means that man's 'essence' cannot be captured under socialism.

In Communist society the formula of distributive justice is 'from each according to his ability, to each according to his needs'. This presumably means that reward will not be in accordance with contribution but with the special needs that each individual has in order to realise his essence. This utopia requires either material abundance, or a change in human nature so that people are motivated to produce goods and services without the incentive of differential reward. If this is so then it is difficult to see what it has got to do with the problems of distributive or social justice because these problems only arise when there is *scarcity* and when there is conflict between the *interests* of individuals.

Those who interpret Marx as a moral positivist would maintain that it was not his intention to evaluate capitalist society by these conceptions since a different morality applies to that order (Tucker, 1970, ch. 2). The 'exploitation' of labour in capitalist society is not technically unjust since it is part of the mechanics of capitalist production and cannot be evaluated by some supposedly external, universal moral criteria. Values, in this view, are relative to the mode of production.

In an interesting article Ziyad I. Husami (1978) has argued that this is mistaken and that Marx did believe that capitalism could be morally evaluated, that the ethics of one class could be used to evaluate a particular social and economic system. Thus he shows how Marx used the two doctrines of justice (socialist and Communist) to deliver a *moral* attack on capitalism. On the first view of justice, capitalism is damned because private ownership means that the exchange between capital and labour is not a fair one. The worker sells his labour power but the capitalist through exploitation is able to appropriate the surplus value created by the worker. Defenders of capitalism have often argued that under perfect competition the worker does get his marginal product and the return on capital is justified because it represents a reward for 'abstinence' (refraining from consumption). Marx, of course would have none of this; and, indeed, this is by no means the only defence of capitalism, nor is it a very satisfactory one.

Capitalism is also condemned by the second version of justice. The dehumanising system of capitalist production destroys man's essence and makes him a slave to so-called immutable economic laws. Its most significant injustice is that it directs production for profit and not for the satisfaction of genuine human needs. At the end of the day the most significant element in Marx's theory is its insistence that justice is concerned with the satisfaction of genuine human needs as opposed to exogenously generated wants.

Contemporary Marxists, to the extent that they are not moral positivists, stress the need factor. Although the expression 'production for need not for profit' has very great emotive appeal it is difficult to make it serviceable as an evaluative concept. In a free economy production for profit means satisfying the desires of consumers. If there are any 'needs' over and above the expressed preferences of individuals as consumers then it is difficult to establish what they are in any objective sense. It is certainly possible to believe that access to the market is unequal, and that redistributive measures ought to be taken to correct this, but the theorists of social justice normally recommend that needs should be catered for by the collective delivery of goods and services. It is difficult to resist the conclusion that the invocation of need is often a device for paternalism: that it is the business of the state to deliver to people what others think they ought to get.

There are a number of difficulties with all theories of social justice which are worth stressing. First, all involve considerable extension of state activity and this requires the careful design of institutions to ensure that the activity proceeds in the desired direction. Marxists themselves are well aware that the state, through its officials, may develop interests contrary to those of the people it is supposed to serve. Curiously enough, on this point there is an unconscious intellectual alliance between Marxists and economic liberals. Secondly, it is an immensely difficult task to determine just what are the appropriate criteria that determine justified departures from equality. The advantage of procedural justice is that it avoids the comparisons that are entailed in the social justice approach but at the cost of tolerating outcomes that often run counter to a commonsense understanding of justice. Thirdly, there is a threat to liberty in the implementation of policies derived from social justice. There is in the pluralist approach no theoretical limit to how much liberty may be traded for a small increase in social justice. What is required here is some explanation of the social decision procedure which determines what the trade-off shall be.

Answers to these and other questions are contained in the most influential book on justice, and political philosophy in general, since the war: John Rawls's *A Theory of Justice*. No account of the subject is adequate without a serious consideration of this important book.

## 5. Rawls's theory of justice

From this vast and imposing work of political and moral philosophy we will pick out only those areas which are relevant to the central problems discussed in this chapter. The first thing to note is that Rawls's theory is a type of procedural theory, but it differs from other procedural theories in several important respects. He wishes to show that justice is about the rules that should govern a social practice, and not about the evaluation of various states of affairs using criteria such as need and desert, but he attempts to counter the main criticism of this approach, which is that the meticulous following of rules may produce outcomes which are inconsistent with our common-sense notions of justice. Therefore he wishes to show that under certain carefully specified conditions rational agents would choose a set of principles which are consistent with our intuitive ideas of distributive justice, and which when followed produce outcomes which, whatever they might be, are morally acceptable.

Despite its procedural features, however, Rawls's theory could be regarded as a contribution to the theory of social justice because he persistently stresses that all departures from equality have to be rationally justified; there is a presumption in favour of equality which contrasts strongly with various versions of the entitlement theory. Allied to this is an implied distinction between production and distribution. Even though Rawls makes great use of marginal productivity theory in the determination of wages, and indeed agrees that the application of it is the only way natural talents can be drawn into their most efficient uses to the benefit of everybody, he does argue that market criteria must always be controlled by the principles of justice.

To elucidate Rawls's theory of justice we must start with his method of approaching moral problems, which is in the 'contractarian' tradition of social philosophy. This involves abstracting individuals from their particular social and economic circumstances and reconstructing the rules, principles and institutions they would adopt in order to maximise their interests in any future society. Thus there are two essential parts of Rawls's programme: the description of the conditions under which rational contractors deliberate and the content of the principles they would choose.

The relationship between the conditions and the adoption of the principles is said to be deductive, that is, rational agents in the situation described by Rawls will of necessity maximise their well-being through the choice of his principles of justice. Thus the principles will be unanimously agreed to and properly universalisable. Of course, it may be the case that the Rawlsian principles might be agreed to but the validity of the deduction denied, or that people may accept what Rawls calls the 'original position', in which individuals are abstracted from their environment, but deduce different principles.

The idea of 'reflective equilibrium' is central to Rawls's methodology (1972, pp. 48–51). This means that we must constantly check the conclusions of our moral reasoning against our intuitive moral notions and possibly readjust the conditions of the original position so as to derive principles which are consistent with these fundamental moral beliefs. There is perhaps a much greater reliance on intuition in the construction of the Rawlsian theorem than is apparent in the formal statement of Rawls's methodology. However, Rawls's method entails also that our intuitive notions of justice be modified by philosophical reasoning.

We will consider first the description of the original position. Rawls places men behind what he calls the 'veil of ignorance' (pp. 36–42). This is an hypothetical situation in which individuals are deprived of basic knowledge of their wants, interests, skills, abilities and so on. They are also deprived of knowledge of the things that generate conflicts in actual societies. Thus knowing that they are white or black, or Protestant or Catholic and so on, will not be of much significance since they do not know, for example, what particular patterns of discrimination operate in society. But they will have an elementary knowledge of economics and psychology, and also what Rawls calls a 'sense of justice'.

Behind the veil of ignorance, then, certain constraints are imposed and these are implied by the idea of having a morality. In Rawls's conception what is excluded is the 'knowledge of those contingencies which sets men at odds and allows them to be guided by their prejudices' (p. 19). While Rawlsian men are self-interested, it is important to note that they are not, strictly speaking, egoists. Egoism, the doctrine that everyone should pursue his own ends on every possible occasion, is precluded by the notion of having one's life restrained by moral rules. A self-interested person can rationally adopt a set of moral rules to guide his conduct even though the application of the rules may not be in his interest, in an egoistic sense, on every particular occasion. Egoism runs counter to Rawls's conception of the *right*, which is 'a set of principles, general in form and universal in application, that is to be publicly recognised as a final court of appeal for ordering the particular claims of moral persons' (p. 135).

This can also conveniently be contrasted with utilitarianism, which takes all wants as initially entitled to satisfaction, including what might be thought of as morally undesirable wants, and then tries to maximise the total amount of want-satisfaction. Rawls excludes undesirable wants by the conditions of the original position and by the constraints of having a morality.

Men behind the veil of ignorance do not have to have a specially elevated conception of the good life; as rational maximisers they will wish to promote their 'primary goods' – liberty, opportunity, income and wealth, and self-respect (pp. 90–5). An increase in these enables individuals to pursue whatever rational plans of life they have. By constructing a theory of justice that enables only primary goods to be maximised Rawls hopes to avoid some of the traditional difficulties that arise when arguments about justice take the form of arguments about needs and deserts and so on; principles that are concerned with the maximisation of the primary goods preclude these sorts of comparisons. Yet it is this refusal to go behind the primary goods and consider particular needs that has provoked strong criticism. It is said that theories of justice have to involve some reference to want-satisfaction (Barry, 1973, pp. 49–51). For example, a given level of income will mean different things to different people depending upon their circumstances. In this matter Rawls is no different from other procedural theorists mentioned earlier in this chapter.

There are two crucially important assumptions that Rawls makes about self-interested rational agents. First, they are not *envious*. This means that they are concerned only with maximising their primary goods and are not affected by the positions of others. Thus non-envious people would rather secure the highest amount possible of primary goods for themselves, even if others have a much larger amount, than have a lower level on the understanding that others have much less too. Secondly, they can be assumed to have a conservative attitude towards risk. That is, since behind the veil of ignorance they do not know their propensity to gamble, in a situation of uncertainty they will opt for the least disadvantageous outcome in any choice presented to them.

Under these circumstances Rawls argues that the two following principles of justice will be chosen:

1. Each person is to have an equal right to the most extensive liberty compatible with a similar liberty to others.
2. Social and economic inequalities are to be arranged so that they are both
   (a) to the greatest benefit of the least advantaged and
   (b) attached to offices and positions open to all under conditions of fair equality of opportunity (1972, p. 302).

The principles are arranged in *lexical* order under the priority rule (pp. 40–5) which states that 1 is prior to 2, and within 2, 2(b) is prior to 2(a). The priority rule can be compared with the pluralist approach of balancing principles. We noted that in this theory there is no way of showing how a conflict between people who weight sets of principles differently could be resolved. Rawls wants to show that it is rational to opt for a priority rule which gives absolute priority of 1 over 2. To be more exact, he says that, given a certain level of economic development, it would never be rational to trade an equal liberty under 1 (for example, the equal right to vote) for some economic advantage.

The equal liberties under the first principle can be concretised as the familiar rights of liberal democratic regimes. They include equal rights to political participation, freedom of expression, religious liberty, equality before the law and so on. Rawls does imply that some equal liberties may be attenuated but only on condition that this leads to an increase in liberty.

Although 2(b) is technically prior to 2(a) Rawls spends a great deal of time on the latter and it is this which has aroused most interest. He calls this the 'difference' principle and it requires some elucidation. Rawls assumes an initial equality and argues that departures from this can only be justified if they result in clear gains. Obviously, the inequalities of income in a market system increase wealth, by drawing labour into its most productive uses, from which, ideally, everybody gains. Rawls's initial interpretation of the principle was that everybody should gain from inequality but this was later clarified to mean that it should be to the benefit of the least advantaged.

How does Rawls demonstrate that justice requires that all inequalities be acceptable only if they are to the benefit of the least advantaged? He reaches this conclusion in the following manner. He agrees that the Pareto or efficiency principle (see above, Chapter 3) is the criterion for the optimal allocation of resources in society. In the absence of externalities, free exchange will produce an efficient allocation in which no change can take place without making someone (at least one) worse off. An optimal position is reached when no further gains from trade are possible. However, an efficient allocation in this sense is consistent with any initial distribution of property holdings. Even a slave society is technically efficient if a move away from it would make the slave-holders worse off. Rawls therefore argues that since the existing distribution of wealth is likely to be determined by luck, political power and past injustices, the Pareto principle *alone* cannot be a satisfactory criterion of justice. There-fore, in the first instance, the competitive market must be regulated by the fair equality of opportunity principle. This principle then sanctions those social policies which are designed to mitigate the effects of social contingencies which give some groups and individuals unfair advantages over others.

This is quite an egalitarian argument in itself, but Rawls goes further and argues that the modified structure 'still permits the distribution of wealth and income to be determined by the natural distribution of abilities and talents' (pp. 73–4). Any given distribution of *natural* talents, which enables some to secure high returns for their skills, is purely arbitrary from a moral point of view and Rawls thinks that the effects of this 'natural lottery' have to be mitigated by the difference principle. Those with natural talents are entitled to high earnings *only* if such inequalities are to the benefit of the least advantaged. However, once those conditions are met, the efficiency criterion can operate in a competitive economy, which Rawls thinks is possible under either private or public ownership, and the traditional principles of resource allocation will operate so that nobody will be made worse off in any economic outcome. However, to the extent that any given structure is unjust, the principles of justice sanction changes that will aid the worst off at the expense of the better endowed and therefore there will be a breach of the strict formulation of the Pareto principle.

Rawls has to show why this set of principles, and the priority rule, would be chosen by self-interested rational agents behind the veil of ignorance. Such individuals would adopt a maximin strategy and it is this that yields the principles of justice (pp. 152–8). Maximin applies in situations of uncertainty when individuals have *no knowledge* of the probabilities of various outcomes occurring. Under these conditions rational agents, not knowing their propensity to gamble, will have a conservative attitude towards risk and will choose those principles which maximise the position of the worst off, just in case it should turn out that they are the worst off, in terms of talents and skills, in any future society.

Rawls's arguments here are directed against the various forms of utilitarianism. Since utilitarianism maximises total utility, irrespective of its distribution, an individual cannot be certain that he will gain from its implementation. If he knew his attitude towards risk and had knowledge of the probabilities of various outcomes it would be rational for him to gamble on the prospect of, say, turning out to be rich in a utility-maximising society. But in a situation of uncertainty he must assume that he has an equal chance of ending up at the bottom of the pile or at the top. While a slave society might maximise a high level of utility, a rational agent, under Rawls's conditions, must assume he has an equal chance of being a slave as a slave-holder and therefore will not take the risk. Of course, in Rawls's system the pleasures of the better off, however great, cannot compensate for the pains of the worst off.

There are considerable advantages in Rawls's approach. He describes it as a system of *pure procedural justice*, which means that if the principles are unanimously agreed upon, whatever distribution emerges is necessarily just. Thus he can eliminate, in the evaluation of a distribution, interpersonal comparisons based upon desert and need. While individuals can agree upon basic principles they do not have the knowledge, nor can they be expected to have the capacity, to make these particular judgements. In fact, the only interpersonal comparison that Rawls makes is that involved in the identification of the least-advantaged representative man.

There is a particular aspect of the Rawlsian system which might be thought questionable. On what grounds is it reasonable for the better endowed to have their talents, in a sense, used for the well-being of the least advantaged? Rawls anticipates this objection and argues that social life cannot be reduced to individual transactions. It is a collaborative activity in which the most talented can only realise their opportunities in co-operation with those less able (p. 103). This point would appear to put Rawls into the school of *social* justice since it involves a collective dimension to actions which goes beyond the making of transactions between individuals within general rules of fair play.

The objections to Rawls's theory have turned partly on technical arguments about the validity of his deductions and partly on the content of his social philosophy. We shall be concerned here mainly with the general properties of the theory as a substantive theory of justice. There is a difficulty in that some critics have interpreted it as quite a radical egalitarian theory while others treat it as a particularly elegant restatement of the social principles of liberal capitalism. There is evidence for both views.

A great deal of attention has been paid to the nature of the difference principle. We noted earlier that Rawls hoped to devise a theory which is congruent with our intuitive notions of justice but it is not clear that the principle does this since it is consistent with some highly peculiar distributions. If inequalities are justified to the extent that they favour the least advantaged then this would logically permit vast inequalities between rich and poor as long as there is the slightest improvement in the prospects of the poor in comparison with any alternative. Yet intuitively we may wish to comment on the inequalities themselves, even though this means making the complex comparisons between individuals that Rawls forbids. By the same token a utilitarian would object to the conclusion of the Rawlsian theorem, which disallows great gains to the better endowed if that entails a minute loss in the expectations of the worst off.

Rawls tries to counter some of these objections by suggesting that such outcomes are unlikely to occur in practice because the application of his principles would bring about a natural tendency towards equality (pp. 100–5). He argues that a 'chain connection' operates between the best and the worst off and that a rise in the expectations of the best off will have the effect of raising everybody else's expectations throughout the system. This has provoked great hostility from collectivists who say that it is a rationalisation of the traditional liberal-capitalist argument that, somehow, people can only gain from an economic process if the better off are allowed freedom to accumulate. Collectivists would argue that the better off are only able to be successful because of past privileges and class advantages which even a rigorous application of Rawls's fair equality of opportunity principle can do little to alleviate. There may, however, be something important in Rawls's idea here. The evidence suggests that an incentives-based market system does raise the well-being of the worst off, at least in comparison with all known and practised alternatives. While it is certainly impossible to eliminate all the advantages that some have over others, short of abolishing the family, it may be the case that the preservation of the more serious inequalities is a product of the granting of privileges by *political* authorities rather than an endogenous feature of the market system itself. In planned economies these privileges lead to very great inequalities of power.

A very difficult problem for Rawls is the identification of the least advantaged. This clearly cannot be literally *the* worst-off person in any society and must refer to some class of persons: Rawls always refers to the representative man of the least-advantaged group. He gives two definitions of such a person (p. 98), but his whole approach here has been heavily criticised. This is because his methodology precludes him from considering the actual disadvantages of individuals and groups and therefore, it is said that many people who are in real need because of special circumstances would be missed out if an abstract criterion based upon an arbitrary measure of income or wealth were to be the lynchpin of social policy.

The nature and justification of the priority rule has been criticised. While in principle this provides a determinate solution to the possible conflicts between principles, the priority of equal liberty over economic advantage has been challenged. While it is true that in liberal democratic regimes, for example, an individual is not allowed to sell his vote, this, and other similar prohibitions, are a consequence of the *mores* of these political systems, and it is difficult to see how they can be derived from the rational choice situation described by Rawls. It is certainly possible to think of cases where it would be rational to trade an equal liberty for an economic improvement.

Collectivist critics of Rawls are particularly concerned about his commitment to the marginal productivity principle of wages; this permits inequalities which they would exclude by reference to other principles of justice. It is true that by describing the problems of justice in terms of what rules would be chosen in an hypothetical state of ignorance Rawls is departing significantly from the view of justice as a backward-looking concept and seems therefore to sidestep the traditional problems of justifying inequalities.

The Marxist would say, of course, that the idea that principles of justice can be demonstrated in the absence of knowledge of economic and social facts is erroneous. Moral systems can only be understood in the context of class relationships and systems of ownership. However, this retreat into the sociology of morals is a way of avoiding rational argument. When Marxists do make generalised ethical statements their dependence on a rather idiosyncratic concept of man makes them inappropriate for the typical problems of justice. The most effective Marxist criticisms are aimed at exposing particular inequalities characteristic of bourgeois society but here what moral force they have derives from an appeal to liberal-democratic principles rather than specifically Marxist ones.

Some penetrating criticisms of Rawls have come from economic liberals. They see it as a strongly egalitarian doctrine and presumably Rawls would not deny this. Specifically they maintain that although it is a procedural theory of justice it does, nevertheless, pick out a particular end-state; that is, that distribution is just which maximises the well-being of the least advantaged. They also object to the presumption in favour of equality and the assumption that natural assets should constitute a 'common pool' to be distributed according to the principles of social justice. Indeed, Nozick's entitlement theory of justice is a reply to the doctrine of social justice and a large part of *Anarchy, State and Utopia* consists of a sophisticated refutation of Rawls.

An analysis of Rawls's theory reveals some of the familiar problems of justice. The emphasis on justice as a system of rules provides a certain kind of rigour in the use of the concept while at the same time it seems to exclude some of our most deeply-held moral convictions about the way income and wealth should be distributed. Yet there seems to be little agreement about what a more expanded notion of justice should consist of, even amongst those who believe that all departures from equality are in need of justification. Such problems may be best approached by trying to understand what implications general distributive principles have for social policy. What is also required is some analysis of the other item on the agenda of social justice − equality.

# 7

# Equality

## 1. The equality principle

In 1931, when R. H. Tawney first published his famous book *Equality*, he lamented what he called 'The Religion of Inequality' in British society. The problem for him, as a strong egalitarian, was not merely that extremes of income and wealth existed and that the system of social stratification preserved outmoded class distinctions, but that they were accepted as inevitable, and even approved of, by those who stood to gain most from their removal – the working classes. The people accepted the *mana* and *karakia* (Tawney, 1969, p. 35) of social and economic inequality in the same way that primitive people accept the ritual of tribal society. According to Tawney there was no rational justification for inequality; its survival was a matter of prejudice.

It would not be too inaccurate to suggest that today the position has been almost exactly reversed. While egalitarians might protest at the expression the 'religion of equality', which suggests that measures to promote more equality lack a rational foundation, it cannot be denied that the concept has been embraced with great enthusiasm in the postwar years. There seems to be a new consensus, at least amongst *all* brands of socialist opinion, that every movement towards equality is necessarily a good thing, and almost all the social reforms in the welfare state are designed to promote by collectivist measures a form of equality that would not have emerged through private transactions. However, it is difficult to say how far the reverence for the equality principle extends throughout society at large.

The pace at which the progress towards equality proceeds varies from one Western country to another, as does the type of equality pursued. In the United States of America, for example, while there has been a considerable amount of legislative and judicial activity to promote social equality and create more equality of opportunity for minority races and groups, progress towards economic equality has been less speedy. Also, many of Tawney's strictures on the British working class's acquiescence in the face of economic and social inequality might well be true of the United States today. Arthur M. Okun, an egalitarian economist, concedes with regret the point that there is in that country a strong moral approval of the inequalities characteristic of a market economy, even by those groups in some considerable state of deprivation (1975, p. 128).

It is not true in social and political theory that egalitarians are having it all their own way. A perennial debate between political philosophers concerns the relationship between equality and liberty and a long tradition in the discipline holds that the use of state power to bring about an equality that does not emerge spontaneously necessarily involves a reduction in personal liberty. This tradition has been reinforced in recent years by the resurgence of the school of political economy which argues that the imposition of egalitarian measures in the economic sphere necessarily disturbs those mechanisms that allocate resources efficiently in society, and that such disturbances will make everyone worse off, including those the egalitarian measures were designed to help. In this economic philosophy there is not just the familiar political theorist's problem of the tension between equality and liberty but also an exploration of the trade-off between liberty, equality and prosperity (Brittan, 1973, p. 128).

It is important to stress that in this chapter we shall be concerned with equality as a justificatory principle in its own right rather than equality as a part of justice. We have already noted that all theories of procedural-rules justice contain a weak sense of equality which means that, whatever their differences, all men, on account perhaps of their common humanity, are entitled to be treated equally by the rules of a social practice. This is of course not especially egalitarian and is quite consistent with a great deal of social and economic inequality. It is also true that someone could accept this moral principle and still not accept the view that all inequalities have to be justified. As we have seen, most theories of justice do maintain that justice is precisely about justifying departures from equality (which is Rawls's procedure). Classical liberals maintain that a movement towards equality would count as unjustified since it might entail paying the same income to individuals who make widely differing contributions to the output of an economy.

Equality can then conflict with the principles of justice (especially desert-based theories of justice) even though the strong sense of equality,

or egalitarianism, is a basic component of *social justice*. The demand for
equality is not a disguised demand for the removal of some unjustified
inequalities so that all economic and social differences may have some
rational foundation; it is an argument for the thing itself (Barry, 1965, p.
120). Political and constitutional rights, such as the equal right to vote in a
democracy, are examples of the application of equality, just as laws
prohibiting sexual and racial discrimination are. People may reasonably
disagree on how far equality may be pushed but to say that egalitarian
policies are reducible to policies that remove arbitrary privileges is to
misunderstand the (prescriptive) meaning of the principle. Berlin makes
this point when he says, of equality, that 'like all human ends it cannot be
rationally justified for it is itself that which justifies other acts...'
(1965–6, p. 326). As a pluralist Berlin thinks that equality has to be
traded off against other values. While accepting the independent status of
equality as a political principle we shall not accept the view that 'ends'
such as equality and liberty cannot be rationally argued about; indeed
some of the most interesting work done in social and political theory in
recent years has been about ends.

The stress on equality as the essential feature of social justice means
that egalitarians do not have to invoke the concept of moral desert to
justify particular income distributions and in this they have something in
common with *laissez-faire* liberals. An egalitarian who retained some
belief in the importance of liberty should be highly sceptical of
centralised institutions determining a person's worth subject only to
political controls. The problem of need is more complicated since the
satisfaction of needs is an essential element in the egalitarian's social
programme. Yet there are grave problems in establishing what needs are
and connecting these to equality. While it is true that people need food,
clothing, shelter and so on, it is obviously not the case that they need
equal shares of these things. The most pressing cases of social justice are
concerned with the justification of the satisfaction of quite different
needs.

## 2. Human nature and equality

Contemporary egalitarians are eager to make two disclaimers in the
presentation of their doctrine. First, they deny that the demand for
equality means a demand for absolute equality. In fact, this has rarely
been demanded by any thinker in the history of egalitarian thought. They
think therefore that a more equal society would not be characterised by

sameness and uniformity but by a certain amount of variety. It is simply argued that the removal of a large number of existing economic and other inequalities would represent a social improvement. Secondly, the argument for more equality is not normally justified by reference to a supposed natural equality in men. It is true that in the past egalitarian arguments did appear to derive from propositions such as 'All men are created equal', but it is generally agreed that such statements are of little use in the generation of egalitarian theories. In political discourse the word has little *descriptive* content because in all their most important aspects men are most certainly not equal. Therefore its use is mainly *prescriptive;* that is, policies are recommended because they promote the ideal of equality, and the justifications for them do not have to depend upon some descriptive properties of human beings.

Egalitarians would be unwise to base their arguments on human nature. Nothing follows logically about how men ought to be treated in an egalitarian sense from a statement about some supposed factual equality. There is an is – ought gap here, as in other problems of normative ethics. An egalitarian might say that men ought to be treated equally in those respects in which they are equal; they are equal in respect of $x$, therefore in respect of $x$ they ought to be treated equally. But even if agreement could be secured on the prescriptive premise it is unlikely that the completed argument would generate the policies desired by the egalitarian since the ways in which men may be factually said to be equal are trivial. The temptation for egalitarians is to say that because men are equal in some respects they are equal in others and therefore ought to be treated equally (Lucas, 1971, p. 140).

The illegitimacy of 'is to ought' arguments also tells against inegalitarians who, from factual premises alone, attempt to derive policies that treat races and sexes differently. The psychologists' discovery that there is a strong correlation between measured intelligence and race, that on average certain races are superior to others in terms of natural abilities, does not entail in any way normative policy conclusions as to how individual members of the races and groups are to be treated. Policy conclusions with regard to matters of discrimination depend ultimately upon moral principles which cannot be derived from facts. The danger of making the egalitarian argument turn upon facts is that this invites the inegalitarian to produce evidence of natural inequality to give some bite to his argument that there is a case for treating people un-equally.

This sort of reasoning underlies arguments for showing that a version of the equality principle does not depend upon natural equality at all. It is argued by some that the principle of equality before the law and the requirement that rules in a legal system should be general and non-discriminatory are the only procedures which can guarantee that fundamentally *unequal people* can conduct their lives with reasonable predictability and security. The inequalities of human beings cannot be a ground for government and the law treating them differently. This equality of treatment is, however, quite consistent with substantial economic and social inequality. In fact it is certain to be accompanied by such inequality since this ideal of equal liberty before the law enjoyed by individuals who are unequal in endowments must lead to some doing better than others. Yet to bring about a more substantial equality must involve treating them differently, which is contrary to formal equality. The most obvious example is in income, where if we wish to move towards the equalisation of incomes we have to treat people differently by the rules of the tax system.

While it is true that prescriptive uses of the concept of equality are more useful in moral and political argument than descriptive uses, nevertheless we still need to know something more about the right to equal freedom which is implicit in our discussion so far. Can this be supported rationally or is the commitment to the principle purely a matter of personal choice? Is there any answer to Hare's fanatic who consistently universalises a principle that Jews should be exterminated even if he himself should turn out to be a Jew? Does the distinction between fact and value mean that all principles are a matter of personal choice or is there some element of *impartiality* built into morality itself? Bernard Williams (1963) seems to imply that there is when he says that the distinction between fact and value cannot be used to smuggle in pure arbitrariness in the guise of moral argument. Thus he says that to argue that someone should be discriminated against purely on grounds of race is not to invoke a special moral principle but to act in an arbitrary manner, that is to say, in a way in which reasons are irrelevant.

The suggestion that morality itself implies an element of impartiality, while it does not yield substantive egalitarian conclusions, is not vacuous. From it we can derive the idea of a 'common humanity' – that minimal, but fundamental notion of equality that unites all men into one reference group for the purposes of moral argument. While men are different from each other in many important respects they are similar in comparison with other species. Thus we treat people equally, in the way that we would not (morally) treat men and dogs equally (Wilson, 1966,

p. 103), yet at the same time we do not treat them as equals, which clearly they are not.

For the egalitarian the price of agreement may be too high since an hierarchical society with no upward mobility or an extreme *laissez-faire* society would both be consistent with this principle. However, it is not trivial because clearly there are societies that do not recognise it and do not treat men as men but solely in terms of some category based on, say, religion or race. Furthermore, the equality which is being referred to is not analytically tied to the entity 'man' because it is certainly possible to deny this property to those whom we would call men on other grounds. What we are referring to in this notion of equality is that it is descriptive of those capable of making rational choices: people are at least equal in the sense that no one person's choices have an *a priori* right to superiority over another's. Yet we would not include within our reference group mental defectives and young children, precisely because morality seems to exclude those either incapable or not yet capable of making rational choices. Of course, this is not to say that we do not have very strong moral duties towards the mentally deranged and others whom we do not call rational choosers.

Despite some heroic attempts by philosophers, it is not possible to derive substantive egalitarian conclusions from the equal right to freedom implicit in the notion of a 'common humanity'. Arguments over equality of opportunity and the appropriate distribution of income and wealth take place between political theorists who accept the idea of impartiality in moral argument and that each human being is entitled to dignity and self-respect. Anti-egalitarians often argue that the imposition of socialist egalitarian measures undermines this dignity and self-respect and that the paternalism that often accompanies such measures negates the idea of man as a rational chooser. Therefore the case for equality in the strong sense has to be argued for independently of appeals to 'common humanity'. The interesting problems centre on the connection between equality and other principles and the consequences of adopting egalitarian policies.

## 3. Equality of opportunity

While it is true that egalitarians disagree on the desirable level of equality in a quantitative sense, there is almost unanimous agreement as to the desirability of the qualitative value of equality of opportunity. It is a value which even some non-egalitarians have found appealing.

Yet it is difficult to see what equality of opportunity has to do with equality at all, and, as has often been pointed out, if it were to be applied rigorously it might well produce a state of affairs with a much greater degree of economic and social stratification than exists at present in most Western democracies.

It is a strictly meritarian doctrine which finds its most coherent expression in the authoritarian political philosophy of Plato. In his *Republic* all those factors which arbitrarily advantaged one person as against another were removed, including the family, so that the social position which men and women (Plato was an early and rigorous exponent of the equality of the sexes) found themselves in was entirely a result of their own abilities and efforts, all elements of chance having been removed from an individual's life-prospects.

While the modern exponent of the doctrine might claim that it is an aspect of the egalitarian creed because it entails the elimination of arbitrary advantages and a general levelling out of the social and economic system, the principle might also be interpreted as an example of the maximisation of an equal liberty. In this view to demand equality of opportunity is to demand the removal of impediments or obstacles that stand in the way of an individual realising his potential; an increase in opportunity is an increase in liberty. There is a certain plausibility in this view since, at least in the original formulation of 'the career open to the talents', the doctrine demanded the removal of *legal* and other unjustifiable privileges that reserved certain social, economic and political positions for classes, races or one particular sex. However, the modern exponent of the doctrine wants to do more than this; he also wants to remove those other factors that advantage some but which are the result of luck rather than legal privilege, such as being born the son of a successful entrepreneur. To remove these privileges is not to maximise equal liberties but to implement a general levelling out which would certainly involve the abrogation of certain liberties, such as the right to bequest.

The intellectual ancestor of modern thinking on equality of opportunity is undoubtedly Rousseau. In his *On the Origins of Inequality in Society* he sought to explain the immorality of eighteenth-century European society by the inequality which made one man dependent on another. While Rousseau did not believe in absolute equality, and indeed on one famous occasion proclaimed the 'sacred right of property', he did say that when men establish extensive private property holdings they create conventional and arbitrary inequalities that reduce some to servility.

It is the supposed distinction between *nature* and *convention* that underlies Rousseau's egalitarianism. Natural inequalities of physical strength, intellect, beauty and so on, are acceptable: social inequalities, because they are a product of pure convention, are not. The distinction between nature and convention seems to turn upon the assumption that conventional inequalities are *alterable*, while natural ones are not, and it is this that seems to lie behind the contemporary doctrine of equality of opportunity (Rees, 1971, pp. 14–26). While Rousseau's solution to the problem of inequality created by industrial society was to retreat into a small agrarian community of equals governed by the popular will, the modern egalitarian is more forward-looking in that he hopes that society can be rationally planned so that all artificial advantages are removed: the only acceptable inequalities are natural, unalterable ones.

The difficulty with this superficially appealing idea concerns the distinction between nature and convention, which is not as clear-cut as egalitarians imply. While there is an obvious distinction between natural inequalities of strength, beauty and intelligence, and the man-made legal distinctions, such as those that prohibit members of racial or religious groups from taking political office, there is a vast area of social life where the words nature and convention are quite irrelevant. Rousseau's argument that inequalities are created by 'society' is really absurd since we have no useful conception of man abstracted from society which can form a touchstone for the legitimacy or otherwise of various distinctions. What might be thought of as a relevant natural distinction, such as that based on intelligence, is relevant only because society has conventionally regarded it as such for many purposes.

In a similar way, what might be thought of as conventional laws and institutions are not *merely* conventional or the product of choice. Can it be said that the English common law system or the parliamentary form of government were deliberately chosen?[1] It is true that such conventions are not natural phenomena, like the weather, but they are certainly not arbitrary. David Hume described the rules of justice that authorise the possession and transfer of property as 'artificial', but he said that it would be perfectly correct to call them fundamental 'laws of nature' in that every society must have some rules of this type which cannot be cast aside or substantially altered at will.

The significance of this for the egalitarian is that while rules can be altered, the proposed distinction between nature and convention does not provide an indisputable criterion for determining what the alterations shall be. The existence of government and the need to enforce general rules means that there will be of necessity some political inequality which may not inaccurately be regarded as 'natural'. It may be said that disparities between individuals in income and wealth are conventional and arbitrary since they rest upon man-made rules which are alterable by will. This is possible but in doing so new rules will have to be found to govern property holdings which may turn out to be the source of new conventional inequalities. This is not to say that there are no arguments for increasing equality of opportunity, but only to suggest that the distinction between nature and convention is an unsatisfactory ground for them.

It is in education that the most substantial arguments for equality of opportunity have been advanced and it is in this area that the familiar problems of the concept can be most easily illustrated. If birth or wealth determine educational opportunity then, superficially, this seems quite conventional or arbitrary (and therefore open to alteration) because we have a perfectly good natural, indeed highly relevant, criterion in intelligence on which a 'rational' educational policy can be based. But in logic intelligence is no better a qualification for educational preferment, since those excluded by this criterion may legitimately claim that it is as arbitrary as birth or wealth. Indeed, in a socialised system of education the parents of less gifted children may legitimately complain that they, as tax-payers, are being unjustly treated since they are being forced to subsidise the unequal education of the newly privileged class of children. It could also be argued that a disproportionate amount of money should be spent on the less gifted precisely because they are less gifted.

All this is not to deny that the advocate of equality of opportunity has a point when he protests at the injustices of a system of education that seems to preclude groups of people on arbitrary grounds. However, just what non-arbitrary or relevant grounds might be is not as easy to determine as some people have supposed.

The problems do not end even if agreement can be secured as to the relevance of intelligence to educational advancement – as a brief look at British educational policy reveals. Under the old system of selection at the age of eleven, the aim was undoubtedly to establish a meritocratic procedure in which equality of opportunity was to be guaranteed by making provision of secondary schooling depend upon measured scores in IQ tests. In fact, as a number of research reports indicated, the system did not work since, although the number of working-class children admitted to grammar schools did reflect the distribution of measured intelligence they did not take advantage of the opportunity, so that the numbers going on to higher education and the professions did not, and does not, reflect the mean distribution of IQ throughout the country as a whole (Crosland, 1962, pp. 169–74). Equality of opportunity was nowhere near fully realised because certain factors, such as parental hostility to education and the desire, and perhaps need, to earn high wages early in life, deterred working-class children from taking advantage of those opportunities to which natural intelligence entitled them.

To eliminate these inequalities of opportunity, however, would require very drastic intervention in society in order to equalise the circumstances of children. But if one takes the view that IQ is itself partly determined by environmental factors (which many psychologists do not) then there is really no limit to what the state may do to make educational opportunity correlate exactly with the natural property of intelligence. The first casualty in a completely rationalistic system of equality of opportunity would be the family, which is unavoidably the source of much inequality. The threat to the family, and personal liberty, makes many people fearful of a rigid application of the doctrine.

As Michael Young has shown in his brilliant parody, *The Rise of the Meritocracy* (1961), a meritarian society would produce a much more rigid, and sinister, system of social stratification than Western democracies have at present. Such a system is likely to be resented, and be the cause of disharmony, precisely because it is so eminently meritocratic. People who finish up at the bottom do not have even the comfort of being justly aggrieved at their lot because that is where they deserve to be. As has often been pointed out, what chance would the notion of a fundamental equality of human personality have of being accepted in such a world?

There is also the problem that some of the 'natural' inequalities may prove to be alterable with the advance of medical science. Genetic engineering may soon make it possible to eliminate hereditary differences so that a genuinely equal starting point in life can be established for everyone. The least successful will no longer be able to complain at the injustice of nature in distributing talents so unfairly.

There is no need to speculate further on this theme to realise that there is something deeply unsatisfactory at the heart of the doctrine of equality of opportunity. It would be unwise to push the doctrine beyond justifying the removal of the most obvious type of arbitrary discrimination based on race, religion and sex, since most of the egalitarian's ideals can be presented in ways that do not require the precarious distinction between nature and convention.

But even in familiar policy areas there are difficulties that raise philosophical issues. For example, it seems on the face of it absurd that university education should be accessible *only* to those who can afford to pay for it. It seems natural that those who reach certain educational standards should receive grants from the state so that opportunity is equalised. However, this clearly involves a breach of justice (procedural and social). This is because those with degrees who earn higher incomes than those without them are clearly being subsidised by the relatively worse off (Maynard, 1975, p. 51). Since *anybody* who enjoys three years at the expense of the state, that is the taxpayer, is clearly in receipt of a considerable privilege, it is often argued in Britain that loans should replace grants. What is not often realised is that this is an argument for justice.

While the existence of *private* school education, available only to the rich, is a denial of equality of opportunity, it does not follow that this is most efficiently modified by the imposition of a complete state monopoly since this puts everybody at the mercy of bureaucracy. To maximise choice it has been suggested that money spent by the state on education should be given back to parents in the form of *vouchers* which could be spent at any school; equality could be catered for by varying the value of the voucher in accordance with the income of the parents. Such a scheme would then combine both liberty and some equality.

## 4. Income and wealth

The egalitarian is disturbed by the fact that while a liberal-democratic system grants equality of political, legal and constitutional rights, and trading in such rights is forbidden, it puts very few restrictions on inequalities of rights in the economic sphere where trading reigns supreme (Okum, 1975, pp. 6–31). Not only are these said to be objectionable in themselves but they are also thought to attenuate equal political rights; wealth can to some extent 'buy' political power. There are two major ways by which these inequalities may be removed; either by redistributive taxation, or by the collective provision of goods and services (and hence the creation of equal 'welfare rights' which are logically equivalent to equal political rights).

Progressive income tax is the most obvious method of equalising spending power. The tax system is not just used to finance government services but also to effect redistribution. A movement towards a more equal post-tax distribution of earnings is an important element in social justice. While progressive income tax is taken for granted in Western countries it has never been without its critics. It is said by some to breach a rule of procedural justice in that it unjustifiably *discriminates* against high earners. The critics propose a *proportional* income tax in which the same rule would apply to everyone. Needless to say it is always a low tax that is recommended, perhaps 25 per cent of whatever a person earns. However, it is argued, even by classical liberals, that some progression can be justified on the ground that the rich should bear a greater burden than the poor.

Under a progressive tax system the fixing of the marginal rates of tax must be arbitrary, and indeed the warnings of the early critics of the method have been amply fulfilled; that is to say, the rates have got inexorably higher. In practice, of course, the redistributive aim may not always succeed. It has been argued that under a democratic system, although there is some distribution from rich to poor, the main beneficiaries are the middle income groups, where the largest numbers of voters are to be found. Also progressive income tax systems are riddled with anomalies which enable accountants to earn high incomes by advising people how to avoid paying taxes. This, the critics maintain, is a misallocation of intellectual resources; under a simple proportional tax system there would be no allowances and few loopholes. Furthermore the tax system is particularly anomalous in that the tax threshold and welfare benefits intersect for low earners producing what is called the 'poverty trap'. If a low wage earner works more so as to increase his income he loses certain welfare benefits, for example, rate and rent subsidies, while at the same time he is drawn into the tax net. Thus the effective marginal rate of tax for him can be over 100 per cent. The effect on incentives to work in this situation is too obvious to require comment.

Apart from the practical problems with steeply progressive income tax there is also the general problem of the effect on efficiency that the system has. While economists are not in agreement as to whether high marginal rates are a disincentive to work, income tax is obviously distortionary. If under high marginal rates people work the same number of hours then they have less to spend on goods and services, but if they work more in order to retain the same level of expenditure then the ratio between work and leisure is disturbed. In fact it is almost impossible to design a completely 'neutral' tax, that is, one that has no effect on economic behaviour. The interesting question for the political theorist is the effect that a highly egalitarian tax structure may have on prosperity and liberty.

To take an example, let us assume that the free market price of labour for getting oil out of the North Sea is £400 a week, while at the same time an egalitarian social policy decrees that no one shall earn a post-tax income of over £180 a week. Now if this is insufficient to draw enough labour into the industry to produce the optimal amount of oil then society will be less prosperous, if at the same time it wishes to maintain freedom of choice in occupation. On the safe assumption that non-pecuniary appeals to such things as 'social duty' are ineffective then an egalitarian has to choose between a loss in output or a loss of liberty. Thus if he wishes to maintain the optimal level of oil output and an egalitarian earnings system he will have to resort to the direction of labour. By the same reasoning if the lowest free market wage is £50 a week and the egalitarian wishes to raise that to £80 then this will increase the demand for those occupations and reduce the supply of jobs – thus causing unemployment. It may even lead to the government allocation of jobs.

The trade-off usually made is between efficiency and equality and democratic societies are normally prepared to sacrifice a considerable loss in productive efficiency rather than resort to the direction of labour. *Laissez-faire* liberals have probably been unduly pessimistic in their prognostication that any interference with the free market economy on behalf of equality will lead to the direction of labour. However, it is worth pointing out that at least one strongly egalitarian social philosopher, Brian Barry, has accepted just this, albeit in a slightly different context. In denying that market forces will allocate labour efficiently he suggests that to 'spread the nastiest jobs around' people entering higher education or the professions should be required 'to do, say, three years of work wherever he or she was directed' (1973, p. 164).

While most egalitarians would accept the loss in efficiency that equality entailed, and might suggest that a more equal society would exhibit other more desirable values, there is another line of attack on high incomes that is worth exploring. It is often said that part of the high earnings of for example, film stars, footballers and other entertainers, consists of 'rent', that is, the income that accrues over and above that income required to make them remain in that occupation, and that this could be taxed away without reducing their productivity. The argument is also applied to lawyers and doctors. This argument has only a superficial plausibility. First, there is the difficulty of establishing how much of the earnings is rent; secondly it would almost certainly require limitations on people leaving the country, and a permanent incomes policy with sanctions. In fact in many cases high earnings do not represent rent but a return for investment in training. Even the enormous sums earned by entertainers may only be temporary so that when these are spread over a lifetime of possibly low earnings the element of rent may be negligible.

A better target might be the virtual monopoly positions enjoyed by some professionals. The high earnings of American doctors are partly explained by the ability of the American Medical Association to control and limit the supply of doctors. The same reasoning can be applied to trade union practices that are designed to restrict entry into certain occupations thereby raising wages and causing inequalities between workers. Other reasons for differential wages include the very important one that differential earnings may reflect non-pecuniary rewards that inhere in some occupations.

Egalitarians, perhaps wary of some of the undesirable consequences that may follow from a bureaucratic interference with wages, have put more stress in recent years on the unequal distribution of *wealth* in Western societies. It is certainly true that in Britain the spread of ownership of personal wealth is more uneven than income, though they both show a tendency towards equality. The fact that substantial inequality remains, however, has led to the demands for a wealth tax, which is an annual tax on personal assets above a certain level. This is thought to have a much less deleterious effect on efficency and would be consistent with the retention of a market allocation of resources.

Before we can properly analyse the case for a wealth tax, however, we must understand the meaning of statistics about wealth ownership: far too often political argument is retarded by slogans such as '5 per cent own 80 per cent of the wealth' which have primarily an emotive appeal. In Britain the Royal Commission on the Distribution of Income and Wealth reported in 1975 that the richest 1 per cent of the population owned 27.6 per cent of the wealth, the top 5 per cent owned 51.3 per cent and the top 10 per cent owned 67.2 per cent (*Financial Times*, 31 July 1975). Although there has been a noticeable equalisation – in 1960, for example, 10 per cent owned 77 per cent and for the period 1911 – 38 the same proportion owned approximately 90 per cent – the figures still appear to require some explanation, if not justification. In fact, since the Inland Revenue figures are based on estate duty figures only, they imply that over half the population owns no wealth at all! Wealth statistics include 'marketable' wealth only and therefore exclude pension rights which, although they cannot be bought and sold, ought to be counted in some form. It has been calculated that if occupational pension rights are included the figure for the top 10 per cent would come down by about 7 per cent, but if state pension rights are included this figure is reduced to about 45 per cent.

It has also been plausibly suggested that wealth inequalities can be accounted for by life-cycle factors: if people accumulate savings during their working life then one would expect a concentration of wealth around the group which is at retirement age. However, this would not explain the very significant concentration of wealth among the top 1 per cent which must be a result of inheritance.

The evidence suggests that there is, in Britain, not much room for manoeuvre for wealth redistribution (Kay and King, 1978, pp. 118–20). Taxing the very rich would not yield much for dispersal and such measures could be interpreted as purely punitive. To secure a significant yield the state would have to tax much less well-off people which would not only be resented but might also produce unintended economic and social consequences.

This is not to say that there are no grounds for increasing equality through the tax system but only to suggest that the costs in terms of almost certain losses in efficiency, and possible losses in liberty, should be borne in mind. With regard to income, most egalitarians would agree that a sharing out of the 'excess' of the top salaries would not increase the spending power of the rest of the population all that much:[2] it would, however, have a serious implication for production and certainly lead to an increase in emigration. In fact, traditional egalitarian arguments for economic equality have depended more on the 'social' benefits of a more equal distribution than on the material advantages it might bring to the less fortunate.

The advantage of redistributing wealth through the tax system (rather than the state promoting equality through the universal provision of such goods as education, health and housing) is that it allows freedom of choice for individuals in expenditure. An egalitarian could logically believe in a very small public sector and a market allocation of resources that reflected individual preferences and yet recommend strongly redistributive economic policies. Most egalitarians are not of this type but hope to promote equality by public provision of specific goods.

There is undoubtedly a paternalistic element in this form of egalitarianism since it implies that individuals cannot be trusted to spend their incomes on welfare goods so that the state has to do it for them via the tax system. There is a justification for some paternalism because of the fact that children may suffer if their parents do not provide for their education and health out of the increased spending power that a redistributive tax system would give them. It is also argued that a welfare system cannot be viewed in purely cash terms and that state provision of goods in kind increases social equality. The case might be strengthened by the arguments of the 'social indicators' school of welfare which suggest that social inequality, revealed by areas in society of chronic bad housing, urban deprivation and so on cannot be overcome by simple cash transfers. What is really being recommended here is an extension of the concept of rights from the political and legal sphere to the economic sphere. There ought, in other words, to be some equalities (for example, in health and education) which the market must not disturb, even if inefficiency may well result. In fact the British experience suggests that the state does not efficiently reflect what people desire in the way of welfare; for example, a smaller proportion of GNP is spent on health in the socialised medical system than in countries that have a mixture of private insurance and public provision.[3]

The foundation of the egalitarian rejection of the achievement of equality by income transfers is really a metaphysical view of man and society. There is a tradition of socialist thought, exemplified in the writings of Tawney and Titmuss, which is concerned about the wider effects of the intrusion of the cash nexus into things like education and health. If these are 'marketed' then, even if incomes are equalised, this will undermine those socially-oriented feelings and attitudes which are required for an altruistic and egalitarian society. The implication seems to be that even if individualistic market societies make even the poorest better off, they are objectionable, because the inequalities they necessarily generate contaminate all social relationships. Equality is not valued in a material sense but for its significance in encouraging the 'gift relationship'. This is not greatly dissimilar from the early writings of Marx in which he was not so much concerned with prophesying the collapse of capitalism as with presenting a moral argument that the cash nexus of capitalism produced alienation and an anti-social individualism.

This is a somewhat romantic view and not a rigorously argued one. There is really no evidence that the public and equal delivery of services generates the desired co-operative feelings and attitudes. The opposite may well be true because of the inevitable politicisation that occurs in the process. Once certain goods and services become the object of pressure group and political activity then even greater divisiveness may emerge than appears in the impersonal market system. There is the fundamental problem that the collectivisation of welfare involves an increased use of political power and there is no guarantee that this will be used in desirable directions, even if it is possible to determine what these directions are.

Those who are critical of contemporary concern with equality claim that it is more important to direct attention to alleviating the lot of those at the bottom of the scale than to establish equality itself. The assumption here is surely the correct one: that the wealth of the few is not necessarily the *cause* of the poverty of others. While a rich society may be able to afford the loss in efficiency that a movement towards equality entails, an increase in equality itself is not the same thing as an improvement in the welfare of the poor. It is also important to note that one of the consequences of economic egalitarianism is that if natural inequalities in man are denied expression in an economic form they will appear in a potentially more harmful guise in the political sphere.

Those who believe that welfare goods should be delivered in kind rather than cash might argue that such provision meets some universal needs which are a part of equality, but these are difficult to state objectively. In fact, most of the pressing cases of need involve *inequality* of provision; although it has been argued that such apparent inequality is consistent with equality since to cater for special circumstances is to establish an equality. However, if it is agreed that directing attention to the poor, rather than establishing equality, is the prime aim of the welfare state then the choice of policies which will most *effectively* guarantee this becomes almost a technical matter. From this point of view it is more important to raise the *absolute* level of well-being of the worst off than worry about *relative* positions within the spread of income and wealth. It is for this reason that special welfare measures to aid deprived groups are preferred to the uniform and egalitarian delivery of welfare goods.

## 5.  Reverse discrimination

One aspect of egalitarianism which has generated fierce philosophical debate in the United States is the policy of giving favoured treatment to members of deprived groups because such groups have suffered systematic discrimination in the past. Favoured treatment includes 'privileged' access to jobs and educational courses (especially law and medical schools), and the recipients tend to be negroes and women. These policies of 'affirmative action' are said to imply reverse discrimination because they embody race (or sex) as a criterion for differential treatment just as overtly racist (and sexist) actions in the past did. The policies could be fairly mild (for example, using race or colour to break ties between equally well-qualified candidates, when spinning a coin might be thought 'fairer'), or strong (for example, reserving places for those of a particular race or sex at lower standards of qualification than everybody else).[4]

There are various justifications for these practices. Some defenders argue that they are examples of *compensatory* justice (to put right past unjustified discrimination against blacks and women); others appear to accept such preferential treatment as necessary for end-state equality; and some, more pragmatically in the case of race, wish to increase the number of black doctors and lawyers for the ghettos. There is also a curious line of justification to the effect that intellectual criteria are not the only relevant factors for appointments (which is, in a special sense, true) and that colour and sex are equally important: women and blacks who are not as intellectually well-qualified as white males nevertheless 'deserve' their preferential treatment.

The social philosophy that lies behind the policy of affirmative action is somewhat confused and many have objected to it without dissenting from the general egalitarian sentiment, or from the idea that social policy ought to take account of the injustices inflicted on blacks and women in the United States in the past. The policy involves injustice at least in the procedural sense (and quite possibly in the substantive sense) since *granting* privileges to individuals *because* of their race or sex is as discriminatory and unjust as *denying* them opportunities and jobs for the same reasons. It is also unjust since whatever wrongs were committed against blacks and women in the past, it is clearly not the case that young white males, the victims of preferential hiring practices, are responsible for them. In fact, since blacks and women are regarded *collectively* as the victims of past injustice it often turns out that rich and socially advantaged blacks get preferential treatment over poor and underprivileged whites: this injustice cannot be avoided if people are treated as members of groups rather than individuals. There would also appear to be a social injustice since the beneficiaries of preferential treatment already have some minimal educational qualifications and therefore may be less in *need* than other members of their race or sex. It is also difficult to see how affirmative action is consistent with the notions of dignity and self-respect which are central to the egalitarian creed, since the knowledge that a person was preferentially treated *because* of race or sex must surely reinforce feelings of inferiority.

The argument about preferential hiring clearly illustrates the differences between methodological individualism and methodological collectivism. For the individualist cases of discrimination must always be interpreted in terms of one individual discriminating against another, while the collectivist argues that systematic patterns of discrimination against a race or sex entitle one to say that that race or sex has suffered collectively and that such wrongs may be remedied at the collective level. The individualist's position is that to admit collective entities into the law will not only produce individual injustice but also undermine the right to equal freedom. If he were an egalitarian he could still justify governmental measures to aid the disadvantaged irrespective of sex, race or social grouping.

# 8

# Liberty

## 1. The meaning of liberty

In ordinary speech we understand liberty or freedom (the two words are taken to have the same meaning even though some writers try to maintain a distinction between them) to mean the absence of constraints or obstacles (Cranston, 1953, ch. I). A person is free to the extent that his actions and choices are not impeded by the actions of others. While most liberal thinkers maintain that it is the *deliberate* actions of others that inhibit the liberty of the individual – and in familiar social and political contexts examples of unfreedom are of this type – this is not *necessarily* so. It has been suggested that a person's liberty can be accidentally limited by the actions of another, as when someone may inadvertently lock another person in a room; the unfortunate victim certainly is unfree although this is not the result of anyone's deliberate contrivance (Parent, 1974, p. 151). However, such cases are not of great interest to the social and political theorist since his main concern is with the *justification* of the limits on liberty imposed by political and other authorities.

The cases of unfreedom that illuminate the concept most clearly are imprisonment, slavery, severe restrictions on choice of consumer goods and any action deterred by a law backed by sanctions. The types of constraints are numerous and various so that statements about liberty are seriously incomplete if they do not specify particular prohibitions. While in political argument men demand 'liberty' itself or a 'free society' these are incoherent slogans until it is indicated what particular restraints it is desirable to remove. Since all societies are characterised by a variety of restraints the demand for complete liberty is meaningless, unless it is the cry of the hermit who wishes to opt out of all social relationships and lead a completely self-sufficient life. But even if this state of affairs were possible the 'liberty' enjoyed in it would be of no interest to the political theorist.

We think of freedom in the context of particular constraints occurring in social relationships. While it is sometimes meaningful to speak of *physical* constraints limiting personal freedom this is not normally at all helpful. One does not normally say that a person is not free to fly like a bird or that one's liberty to travel to the United States of America from Britain is impeded by the existence of the Atlantic Ocean (Lucas, 1966, p. 146); in such cases it is the *power* that we lack. The point of labouring this rather obvious fact is that it directs attention to the most important aspect of freedom, which is that it is concerned with circumstances that are alterable. We speak of individual liberty being constrained when the particular constraint is removable. If certain features of social life can be altered then freedom may be increased.

Free action is then voluntary action. It is action which is a product of individual choice and not dictated or determined by threats and other forms of coercion. Of course, this does not take us very far since there is the vexed question of what is to count as a constraint. Do the examples of influences in the form of psychological pressures on individuals, in the case perhaps of advertising, count as causes of unfreedom? Also, although most theorists of liberty say that the existence of law implies the absence of freedom, it is undoubtedly meaningful to say that people do *freely* choose to break the law and are therefore, strictly speaking, not impeded. By reasoning which appears odd to the modern mind, Hobbes maintained that freedom and 'threat' were not antithetical, that someone motivated by fear was nevertheless free. The problems that surround freedom and choice will be discussed below.

When freedom is understood as voluntary, uncoerced action it enables some kind of ethical evaluation to be made of human conduct: there is an intimate connection here between freedom and responsibility. It would be meaningless to distribute praise or blame to actions that were not voluntary. To say that a person's action is the product of choice is to say that he could have acted otherwise than as he did, and to say that is to attribute rationality and responsibility to agents. There are severe difficulties in the notion of a responsible rational agent which cannot be discussed here, but without such a notion the idea of a free society would be incomprehensible. Of course, all theorists of liberty exclude certain categories of persons, children and mental defectives for example, but restrict this to as small a number as possible. At the heart of traditional liberal theory is an objection to *paternalism*, the belief that some people can have a better idea of others' wants than they can themselves. Liberal theorists, including John Stuart Mill, have also thought that freedom could only be enjoyed by citizens of reasonably advanced societies.

A most important feature of freedom as the absence of constraints is that it distinguishes free acts from right or virtuous acts. Unlike some 'positive' theories of liberty which imply that the only proper freedom is doing the right thing or pursuing worthy aims, the common usage conception of freedom is not concerned with the *content* of an action, but only whether it is prevented or not. A person who wastes his freedom on worthless activities is just as free as a person who develops his potentialities to their highest point. The traditional liberal was concerned precisely to stress the fact that freedom necessarily involves the freedom to do wrong and to make mistakes. The justification for so wide a range of freedoms in his doctrine depends upon the idea that men can learn from their mistakes and that social progress depends upon this. The problem here is that freedoms can conflict, that one man's liberty to write, publish and display certain kinds of literature may collide with another's freedom to suppress these things. Just what the relationship should be between law and liberty is one of the most complex and delicate problems for liberal theorists.

The account of freedom given so far should not be confused with a superficially similar definition. This approach identifies freedom with the absence of impediments to the *satisfaction of desires*. In this view a person is free when he can do what he wants to do, when he is not frustrated. This identifies freedom with contentment or want-satisfaction.[1] It is misleading because it implies that a person is still free even though there are impediments preventing him from doing that which he does not want to do. From this it would follow that a slave was free simply because all his desires were satisfied and he had no wish to be burdened with the kind of choices that a free man has to make. We can only make comparative judgements about freedom by looking at the range of alternatives available in one situation or another; whether individuals actually want the liberties that exist is not strictly relevant to the *analysis* of freedom.

It would also follow from this mistaken definition of freedom that freedom could be increased by actually suppressing or manipulating desires so that only desires which can easily be satisfied remain. The important point about freedom as the absence of constraints is that it accommodates a *potentiality* for the satisfaction of desire. A person may be forbidden from doing that which he does not want to do anyway but we do not describe him as free, however contented he is, since the prohibition cuts off a possible future course of action. A free society is not one which allows individuals to have their desires satisfied but one which, by reducing coercive law to the minimum, allows for an ever widening range of choices. For this reason it is sometimes said that freedom may not always be congenial; the necessity of making choices may indeed be burdensome to some. We can distinguish between 'feeling free', a state of contentment, and 'being free', a state in which the major impediments to making choices have been removed. The old lag may deliberately commit a crime in order to recapture the security of prison life but it would be absurd to describe his resulting condition as one of liberty.

A distinction is commonly made, although not universally accepted by political theorists, between being *free* to do something and being *able* to do something (Cranston, 1953, pp. 25–7). To be free to do something is not to be restrained, while to be able is to have the capacity, financial or otherwise, to do something. Thus I am free to go to France if there is no law preventing me from travel but I am unable to take advantage of this freedom if I cannot afford to do so. Liberals who uphold this distinction want to make clear a conceptual distinction between liberty (not being restrained) and the conditions which make liberty worthwhile.

Those who oppose this maintain that there is a distinction between freedom *from* and freedom *to*. It is not merely the fact that a starving person who is not *legally* prevented from eating in an expensive restaurant enjoys only a derisory liberty, but that freedom itself requires positive action by the state. It is this reasoning that has been used to justify social legislation designed to increase the opportunities of individuals. State action is said to increase liberty and not merely to reduce inequality. Undoubtedly there is an attempt to capture the favourable overtones that freedom has for some policies which may in fact involve a loss of liberty. It must be stressed, then, that those who object to the assimilation of being free with being able are not necessarily objecting to the policies but to the description of their purpose.

It has often been pointed out that one of the disadvantages of this assimilation is that it destroys the special significance of freedom. How are we to describe a situation in which a rich negro is denied entry to a restaurant in a country where a colour bar operates, if freedom *means* having a certain capacity? Freedom is intimately connected with rights and in one important sense (see Chapter 9) rights are held against governments. These rights may very well be lost sight of if intervention to correct an unacceptable inequality is presented as an increase in liberty. The assimilation would prevent us drawing the important distinction between the situation of a poor man in a free society who enjoyed the traditional liberties – freedom of movement, freedom from arbitrary arrest, free choice in occupation and so on – and that of someone who was well cared for by the state in an economic sense but lacked these liberties.

It is also important to examine the connection between liberty and political liberty. Many writers do not clearly separate the two concepts but it is certainly the case that many important freedoms could obtain in the absence of political liberty. We normally associate political liberty with democratic regimes, and it includes the right to vote, to participate in politics and to influence government. While it would be odd to describe a society as free which did not grant political liberty, it is true that democracies, characterised by participation and responsive to the popular will, may suppress individual freedoms. But it is also true that non-democratic societies, and even mild dictatorships, may leave their citizens well alone in certain important areas. The connection between democracy and personal freedom is a contingent and not a necessary one. However, it is important to note that the *competitive* party democracies in the West *must* grant some considerable freedom to people to associate, communicate ideas and to oppose government if they are to survive and this of itself ensures the maintenance of important freedoms (including a free press).

We understand freedom to mean the absence of coercion. The actions of free persons are actions that are not determined deliberately by others. One of the clearest cases of a person's unfreedom is when he is limited and restricted in his behaviour by the existence of laws backed by sanctions. Law and liberty are commonly thought to be antithetical. The precise relationship between law and liberty is, however, in need of some clarification.

We say that someone is not free to do $x$ if a law, backed by a sanction, prohibits it, but if freedom means the absence of impediments it seems, paradoxically, that the existence of a law does not render a person unfree. One can still choose to break the law and it would indeed be most odd to say that criminal acts are not free acts (Benn and Weinstein, 1971, p. 206). Also some laws hardly limit freedom at all since the penalties that accompany them are so slight that they function like taxes rather than instruments of coercion; parking fines may be viewed in this way. Similar problems arise in the case of someone who obeys the law because the penalties of disobedience are extremely painful. In such a situation a person still chooses to obey when he could have done otherwise; is he not therefore free? From this it would follow that if freedom means the absence of impediments or obstacles to actions and choices imposed by others, then the only genuine case of unfreedom would be where a person is imprisoned, or to put it more exactly, when he is literally bound and chained. This seems to be the position taken by Hobbes in his attempt to demonstrate the consistency of freedom and 'threat'.

There is, however, another reason for wishing to retain the idea that there is some element of freedom of choice in the action of an individual when faced by a law backed by a sanction. Occasionally we want to say that a man ought to have disobeyed an order even though penalties were attached to it. Sometimes it is no defence (morally) to say that 'I was only obeying orders' when, say, a person is ordered to shoot innocent civilians. There are occasions when moral considerations are thought to override the normal prudential calculations that are made by a person when faced by a law or command backed by a sanction: a person cannot say, 'I was unfree to do otherwise, I had no choice.' If moral evaluations of this kind are made then obviously freedom, in the sense of making a choice, is presupposed. Of course, circumstances in which this problem arises are rare.

However, we still want to maintain that freedom is attenuated by the existence of laws with sanctions. The liberal is not impressed by the argument that a person still chooses under such conditions. It is not that unfreedom means not being able to choose, since we have already shown that in circumstances normally described as unfree a person still *technically* chooses; unfreedom really describes situations in which the conditions of choice have been so manipulated by external factors that the choices become limited solely to those determined by the coercer. The paradigm case of unfreedom is therefore that of being told to do something by someone who disposes of overwhelming force.

It is obvious that for the benefits of liberty to be enjoyed there must be a legal framework within which action can take place. To avoid disputes being settled by recourse to violence a legal system grants $A$ liberty to do $x$ and this is only meaningful if $A$ has a right against $B$; that is, $B$ is under an obligation not to impede $A$ in the exercise of his liberty. The existence of a legal system means that one person's liberty is another's restraint. Bentham believed that law and liberty were antithetical, that every law was 'an infraction of liberty', and thought that the necessary balance could be reached by reference to social utility. A legal restraint could only be justified if it produced a net increase in utility for the community as a whole.

There is, however, a different liberal tradition that does not necessarily understand law and liberty as being antithetical; at least, not when the two concepts are understood in certain specified ways. This tradition derives from Locke, who, in a famous phrase said that: 'The end of the law is, not to abolish or restrain, but to preserve and enlarge freedom' (1960, p. 348). In an equally notable passage he said, of law, 'that ill deserves the name of confinement which hedges us in only from bogs and precipices'. Thus not every law is an evil, and a legal framework is a logical necessity for freedom since free action is only possible within a framework of known rules.

The modern versions of this doctrine hold that an individual's liberty is only limited to the extent that a coercive law dictates that he perform a particular action. A legal system such as the common law, which merely sets necessary limits to individual action, does not inhibit freedom because an individual can plan his life so as to avoid them. If the rules are perfectly general, non-discriminatory and predictable they can be treated as equivalent to natural phenomena and are therefore not destructive of liberty. Laws couched in the form of commands which direct individuals to do certain things are, however, inconsistent with liberty since they are not impersonal but proceed from particular wills, and cannot be planned for and avoided in the way that general rules can. To the extent that general rules are predictable, more or less unalterable and not the deliberate product of centralised authority, they are consistent with liberty even though they prohibit certain courses of action.

This theory is clearly directed at the command theory of law and utilitarianism. It holds that since freedom is limited only by particular commands these should be reduced to the absolute minimum and also that, because no social utility function can be derived from individual preferences, the justification for law cannot be that it produces more utility. Since liberty is the highest principle, laws and policies are evaluated for their consistency with this and not with utility.

It is true that in some respects the existence of general rules does not appear as a restraint on individual freedom and 'free societies' do exhibit the major features of the above theory, but the theory is defective. By defining freedom as not being directed towards particular ends it ignores the fact that freedom is still limited when courses of action are closed, even though the individual is not actually ordered to do anything.[2] There are many examples of perfectly general laws in Western democracies which impose severe constraints on individual liberty. Any theory of liberty must take account of the range of alternatives that are open to the individual, so that the wider the range the more free an individual is.

While threats posed by others constitute the standard case of constraints on choice, attention in recent years has been directed to a different type of limitation on individual liberty; that which occurs when an individual's choices are determined by psychological forces over which he has no control (see Chapter 4). Since freedom and rationality are so closely connected it would indeed be disturbing for the traditional concept of liberty, which deals mainly, but not exclusively, with external, observable restraints, if, say, the effects of advertising were to make consumers subservient to producers. In fact, the effects of psychological pressures have probably been exaggerated and indeed, an important element in the liberal's creed is that rational agents should be able to resist such pressures. However, the existence of psychological techniques, even those which fall short of brainwashing, should always be considered as one of the many possible ways in which the autonomy of the individual may be undermined (Benn, 1967).

## 2. Negative and positive liberty

It was maintained in the previous section that there is only *one* concept of liberty, absence of constraints; we say that a person acted freely when he could reasonably have chosen some other course of action. Arguments about freedom in this view turn upon what can be counted as constraints and what justifications can be given for political and legal constraints. There is, however, another argument in political theory to the effect that there are two logically distinct concepts of liberty, both of which are equally valid yet which lead to radically different social philosophies. This interpretation is expressed in Sir Isaiah Berlin's now classic *Two Concepts of Liberty* (1969).[3]

Berlin distinguished between a 'negative' and a 'positive' conception. The negative sense is contained in the answer to the question: 'what is the area within which the subject – a person or group of persons – is or should be left to do or be what he is able to be, without interference by other persons?' (1969, p.121). The positive sense is concerned with the answer to the question: 'what, or who, is the source of control or interference that can determine someone to do, or be, this rather than that?' (1969, p. 122).

The negative conception is clearly not dissimilar from the account given in the preceding section. It is characteristic of the strongly anti-metaphysical utilitarian tradition in English political thought and is a marked feature of the writings of Jeremy Bentham, James Mill, John Stuart Mill (although he was not an entirely consistent spokesman of negative liberty), Henry Sidgwick, Herbert Spencer and the classical and neo-classical economists. It flourished at a time when individuals were struggling to be free from the unnecessary restraints of arbitrary government and when individual choice determined the allocation of resources. The main political axiom of the negative liberty doctrine was that 'everyone knows his own interest best' and that the state should not decide his ends and purposes.

Essential to the doctrine was the sanctity of contract. In Sidgwick's uncomplicated view of the 'self', for example, a person who freely negotiated a contract, even if the terms were particularly onerous to him, thereby expressed his individual choice. The law must enforce all contracts (with some exceptions, for example, contracts of slavery), since not to do so would imply that the state knew what was good for the individual. A person's liberty was a function of that area in which he was left alone and not related to the *quality* of the action.

This is best understood as a doctrine about the *meaning* of liberty. Although negative freedom is often condemned as 'freedom to starve' this is somewhat misleading. It does not necessarily put a prohibition on state intervention but merely holds that this cannot be justified on the ground that it increases freedom; although arguments from equality (or more often utility) might well sanction such action. However, the historical connection between negative liberty and *laissez-faire* economics cannot be denied, and most of its advocates favoured a minimal state.

Positive liberty, on the other hand, does not interpret freedom as simply being left alone but as 'self-mastery'. The theory is a special theory of the self – the personality is divided into a higher and lower self and a person is free to the extent that his higher self, the source of his genuinely rational and long-term ends, is in command of his lower self, wherein lie his ephemeral and irrational desires. Thus a person might be free in the sense of not being restrained by external forces but remain a slave to irrational appetites; as a drug-addict, an alcoholic or a compulsive gambler might be said to be unfree. Since true freedom consists in doing what you ought to do then law, if it directs an individual towards rational ends, may be said not to oppress but to liberate the personality. If a law that appears to restrain us meets with the rational approval of the individual then positive liberty appears to retain a toe-hold on our ordinary concept of liberty.

Of the many political theorists who have held this doctrine, Rousseau (1913) may be briefly mentioned. Rousseau maintained that true liberty consists in obedience to a moral law which we impose upon ourselves. We are not free by maximising selfish interests but by promoting those interests which we share with others. Rousseau's argument does not depend upon a naive altruism but rather on democratic institutions being so designed that we have an incentive to impose laws on ourselves that advance common interests. One essential requirement is a significant measure of social and economic equality. The problem is, of course, determining what these common interests are, and ultimately Rousseau has to admit that if, even after participation in a democratic assembly, an individual finds himself at odds with the General Will he must be enslaved by his lower self and therefore unfree. The individual may be 'forced to be free' by coercive laws.

A particularly pernicious modern version of positive liberty can be found in the philosophy of the neo-Marxist, Herbert Marcuse. In a number of works (Marcuse, 1964; 1967; 1969), he has maintained that although Western capitalist democracies have removed traditional impediments to liberty they have managed to stifle freedom and rationality by new forms of *repression* and *domination*. The masses do not enjoy 'true liberty' since their tastes and wants have been manipulated by the techniques of modern capitalism. Furthermore, their revolutionary zeal has been blunted by a constant supply of consumer goods. The formal provision of civil liberties does not indicate that genuine freedom of expression exists since opinion has been successfully moulded by the 'system'. Indeed, dissent is tolerated precisely because it is no threat to capitalist domination. True 'freedom' would appear to consist not in the making of choices but in the pursuit of 'rational' ends.

It is here that Marcuse's anti-Marxism and fundamentally cynical view of the human condition becomes apparent because he believes that the working class are incapable of seeing their true ends and have to be 'liberated' by a revolutionary élite of radical students, dissident intellectuals and racial minorities. Furthermore, Marcuse does not hide the illiberal nature of post-revolutionary society. Traditional liberal institutions must be abolished since they may encourage the re-emergence of the old repressive order. The masses must be re-educated and forced to be free.

Even if Marcuse's ideas are presented in the most favourable light they seriously distort the facts of the modern world and our notions of freedom and reason. At the most he is saying that modern commercial practices may undermine consumer sovereignty (a point we have considered earlier) but the effects of these have been exaggerated. What is remarkable is his contempt for the majority of mankind; most people are incapable of resisting the pressures of modern civilisation and must be liberated by an enlightened minority. While it is true that many of the consumption habits of individuals in liberal societies may not be desirable, this in itself illustrates an essential property of freedom; that is, freedom involves the making of choices, many of which may turn out to be mistaken. Marcuse merely equates freedom with pursuing activities which he regards as desirable. Furthermore, his intolerance of other philosophical and political ideas removes the essential element required for human progress – rational criticism. Equally sinister is his critique of the freedom of expression and opinion in Western liberal democracies as a system of 'repressive tolerance' since it removes the distinction between societies which have clear and genuine impediments to freedom of thought, discussion and communication, and those which do not. His identification of freedom and 'truth' prevents that competition between ideas which is the mark of a free society.

Berlin easily exposes the trickery involved in the argument for positive liberty. It depends crucially on a special interpretation of the self; it assumes not just that there is a realm of activity towards which the individual ought to direct himself but that he is being liberated when he is directed towards it. The route to totalitarianism is plainly laid out when the higher purposes of the individual are made equivalent to those of collectivities such as classes, nations and races. According to Berlin, a belief in positive liberty entails a *monist* social philosophy; the idea that all other values – equality, rights, justice and so on – are subordinate to the supreme value of higher liberty. However, it is not clear that positive liberty *necessarily* implies monism, although the examples chosen by Berlin do exhibit this feature.

A further implication of positive liberty exposed by Berlin is the argument that liberty is increased when sovereignty is put into the 'right hands' (1969, pp. 162–6). Negative theorists correctly maintain that liberty is reduced whenever the circle within which individuals are free to choose is diminished, and it can be diminished by democratic as well as despotic government. Indeed, a great deal of personal freedom is possible under authoritarian regimes. For Rousseau and Marx, however, it appears to be the case that freedom is a function of the will of the enlightened people or exists only when the rule of the bourgeoisie is replaced by that of the proletariat.

While Berlin has produced convincing arguments to show that certain political theorists have misused the concept of liberty, and indeed blurred obvious differences between restraint and autonomy, it is open to doubt as to whether he has distinguished two *different* concepts of freedom. He says himself that the two terms 'start at no great logical distance from each other' (p. x ii): the difference is that theories built on them develop in different directions and reveal strikingly different attitudes to social and political life. But true though this is it does not follow that statements about 'self-mastery' and 'self-realisation' may not be reinterpreted as statements about restraints on individuals. One person may be as constrained by internal factors, such as uncontrollable desires, as another is by external laws.

Gerald MacCallum (1972) has argued that freedom must always be understood as a 'triadic' relationship. When we talk of an individual's freedom it is always a question of what constraint he is free from in order to do or become something. Claims about liberty have to be analysed in the following way: $X$ is (or ought to be) free from $Y$ to do or become (or refrain from doing or becoming) $Z$. Differences between normative theories turn upon how the three 'term variables' are filled; they will depend on the accounts given of the self, the nature of the obstacles, and the activity in question. What is not at issue is the nature of freedom itself. It might also be said that theorists of positive liberty were really talking about the desirability of things like equality and social justice, and trying to capture the emotive appeal that liberty has for values which are logically distinct.

Using MacCallum's apparatus we are in fact able to treat some of the traditional problems of liberty within the same, single account of the concept; and in using it we are not committed to a particular set of values or ideology. Many of the things that positive theorists wanted to say can be encompassed within it. State intervention may be justified in order to free people from hunger and so on as long as it is borne in mind that such action involves restraints *on others*; a point not appreciated by collectivists. The argument will then be about the merits of state action itself rather than about the concept of liberty. Some writers might say that it is meaningful to speak of economic deprivation preventing a person from doing something (or realising his potentialities) but stress that state action to remove such impediments creates the conditions for the full exercise of liberty rather than liberty itself. Otherwise being free may be confused with being 'able'.

An important way in which rival theories of liberty differ is over the extent to which certain impediments to individual action are alterable, since we only speak of a person being unfree when the constraints are removable. The classical liberal's objection to the idea that state action could increase liberty turned on the argument that the laws of economics were as unalterable as physical laws and that there was therefore little that government action could accomplish in the way of relieving economic deprivation without upsetting the delicate mechanism of the market and producing worse conditions for all. Against this Marxists (and to some extent non-Marxist socialists) regarded these 'laws' (and the laws of property and commerce that accompanied them) as being true of only a particular historical period and that not to alter them, in appropriate circumstances, would be to acquiesce in a form of enslavement. In this view economic freedom meant the removal of those constraints that prevented man shaping his own destiny.

Once again this may not be an argument about the concept of liberty but about the possibility of social control. Classical liberals and their successors maintain that personal liberty is only possible in a free market economy since this is concerned solely with satisfying individual wants. They would stress that a free economy is a necessary but not a sufficient condition for individual liberty, since a system of general rules guaranteeing freedom from political oppression is also required. A further crucially important requirement is a wide dispersal of private property since only this can guarantee the individual independence from the state. Governments may be able to act to prevent *severe* economic depressions, eliminate those monopolies that significantly reduce consumer choice, and provide a measure of welfare without threatening liberty. But to attempt to plan an economy comprehensively must ultimately lead to the destruction of freedom since economic control is only possible with a centralised system of coercion. In fact, the experience of centralised planning in Communist regimes has amply borne this out.

Even the milder forms of planning associated with Keynesian demand management policies are not as effective as they once were; indeed they may only be appropriate in special economic circumstances, and are only properly workable in regimes where democratic political freedoms are absent. All this suggests that while there are respectable moral arguments which justify limitations on the economic freedom of some to create conditions for the well-being of others it is a mistake to identify liberty with economic control.

### 3. John Stuart Mill and the value of liberty

*On Liberty* is justly praised as the most eloquent expression of the libertarian approach to morals and society and although it has been much criticised, and subjected to a great number of differing interpretations, it is still quoted today in arguments for individual freedom. Yet curiously enough, despite Mill's contempt for custom, and for rules that could not rationally be justified, and his encouragement of spontaneity, individuality and 'experiments in living', his work had very little influence over those radical political movements which propagated these very same things. Mill's ideas were extremely influential in the academic debate in the 1960s over the relationship between law and morality, but elsewhere it was Marcuse's voice that was dominant. The reason for this must surely be that liberation in the latter's doctrine does *not* include the traditional economic freedoms of the free enterprise economy. Mill himself argued that in Victorian Britain business was the only outlet for individual expression which a stifling and conformist public opinion regarded as legitimate. It would be no exaggeration to say that the position of the New Left spokesmen today is the exact reverse.

Mill has often been accused of thinking that any free action, no matter how immoral, at least had some value in virtue of the fact that it was freely performed. Against the view that liberty in principle is always a good thing many writers have echoed the views of Mill's sternest contemporary critic, Sir James Fitzjames Stephen, who said that fire and liberty could not be said to be good or bad but were 'both good and bad according to time, place and circumstance' (1967, p. 85). It is true that Mill thought that 'all restraint qua restraint is an evil' but he did not think it was unjustifiable; he merely thought that there was a presumption in favour of liberty and that the onus of justification always lay on those who would restrict liberty.

Mill is frequently cited as a theorist of 'negative' liberty (in Berlin's sense of the term) but this requires some explication since he was less interested in discussing the traditional restraints on liberty imposed by despotic governments – which had been removed in parts of Western Europe and North America in Mill's time – than new ones in the form of the pressures of public opinion and social convention. It was this that was severely threatening 'individuality'. By individuality Mill meant the property in human beings that made them *active*, rather than passive, and critical of existing modes of social behaviour so that they refused to accept conventions without submitting them to the test of reason. Freedom appears to be not simply the absence of restraint but the deliberate cultivation of certain desirable attitudes. It is because of this that it has been suggested that Mill had a rationalistic view of liberty. It is also said that he was an elitist in that on more than one occasion he said that only a minority were capable of enjoying freedom as individuality. Nevertheless, his conception of liberty is firmly anchored to the notion of *choice*:

> He who lets the world, or his own portion of it, choose his plan of life for him, has no need of any other faculty than the apelike one of imitation. He who chooses to plan for himself employs all his faculties. (1974, p. 123)

Mill's views on the value of liberty can be illustrated by comparing them with the orthodox utilitarian approach. To Bentham, happiness, understood as a measurable psychological property, was the supreme value and all other values, including liberty, were good only in so far as they contributed to the maximisation of the general happiness. There was no *right* to liberty; in fact, this could be taken to mean that if a legislator could increase people's happiness by the use of drugs or psychological techniques, then the values of personal independence and individuality should not, theoretically, be counted as an argument against this. While Mill claimed that he eschewed any appeal to abstract right in the justification for individual liberty, but relied solely on utility (pp. 69–70), he interpreted this in such a way that the connection between it and Benthamism was remote. Mill's argument was not merely that there is a contingent relationship between liberty and utility, that freedom of opinion and enquiry is conducive to social and scientific progress, but that a proper conception of happiness necessarily includes freedom as individuality.

Mill implies that freedom consists in actually challenging accepted rules, but one could argue that a person who follows customary rules of behaviour, even if he does so unreflectively, is not necessarily unfree. Indeed, customary rules may be indispensable conditions for the exercise of liberty and there are arguments, not necessarily utilitarian, to the effect that the cultivation of the personality traits favoured by Mill are not conducive to the *order* of a free society. It is the virtual identification between individuality and liberty that leads Mill to suggest that the great bulk of the population is incapable of appreciating it: 'they have no tastes or wishes strong enough to incline them to do anything unusual, and they consequently do not understand those who have . . .' (p. 134). The masses are unfree precisely because they are the slaves of custom.

There are, then, elitist elements in Mill's account of liberty, but the principle that he uses to determine the boundary between the individual and society seems, superficially, to be uncompromisingly libertarian. This is the famous 'harm' principle. The *only* ground for interfering with an individual is to prevent harm to others; over actions that affect only himself the individual is sovereign (p. 69). This rules out paternalism, the idea that law (and society) can intervene to promote what are considered to be a person's best interests; 'moralism', the idea that some acts are intrinsically immoral and therefore must be punished irrespective of whether they affect anyone else; and even utilitarianism, of the Benthamite kind, which would license interference in order to maximise the general happiness. Of course, Mill's principle is capable of a libertarian or an authoritarian interpretation. Since all but the most trivial acts affect somebody in some way, then, could this not allow the law to protect the public from certain immoral acts which, although they do not cause injury in a direct sense, nevertheless cause offence? Furthermore, Mill himself certainly believed that his principle did not imply moral indifference towards the self-regarding behaviour of others and that it was permissible to use persuasion (though obviously not coercion) to discourage someone from immorality.

To preserve the libertarian elements in Mill's theory his principle has been interpreted in a number of ways. It has been suggested that Mill meant that intervention is legitimate only when an individual's actions affect the *interests* of another, as opposed to merely affecting himself, or that there is a distinction between *direct* and *indirect* effects of action. Modern versions of Mill's doctrine make a distinction between causing *offence* and causing *injury*. It is recognised that the effects of individual liberty may well cause offence, especially to people with strongly held moral beliefs about appropriate forms of social behaviour, but no one has a right to protection from this in the way that every person has a right to the protection of his person and property. What Mill is clear about is that the repugnance that the majority may feel for immoral acts that do not cause injury could never constitute a reason for prohibiting such acts. This runs counter to Benthamite utilitarianism because the latter allows for the pleasures of *malevolence* in the measurement of social utility, so that the abhorrence the majority may feel for particular sorts of private conduct has to be considered along with the pain that would be caused to individuals if such conduct were to be prohibited. Mill, in effect, established the modern libertarian view that there is a right to liberty which cannot be overridden by orthodox utilitarian considerations; an individual's freedom cannot be sacrificed in the interests of public policy, but only for some other right. We shall consider some of the problems raised by contemporary versions of Mill's principle in the final section of this chapter.

Even if Mill's particular statement of the connection between liberty and individuality is not accepted by all libertarians his argument for the instrumental value of freedom in the promotion of social goods features strongly in contemporary discussion. This is especially true of Mill's celebrated argument for the complete liberty of thought, discussion and expression (ch. 11). Mill's major argument for freedom of expression follows from his empiricist epistemology. Since all knowledge is a product of experience, even our most firmly-held convictions as to truth and falsehood are corrigible and may be overturned. Therefore competition between ideas (and the prohibition of claims to infallibility) is the only means of guaranteeing that truth will prevail. Mill did believe that the number of disputed doctrines, including those in the social sciences, would decline but this could only come about through free intellectual debate. Mill argued that the suppression of opinion may blot out truth, that society benefits from even the free expression of false doctrines since truth is served by refuting them, and, perhaps most importantly of all, that truth is many-sided and likely to emerge from conflicting ideas (even the most obviously false theories are likely to contain some hidden truths) (pp. 108–11).

These arguments are not strictly utilitarian. It is easy to show that there could be arguments for suppressing opinion if that would increase happiness (as would be the case in a society where the bulk of the population were of a particular religious persuasion). Even Mill's principle that progress is advanced by unrestricted freedom may not always be applicable in some aspects of scientific research, especially in such obviously potentially dangerous areas as nuclear research and microbiology. Of course, it is the harm that results from the misapplication of scientific discoveries that is wrong, not the activity of free scientific enquiry, but it is surely not difficult in some areas to establish a very strong connection between the two. What is true is that scientific truth can only be established on an *objective* basis in a community in which claims to infallibility are abjured and the canons of rational argument are accepted, but this is only one aspect of Mill's argument.

There are major problems of free expression in the question of the propagation of ideas which may have dangerous consequences and which deliberately treat certain groups in an insulting and degrading manner.

Racist propaganda is a clear example of this. Should there be legal restrictions on the dissemination of such ideas?

In many cases there is no problem. The use of words which are deliberately designed to incite people to commit acts of violence would clearly be prohibited by most interpretations of the harm principle. In fact it is doubtful if special legislation is required to protect minority groups from insulting comments since the common law provides such protection for individuals. Some people have argued for a prohibition on the right of free speech to political parties whose doctrines may well stir up racial hatred, on the ground that freedom should not be extended to those who preach intolerance. It is true that a liberal society must take steps to protect itself from groups whose ideas, if put into practice, would destroy the liberal order, but the danger is that it may lose its liberal credentials in doing so. The main principle that liberals stress is that a person should only be punished for his actions if they breach the rights of others, and not because of the opinions he holds; they would be wary of coercive legislation, the justification of which might depend only upon a contingent relationship between opinion and action.

The problem is particularly acute in connection with the right to free assembly and association. Are the authorities morally entitled to ban meetings of groups whose professed ends are antithetical to the idea of an open and tolerant society? The difficulty exists because such meetings are normally held in publicly-owned halls and collective decisions therefore have to be taken on issues on which it is highly unlikely that there will exist anything like unanimous agreement. Presumably, very few would deny the right of a private owner of property to let it to whom he liked. The danger is that the authorities may ban public meetings which are for the expression of views of which they disapprove, when the libertarian principle is that only considerations of harm and injury to private rights and public order should affect the decision.

Mill was probably much too optimistic in thinking that all restrictions on free discussion should be removed because truth would emerge from the free competition of ideas since, in a utilitarian sense, much harm may be caused by the spread of dangerous doctrines before truth finally triumphs (if it ever does). Discussion and expression cannot be literally unrestricted (as laws against libel and slander indicate) but the rationale of restriction is difficult to formulate. The danger in the Benthamite justification for restriction is that it may reduce freedom to a vanishing point. A different way of treating free expression is to regard it as a type of personal and property right; the limitations on its exercise by one person being determined by the fact that others have similar rights. Questions of justifiable restrictions on liberty would then depend upon judicial interpretation within general rules rather than legislation.

In today's 'catalogue' of liberties, freedom of expression is probably valued more than economic liberty (when this is interpreted as freedom to exchange without direct government interference); indeed the connection between economic freedom and other civil liberties is seldom appreciated. Yet free exchange between individuals is undoubtedly an important exercise of liberty and a society which forbade all other liberties but allowed this would still be free to this extent. The market economy is the only social device man has developed which combines freedom, in the sense of personal choice, and efficiency. In the absence of monopoly (and, it is not often appreciated that most monopolies are a consequence of government privilege) an exchange system increases liberty by ensuring that what is produced reflects individual choice.

An important justification for economic liberty is that decentralised economic decision-making guarantees that a greater amount of knowledge is utilised than is the case under central planning (Hayek, 1960, ch. 2). The major *economic* disadvantage of centralised planning is that the planner does not have access to the knowledge of consumer tastes and production costs that is automatically signalled to the participants in a market process. Even if freedom is considered as an instrumental value only, rather than as constitutive of individuality, it is difficult to deny that it is essential for the handling of ignorance and uncertainty that characterise all social and economic processes.

Economic freedom does, however, throw up some interesting problems for the political theorist. One is that the process of exchange between individuals may not produce a state of affairs which would be called 'free'. One example is the closed shop in industrial relations. If an employer *voluntarily* makes an agreement with a trade union to employ union members only, should it be prohibited by law? Is it consistent with liberty for the law to reproduce those characteristics of a free society which have not emerged through the voluntary transactions of individuals? It could be said that the conditions of employment are a matter for individual negotiation and not coercive law and that as long as a variety of employment prospects exists, individuals who do not wish to join trade unions would not be harmed. It is certainly not the case that voluntary closed shop agreements have the same coercive features as, say, some aspects of picketing. It is not often noticed that the arguments which say that it should be illegal for union membership to be a condition of employment have exactly the same logic as arguments for the legal enforcement on employers of non-discrimination practices in respect of race or sex. It is curious that Conservatives in Britain tend to oppose the latter but support the former.

## 4. Law, morality and paternalism

The issues raised by Mill in the defence of individual liberty have reappeared in the extremely interesting debate occasioned by the emergence of the 'permissive society'. In the last twenty years or so in many Western democracies laws governing personal conduct have been significantly relaxed so that individuals now enjoy more freedom with regard to sexual habits, choice of literature and life-styles than ever before. It is curious that the demands for liberty in personal morals have not normally been accompanied by a demand for economic freedom from the state, though the theoretical and empirical connection between economic and personal liberty is very close. It is also interesting that the debate on permissiveness illustrates the point that the connection between democracy and personal liberty is a *contingent* and not a necessary one; for example, the Republic of Ireland has impeccable democratic credentials yet it also has illiberal laws in relation to divorce, contraception and censorship.

In Britain the libertarian principles that should determine the relationship between liberty and the law were set out in the Wolfenden Report, published in 1957. Echoing Mill, the Report said that there ought to be a sphere of personal conduct which should be immune from the law. Alluding to a distinction between the *private* and *public* realms the Report maintained that the criminal law should only be concerned to protect the public from outward displays of immorality and with the prevention of corruption and exploitation. Thus it was recommended that homosexual relations between consenting adults be legalised and that while prostitution itself should still remain legal the law should be made stricter on the outward manifestations of the activity, such as soliciting.

The libertarian position with regard to law and morality is that where no harm is involved and all parties consent to the activity then the fact that the activity is immoral should not be a reason for legal interference (in fact, some libertarians would maintain that the activity itself could not be called immoral if it involves no harm). The application of the injury principle is restricted so as to exclude the 'injury' experienced by a bystander who might feel aggrieved at the thought of some immoral act taking place since if this were to be relevant then there is no limit to the reach of the law into people's private lives.

It is argued that all coercion requires justification and that the frustration and pain experienced by those denied the liberty to practice unconventional sexual activities, the risks involved in entrusting the police with the task of enforcing 'moral' laws, and the possibility of blackmail, all combine to make legal prohibitions of private immorality productive of great misery.

But this view has never been without its critics. In the nineteenth century the great common law judge Sir James Fitzjames Stephen in his *Liberty, Equality, Fraternity* was of the opinion that certain sorts of immoral acts are so degrading that 'society' must express its disgust and abhorrence of them by punishing the perpetrators irrespective of the fact that the acts in question rest on consent and harm no one (1967, ch. IV). Punishment is required to 'denounce' certain crimes for their depravity. This particularly harsh view might be more plausible in relation to crimes involving victims and direct injuries. Stephen had a very much less optimistic view of man than Mill and was deeply sceptical of the value of personal liberty in the formation of character. His belief that moral standards had to be constantly reaffirmed by coercive law revealed a rather Hobbesian conception of social order.

The contemporary exponent of the Stephen argument is Lord Devlin, who, in his Maccabean Lecture *The Enforcement of Morals*[4] challenged the rationale of the Wolfenden Report. Like Stephen he believes that society has an interest in preventing private immorality, that no clear distinction can be drawn between private and public, and that the proper relationship between liberty and law cannot be determined by the abstract principles of the rationalist philosopher. His justification for the law's punishment of immorality is, however, slightly different from Stephen's. Devlin maintains that society is held together by a belief in certain moral standards and that although departures from these may harm no assignable individuals a generalised flouting of them will lead to the collapse of society. In a famous analogy he likened immorality to treason in his justification for legal action against it.

Much of his argument rests upon the assumption that certain sorts of criminal offences can only be explained in terms of a moral principle. For example, the criminal law prohibits a person from consenting to his own murder, which reflects the principle of the sanctity of life; bigamy is a criminal offence because the principle of monogamous marriage (in Western societies) has to be enforced by the law. Thus law is not merely a device to protect individuals from harm but represents the concrete expression of a set of *integrated* moral ideals, and seemingly minor disturbances are to be forbidden because they threaten the whole structure.

In a famous reply to Devlin, H. L. A. Hart (1963) presented a modern version of Mill's attempt to determine *theoretically* the limits of the law in personal morals and refute the argument that an act may be punished because it is immoral. He said that those cases where the law forbids an act even when consent is involved can be explained on other grounds than the enforcement of morality. His argument is that simple paternalism (a consideration forbidden by Mill) can justify the criminal law forbidding a person consenting to his own murder or the trade in hard drugs. Since the liberal philosophy of learning from mistakes can hardly be said to be appropriate in these cases the state has to take a decision to protect people from themselves. To disallow this, says Hart, would preclude the state from many areas where its presence is thought to be desirable.

In fact many libertarians would object to this precisely on the ground that paternalism could be as destructive of individual liberty as Devlin's legal moralism. Both justifications require the state, through its officials, to take a decision as to what is best for a person whose actions harm no one else. If paternalism justifies the outlawing of duelling does it also outlaw certain private sexual acts, such as sado-masochism? In fact, there are many acts about which it is impossible to make an unambiguous judgement within the terms of Hart's theory.

The example of the trade in and consumption of narcotics is interesting because Hart's justification of legal intervention on paternalist grounds could easily be challenged by strict libertarians *and* utilitarians. A libertarian might argue that even though the consequences of taking hard drugs usually mean a diminution of rationality and individuality (in Mill's sense) this does not justify the use of coercive law to prohibit what is, in a technical sense at least, a free act. The more plausible utilitarian argument is that, whatever people's views about the morality or immorality of drug-taking, the consequences of preventing it are much worse for society than the consequences of allowing it. This is because in the absence of a free market for a wanted good gangsters and racketeers will always provide it. Furthermore, the very high price of a banned good leads desperate addicts to crimes they would not otherwise commit. The additional suffering brought about by the small increase in addicts that undoubtedly would occur if restrictions were lifted would be easily outweighed by the increase in security that society would enjoy because of the removal of a major incentive to crime. It is ironic that this argument could logically be accepted by those who believe, along with Devlin, that the law ought to enforce moral standards.

This utilitarian argument is particularly damaging to Hart's case since his view of law and morality depends partly on the *liberal* utilitarian contention that the misery and frustration suffered by individuals whose sexual outlets, even when based on consent, are denied by law, far outweights the benefits that accrue to society from the enforcement of moral standards.

Hart is on much stronger ground when he makes an important distinction between immorality and indecency (pp. 38–48). The law can intervene when someone's actions cause public offence, so that it is the public display of the act that invites legal sanction, not its immorality. Thus it would be punishable to display an obscene poster in a main shopping precinct but quite legal to enjoy the same picture in the privacy of one's own home. Under Devlin's criterion, if something is to be forbidden because it is morally wrong then it is always wrong, whether performed in public or private. The implications of this for liberty are alarming; it implies that the only limitations on the authority of the law to enforce moral standards crucial to society's existence are the practical ones of enforcement.

Liberals do not deny that a society's existence depends upon some agreement on moral rules but they insist that this agreement is compatible with a plurality of moral ideals and that there is no evidence that a society will collapse if people experiment with different moral practices. The freedom to indulge in minority practices should be limited by reference to a rational principle and not by popular opinion, no matter how deeply felt and widespread that may be. Devlin does not think that the decision as to what is morally right or wrong is mere majoritarianism; indeed it must be a product of something approaching unanimity. Nevertheless, he has been criticised, with some justification, for allowing brute prejudice rather than reasoned moral argument to determine the extent of legal interference with personal liberty (Dworkin, 1977, ch. 10). It is also misleading for Devlin to suggest that a society's morality is reinforced by the coercive sanctions of the law. The liberal, and more plausible, view is that rational argument and the critical discussion of values provide a surer basis for morality than the symbolic and denunciatory use of punishment.

There have been in recent years, however, some other questions concerning the role of the state in personal conduct. Should the state enforce the wearing of seat-belts by motorists (wearing crash helmets is already obligatory for motor cyclists in Britain and most American states)? It would appear that the only justification can be the paternalist one, since the harm caused by not wearing a seat-belt is to the driver himself, and this, of course, illustrates the illiberality of paternalism. It is often said that the justification for coercion in the wearing of seat-belts and crash helmets is not paternalist and comes within the harm principle because other people are affected in that the health services have to treat persons unnecessarily injured in road crashes. In logic this argument is quite fallacious and only gains whatever plausibility it has from the existence of welfare states which provide for the collective delivery of health services. The strict libertarian would argue that under a private medical insurance system a road crash victim would be *entitled* to treatment for his injuries. The extra costs incurred by drivers who failed to wear seat-belts would automatically be accounted for in the premiums charged, and the driver might therefore be encouraged to wear a seat-belt by the costs of not doing so – but he would not be compelled to do so by the state. Once a service is collectively delivered its benefits are separated from individual contributions (although the service is, of course, financed by coercively collected contributions from individuals). Those who run the service acquire the moral authority to decide how its benefits shall be allocated. Indeed, quite horrifying consequences follow from universalising the principle implicit in the justification of a law making the wearing of seat-belts obligatory: since there is a very strong connection between excessive smoking, eating and drinking and various diseases, all of which impose high costs on the health service, should not the state take action to prevent this in exactly the same way that it already has done over the wearing of crash helmets for motor cyclists and possibly will do over seat-belts?

The *general* objection that libertarians have made to the welfare state is not dissimilar to the reasoning embodied in the above example. The collective delivery of welfare services necessarily reduces individual choice and increases the power of centralised bureaucracies to determine how much should be spent, and in what way, on services that people desire. Once again it should be clear that the libertarian approach to these matters does not necessarily imply a hostility to egalitarianism; the strict liberal might concede that access to health, education and welfare is unequal and that measures should be taken to correct this, but he would still maintain that freedom of choice ought to be preserved. One of the tasks of the social and political theorist is to explore the implications that social policies have for a more basic structure of values, but it would appear that the connection between welfare and liberty is one that has received little systematic analysis.

# 9

# Human Rights

## 1. Rights in political theory

Implicit in the preceding discussion of evaluative problems has been the notion of a 'right'. Underlying the arguments for equality, even in the minimal sense, is the proposition that individuals are entitled to respect as moral agents capable of choice, and that to use them for collective ends, as some critics maintain utilitarianism does, is to deny a basic right of equal liberty. While it is true that some systems of political philosophy make no use of human rights, and indeed may openly reject them, they feature prominently in all discussions concerning the individual and the state. In contemporary Western political theory the dispute is more likely to be about the purported *content* of the various statements about rights than about the intelligibility of the concept of rights itself. This is aptly illustrated by the differences between the two sorts of liberalism we discussed earlier. An extreme individualistic liberal (or libertarian) believes that individuals have rights, whether recognised or not by the legal system, which political authorities ought not to transgress, and uses a natural rights argument to limit severely the role of the state. By contrast, the liberal who recommends a more active role for government in society and the economy frequently justifies this by reference to a revised and more expansive conception of human rights.

In the history of political theory, natural rights have often been linked to the concept of natural law. As we have seen, natural lawyers maintain that there is a moral order against which positive laws can be tested for their validity, and it is a short step from this to assert that individuals have rights against political authorities which are sanctioned by natural law. John Locke, perhaps the earliest modern exponent of rights, connected these to natural law, and the famous eighteenth-century political statements of the rights of man were rooted firmly in this tradition. However, the link is not a necessary one. The medieval concept of natural law, best exemplified in the jurisprudence of Aquinas, while it presented a framework of morality by which the realm of politics could be justified, did not grant rights to the citizen against political authorities; rather it imposed on everybody, including rulers, a coherent set of moral duties. It is only with the secularisation of natural law that we find the emergence of the potentially revolutionary doctrine of the rights of man. Modern moral arguments for the rights of man can be presented independently of natural law arguments of the traditional type.

Historically, the doctrine of natural rights has suffered from the vagaries of political and intellectual fashion. It was popular in the seventeenth century but suffered at the hands of utilitarianism and Marxism in the nineteenth century and in the early part of this century. Utilitarians always thought that the logical structure of the arguments for natural rights was fallacious and that the social values implicit in the various doctrines could be more coherently encompassed within the utilitarian calculus. Marxists have specifically criticised the ahistorical and absolute nature of statements of rights and argued that they can only be properly understood within the context of particular economic and social circumstances.

In this century statements about natural rights suffered at the hands of the Logical Positivists. Their explicitly normative character meant that they were vulnerable to the charge of being 'meaningless' and therefore of no interest to the analytical philosopher. Politically, however, the horrific experience of the last war, and of various brands of totali-tarianism, heightened interest in natural rights and brought about a new sense of urgency in the desire to see some form of international pro-tection of them. Furthermore, the demise of Logical Positivism and the renewed interest shown in the meaning of statements of rights and the implications they have for other values, and in the possibility of rational justification (as opposed to absolute demonstration), has brought about a nice combination of practical and theoretical concerns for the political philosopher to handle.[1]

The history of theoretical speculation about rights reveals significant changes in their character. In the traditional doctrine rights were always asserted *defensively* against some invasion of the individual's private interests. The invasion of most direct concern to the rights theorist was that brought about by the state. In the theories of limited government that invariably accompanied the doctrine of natural rights the state was morally forbidden to cross the boundary lines, around the individual, established by these rights. In Locke's theory the state was not the creator of rights but was limited to the enforcement of those individual rights which were inalienable. The authenticity of these rights – in Locke's case, the rights to life, liberty and property – could be demonstrated by reference to natural law and reason. Indeed, the essentially negative nature of traditional rights meant that they changed from being radical anti-statist claims in the seventeenth and eighteenth centuries to rather conservative ideas, in the nineteenth century, which were used to disallow a more active role for the state in economic and social life. This is especially true of the right to property in American political thought and political practice. Also, libertarian anarchists, who certainly believe that individuals have rights, have been eager to point out the danger of granting the state a monopoly in the enforcement of these rights.

In contrast, in the last thirty years there has been a marked tendency to inflate the notion of rights. Rights are now not merely asserted defensively against state action but are interpreted as legitimate claims on government to satisfy human needs. Whereas traditional rights statements consisted of the right to life, free expression, property, free association, free movement and so on, they are today likely to include the right to medical care, a minimum wage and holidays with pay. The Universal Declaration of Human Rights, issued by the United Nations in 1948, consisted of both the familiar 'negative' rights and the new economic and social rights. The controversy surrounding this will be considered later in the chapter. Furthermore, not only has the content of rights changed but the range of entities considered as rights-holders has been significantly extended so that we now read of animal rights, where once only human beings were considered capable of possessing rights.

## 2. Analysis of rights

While there are a number of types of rights any analysis must begin with a simple distinction between legal and moral rights (Cranston, 1973, pp. 9–17). The existence of legal rights can be established quite easily by reference to a system of law; indeed, positivists maintain that the only genuine right is a claim which can be enforced by a court and that any other account of a right is entirely subjective and metaphysical. In contrast, moral rights cannot be established by reference to an ongoing legal system (although some moral rights are given specific protection in the law) but depend for their validity on their consistency with social and moral practices and on how they can be morally justified.

There is a great variety of moral rights, the most familiar being those that occur in social relationships; parents have rights against their children and patients have a right to be told the true state of their health by their doctors. The paradigm case of the creation of rights and duties is a *promise* (Melden, 1977, ch. 2). Promises are made by rational moral agents, capable of choice, and they create entitlements to persons such that they have the *right* to limit the freedom of other parties. To break a promise is then to deprive a person of his rights and undermine his status as an autonomous moral agent.

Human or natural rights are a type of moral right in that they do not depend for their validity on enforcement by the legal system, but they are a special sort of moral right in that they do not emanate from specific promises or agreements but are said to belong to all men, irrespective of what nation, community or social practice they may be a member of (Hart, 1967, pp. 63–4). However, this claim to universality which is made by theorists of natural rights poses some problems in the justification of rights.

Of course, some countries have incorporated the traditional rights into their legal systems and made them immune from ordinary political and legal change. Thus the actions of government are limited by the existence of these constitutional rights. It is the aim of active movements for human rights to turn all universal moral rights into positive rights, and to secure international institutions that protect the rights of the individual against the invasions of the state.

While the differences between legal and moral rights are clear, it must be stressed that *all* statements about rights exhibit structural similarities. There are some common features of rights which must be elucidated before we can consider the specific political philosophy of human rights.

Political and legal theorists are interested in the many different senses in which the word 'right' is used. In jurisprudence the classic analysis of the complex nature of statements about rights is to be found in Wesley Hohfeld's *Fundamental Legal Conceptions* (1919), and, although this work is concerned exclusively with the meaning of rights in legal systems, much of what Hohfeld says is of relevance to a wider context of 'rights-talk'. The most important distinction for social and political theory is that between rights as 'liberties' and rights as 'claims' (see also, Raphael, 1967, pp. 56–7; Feinberg, 1973, ch. 4).

To have a right in the sense of a liberty means that the individual is under no obligation *not* to perform a certain act. To have a right to free speech simply means that one is at liberty to speak one's mind; one is under no duty to refrain from the expression of one's views. Liberties are not correlative with duties, that is they do not require the performance of a duty on the part of another. In Hohfeld's analysis liberties are correlative with 'no rights'; that is, in the example given, other persons have no right to interfere with the individual's liberty of free speech. In Hart's famous example of two people walking down a street and seeing a coin, each has a right to the coin in the sense that neither is under a duty to allow the other to pick it up (though each is under a duty not to use force in the process). Where rights are understood as liberties, then, the possession of a right by one person does not entail the restriction on the liberty of another in the sense of him being under a correlative duty.

Hobbes's 'right of nature' is an example of this from the history of political thought. In a state of nature, characterised by the absence of law and government, each person has a right to do anything which is conducive to his own survival (Hobbes, 1968, p. 189). Since the right of one man cannot infringe the liberty of another, the state of nature is highly insecure. For Hobbes, this necessitates the existence of an absolute sovereign who is the source of all positive law. In Hobbes's system the right of nature is the only natural right and its exercise, under the conditions described, would make orderly social life impossible. Other political theorists, who do not share Hobbes's assumptions about human nature, deny that his is the only possible version of a natural right.

Since most important uses of the word 'right' occur in situations where the holder of the right is entitled to limit the freedom of others it might be thought that the isolation of a right as a liberty is not very significant. All theories of rights 'fill out' the notion of a right with an account of the conditions under which one person's right entails a duty upon another. However, the idea of a liberty does indicate that individuals have a prima facie right to have their desires satisfied and that the violation of this requires justification (Flathman, 1976, pp. 42–3). It is perhaps best exemplified in a competitive market economy, correctly described as a system of 'natural liberty', in which each person has the right to maximise his interests, in the sense of not being under a duty to refrain from doing so. But these systems require structures of rules which allow individuals to make legitimate claims against each other, and which supplement liberties.

In the more usual sense of the word 'right' it is understood as a type of claim. Claim-rights entitle their holder to limit the liberty of another person. $A$ has a right against $B$, deriving either from a moral or legal rule, which puts $B$ under a duty. It is not the moral quality of the act that entitles

*A* to limit *B*'s liberty but simply the fact that he possesses the right (Hart, 1967, p. 56). Indeed, there may be occasions when some other moral consideration may compel *A* to waive his right against *B*. Situations can easily occur in which it would be right to break a promise and therefore violate someone's rights. It is crucial, then, to distinguish between doing the right thing and having a right, since these usages describe quite different moral situations.

Claim-rights possessed by persons are quite different from favours or concessions granted to individuals by authorities. A person may be allowed to do something by another, and indeed his welfare may be significantly improved by the actions of others, but that is very different from saying that he has a right, in the sense of a claim. When someone has a right, by the rules of a practice, by an agreement or promise and so on, he acquires a kind of sovereignty over another, against whom he has a legitimate claim. It might be thought that *A* is in a privileged position with regard to *B* by virtue of his possession of the right, but a system of rights receives some justification from the fact that, at least in the liberal-individualist system, everyone is likely to be the possessor of a right on some occasions (Flathman, 1976, pp. 81–2). To say that someone has a right is to acknowledge his autonomy as a moral agent capable of making choices, and while it is possible that moral and legal systems may exist which do not recognise rights, such systems are deficient, from the individualist's point of view, for this very reason. The individualistic feature of statements about claim-rights is revealed by the crucial point that only the holder of a right can waive it or suspend it (Melden, 1977, pp. 99–101).

A perennial question asked of rights is whether duties and rights are correlative in a logical sense. We have already shown in the analysis of rights as liberties that a person can have a right without there being a corresponding duty upon anyone else, but we must also consider the question of whether all duties imply corresponding rights. In the case of claim-rights, the argument that duties and rights are logically linked seems to be watertight, but there are uses of the word duty which do not imply correlative rights. We can speak of individuals being under duties without there being corresponding rights against them held by others. This is especially so in non-legal contexts. We speak of duties to relieve suffering, to be charitable and so on where it would be odd to speak of others having a right in the strict sense. This is because in moral discourse the word duty has come to have a wide range of application, one that extends beyond the simple duties – rights correspondence that is characteristic of legal relationships. This is not to deny that the moral demands of duty may be extremely pressing but only to suggest that this describes a logically different situation from that in which one person, through the possession of a right, may legitimately limit the freedom of another.

This distinction becomes crucially important in considering whether it is permissible to attribute rights not only to infants and animals but also to adults who may not satisfy the minimal criteria of rationality normally associated with the possession of rights. It seems more plausible to speak of duties towards infants than to say that they have rights. This is because the attribution of rights depends upon a certain concept of a person that incorporates autonomy, rationality and the faculty of making choices and entering into agreements within the confines of rule-governed relationships. That infants obviously have the potentiality for conduct appropriate to this concept of a person seems insufficient a reason for saying that they have rights as infants. The same reasoning indicates that it would be improper to speak of the rights of the higher animals, even those that may satisfy some minimal criteria of rational behaviour and towards which human beings have strong feelings of affection. One of the important aspects of someone having a right is that he, and only he, can choose to waive the right, and it would be odd to attribute rights to species manifestly incapable of this.

More difficult problems are posed by the case of the mentally ill, especially as the definition of insanity is itself in dispute. There are many cases of people being forcibly detained in institutions who are quite capable of shouldering the responsibilities that necessarily accompany the possession of rights.[2] It would, however, be difficult to say that psychopaths have rights, for example, since their mental condition does not seem to include those properties of the human personality which are essential to the concept of a moral agent. If the mentally deranged do not have the capacity to understand the purpose of rules, the meaning of promises and agreements, and to feel guilt and remorse, it severely undermines the possibility that they may behave in accordance with the dictates of morality.

A social and legal order in which individuals have rights to that extent recognises their autonomy and self-respect as moral agents. A society that recognised the needs of individuals and promoted policies that maximised their welfare would be a benevolent society but it would not for that reason alone accord them rights. Indeed there are many examples in history of minorities being favourably treated by a dominant class but not granted the freedom which comes with having rights (Wasserstrom, 1971, pp. 109–22).

So far we have been talking of rights in general but natural or human rights have certain features which distinguish them from other sorts of rights. The logic of rights that derive from institutional frameworks, moral and legal practices, family and personal relationships, and promises and undertakings seems, on the face of it, to be different from that of the traditional declarations of human rights. In these documents individuals are said to have rights in whatever society they may find themselves. These are thought of as claim-rights but they belong to men as men and not as members of particular states, societies or social groupings, and do not derive from promises and undertakings.

While few political theorists would deny that individuals have natural rights (with the exception of those sceptics who maintain that philosophy has nothing at all to say about the relationship between the individual and the state), the justification of the more general rights has always been difficult. Central to many discussions of this problem is the argument that implicit in the idea of a morality is the notion of rights. While it is certainly possible that a moral code can be coherent without such a notion, one that recognises individual autonomy is scarcely conceivable without the idea of rights, the violation of which requires considerable justification.

H. L. A. Hart distinguishes between *special* rights and *general* rights (1967, pp. 60–4). Special rights, which arise out of specific undertakings and agreements between individuals, presuppose the existence of general rights because one needs a special right (or claim) to justify a limitation on another's freedom, and in the absence of such a right everyone has the general right not to be coerced. If there are any natural rights, he says, then there is at least the equal right to be free, a right which is possessed by all men capable of choice. The recognition that there is such a right is implicit in the moral justification of its abrogation. Of course, justifications have always been found for the violation of this right but it is a significant practical point that many tyrannical regimes while systematically violating rights nevertheless formally acknowledge their existence. In the contemporary world the real problems are about the content of rights and establishing machinery for their enforcement.

When social and political theorists maintain that human beings possess rights as human beings rather than as members of a social practice, or as participants in a moral or legal relationship, they actually mean that there is a minimum concept of human equality at work in moral argument. This view was considered in a previous chapter and can be restated here in the context of rights. When we say that each person has an equal right to freedom, to be left alone (unless there are substantial grounds for interference), to choose his own course of action, to exchange values with others, and not therefore to be used as a thing or an instrument for the advantage of the 'community' or 'society at large', we mean that irrespective of his merit as an individual in his personal and moral capacity, he is at least equal to others in human worth (Feinberg, 1973, pp. 94–7). Even convicted criminals, who have violated the rights of others and therefore do not score highly in moral grading, still have the right not to be treated in cruel or humiliating ways by their gaolers.

The equal right to freedom, however, needs to be filled out by other considerations in political argument. It might be used by extreme liberals as a barrier against interference in freely-negotiated contracts between individuals and against the state using the property of individuals to advance social purposes. But since morality permits the justification of limitations on this right, a more collectivist conception of society would be consistent with it. However, the argument then would be about the justification of the proposed intervention, not about the existence of the right itself.

There are differences amongst political theorists concerning the content of rights and their supposed 'absolute' nature. The concept of human rights has been expanded in recent years to include economic and social rights and the controversy surrounding this topic is of major importance today. However, the traditional statements have not differed greatly; rights to life, liberty, property, free expression, freedom of movement and a fair trial figure prominently. All of them appear to require little positive action by the state. Political authorities do not create rights and are limited to the enforcement of those rights that already exist.

A criticism often made of the traditional statements about rights is that the rights listed conflict, and that in the absence of some ordering principle or priority rule, they present a somewhat incoherent and muddled set of demands. Does not the right to property conflict with the right to life in a famine, when a person might justifiably claim that another individual's property rights are not inviolable? In fact, in this particular example, Locke would maintain that there is no conflict; since no person can take another's property without his consent, even a starving person has no right to someone else's legitimately acquired property; rather it is the *duty*, under natural law, of the rich to relieve the suffering of the indigent. Locke's real problem is that of making his belief that a man's property cannot be taken from him without his consent consistent with the obvious fact that there has to be coercion in order to raise taxes for essential government services, including the enforcement of rights.

Contemporary exponents of Locke's doctrine of natural rights do argue that statements about rights can be constructed without any inconsistency between the various rights. In fact they would argue that rights do not have to be *specified* or enumerated but that all the basic rights can be derived from the equal right to freedom where that is interpreted to mean that each individual has an inviolable right to person and property. Restrictions on one person's freedom would not count as a violation of his rights if they were designed solely to prevent the use of force or fraud against someone else. Similarly, libel laws would not count as a limitation on anyone's rights to free expression since they protect what are, in effect, property rights that individuals have in their personal reputations. The state would then be limited by the existence of one basic human right.

Collectivists argue, however, that this interpretation of human rights is far too narrow in that it merely gives an ideological justification of the existing set of property rights, which are quite arbitrary from a moral point of view. Instead of being a universal set of claims which are not necessarily tied to any political ideology, rights end up as out-growths of the social philosophy of individualism. In the radical collectivist view, truly human rights must include a welfare element (see below, Section 4).

The other main difficulty with the doctrine of human rights is over the question of whether they are absolute, where this means that they are to be honoured *without exception* (see, Feinberg, 1973, pp. 94–7). For example, does the right to life put a prohibition on capital punishment? The statement that each person has an equal right to liberty offers little guidance here. It is possible to argue that an absolute right to life does not preclude the taking of life if that action is essential to secure the protection of life generally. Clearly, the killing of a terrorist, if that is the only way that he can be prevented from indiscriminate slaughter, would not be thought of as a breach of rights. The case of capital punishment is more difficult but it could be maintained by a natural rights theorist that the institution is morally permissible since it is the convicted murderer who has breached the right to life. It might be argued, however, that there are no absolute rights as such and that situations can be envisaged in which a human right may be overridden. There is nevertheless a meta-ethical right, the right to equal consideration, which requires that justification must be given when individuals are treated in certain ways if they are to be accorded the status of moral agents. But of course this right has no specific content in the way that typical human rights have.

Human rights are also thought to be *inalienable*, that is, they cannot be given up or traded away. Thus slavery is always illegitimate since it violates a person's right to freedom, and makes him a tool of another (no matter how beneficently the slave-owner treats the slave). Unlike non-universal moral rights, which can be waived, the rights that every person has against unjustified interference cannot be simply renounced. The point of saying that certain natural rights are inalienable is that if a person voluntarily gives them up he, in a sense, resigns from the moral community and puts the determination of his future into the hands of somebody else. Voluntary contracts of slavery involve the attempted surrender of the right to freedom and choice. To argue that natural rights are inalienable is to argue that such contracts do not take away the right; a person may, for various reasons, wish to abandon his control over his own future, but this does not mean that he has extinguished a right in the way that one might waive the right to be repaid a £5 loan to a friend.

A perplexing problem that concerns the supposed inalienability of rights is that of euthanasia. In effect, does a person have the right to renounce his own right to life? If this is so, it implies that perhaps the most fundamental of the specific rights is, in principle, waivable. In fact there are many cases, involving painful and terminal illnesses, where the legal *impossibility* of the patient choosing to end his own life itself constitutes an abrogation of his rights. Indeed, to allow the person to decide whether to continue living or not is to pay tribute to him as a rational moral agent capable of choice. Of course, it has to be established that a person is a rational agent when he makes such a decision and is fully aware of the consequences, but to prohibit euthanasia, and in doing so prolong needless agony, seems to reflect the dominance of a particular sort of moral code over the sanctity of individual autonomy and the rights that go with it.

## 3. Critics of rights

The doctrine of natural rights has never been without its critics and it has been rejected both on philosophical and political grounds. It has been suggested that statements about rights are incurably metaphysical and that the social and political ends of the theorists of rights can be formulated in more philosophically respectable concepts. Politically they have been interpreted as radical ideas potentially subversive of the social order, or as reactionary obstacles that prevent the radical transformation of society based on 'scientific' principles.[3] The basic point that underlies all collectivist criticisms of human rights is that they are excessively individualistic and ahistorical. There are other important refutations of the doctrine but those provided by utilitarianism and the varieties of Marxism and socialism are perhaps of most interest to contemporary political theorists.

Bentham's (1843) objection to natural rights was both philosophical and political. As a legal positivist of the command school, Bentham could not accept that statements about natural rights were even meaningful. Rights were correlated with duties and to be under a duty was to be liable to sanctions in the event of failure to perform an action. Thus statements about rights, duties and obligations could be reduced to statements about the facts of a system of law. In Bentham's philosophy it would also be possible to speak of moral rights and duties where failure to perform an action is met by the sanction of popular disapproval. But it would not be possible to speak sensibly of the abstract rights of man which are said to exist independently of legal systems with sanctions. In a famous phrase he described them as 'nonsense upon stilts'. At most, Bentham would concede that natural rights were no more than expressions of what legal rights men *ought* to have; but even here the justification for such rights must be in terms of social utility and not in terms of any other moral principle.

Bentham's political objection to natural rights was that they were in fact reactionary, and that their alleged existence retarded the application of science to social reform. Armed with the felicific calculus the sovereign could derive a collective welfare judgement from the (observable) preferences of individuals, and policies could therefore be evaluated according to their consistency with this rather than their conformity to abstract principles of rights and justice, the validity of which depended on intuition and subjective opinion.

We have seen earlier how utilitarianism fails to provide an objective morality because the derivation of a collective welfare judgement from individual preference requires that utility can be measured, and that the legislator can make interpersonal comparisons of utility. Since these things cannot be done, statements about utility are logically no different from statements about natural rights in that they rest upon sentiment, intuition and subjective judgement. We do, of course, make utilitarian-type judgements about the interests of the community but these are ultimately moral judgements and must therefore be evaluated on moral and not scientific grounds.

By concentrating exclusively on the beneficial consequences of action as the source of value, utilitarianism ignores the rights that come from the past actions of individuals, and the rights that arise independently of social utility from the agreements they make and from their dignity and autonomy as human beings. To say that someone has a right to something entails quite a different justification from that involved in utilitarianism. In pure Benthamism the individual disappears once his preferences are known and incorporated into the utilitarian calculus, and since in a Benthamite legal order the legislator is unlimited in his authority, individual rights may well be abrogated in the construction of the social welfare function. In fact, rights are most often asserted defensively against the general interests of the community. If people do have rights which do not depend upon political enactment for their existence then these cannot be violated merely on grounds of utility for, apart from the difficulty of determining what the general interest is, this would destroy the whole purpose of rights, which are the possessions of individuals for their protection against the 'public'. It is possible to conceive of situations where utilitarian arguments which justify the abrogation of a right might be compelling, but the strong conception of rights involves the idea that the individual can be coerced only when his actions threaten or damage the *rights of others* and not merely when they appear to be against the interests of the community.

It is misleading to suggest that Marxists are as systematically hostile to the idea of natural rights as some utilitarians have been. In fact, contemporary Marxists and collectivists are ambivalent towards human rights, as Marx himself was. On the one hand, for example, they are eager to wage revolutionary struggle against colonialism on behalf of the rights of man, but on the other they are extremely critical of the individualism of the traditional theory of rights, especially its commitment to personal property.

Marx, in *On the Jewish Question* (1971, pp. 85–114), saw the rise of human rights in historical context. The liberation of man from the oppressive and restrictive feudal economic and social structure was a stupendous achievement which realised the major aims of the natural rights thinkers. However, he was insistent that the so-called rights of man 'are nothing but the rights of the member of civil society, i.e. egoistic man, man separated from other men and the community' (Marx, 1971, p. 102). True to historical materialism, Marx rejected the claim to universalism made by liberal theorists of rights. The emancipation of man required the transcendence of *all* oppressive social and economic institutions, not merely those of feudalism; and the bourgeois period of history, for all its many virtues, established mainly legal and political protection for the individual right to appropriate property. The liberal right to freedom separated the private world from the public and undermined those social and co-operative aspects of humanity which are essential for the true nature of man (p. 104). For Marx, rights were anti-social, individualistic and divisive.

Nevertheless, formal acknowledgement of the universal importance of human rights is a feature of existing Marxist regimes. The 1936 Soviet constitution, a product of Stalinism, while including economic and social rights, did also include the traditional liberal rights to freedom of association, free movement, a free press, a fair trial and so on, as does its 1977 successor. However, even these formal concessions are qualified by the existence of strict social obligations. Even in Soviet theory the familiar civil rights can only be exercised in the interests of the proletariat and cannot be held against the socialist state.

In practice, of course, the history of the Soviet Union has been characterised by a persistent and systematic violation of human rights which, according to the evidence of dissidents, has only lessened in scale during the last twenty years. During the height of the Stalinist terror Soviet cruelty is thought to have been unequalled outside Nazism. It may be the case that such occurrences were historical aberrations, or that they proceeded from the personality of Stalin, but it is worth asking whether some explanation can be found in the Marxist conception of human rights.

It is clear that by consigning human rights to the bourgeois mode of production Marxists have systematically underestimated the need for protection against unwarranted interference that men have always required and always will, if the liberal assumptions about human nature are true. In Marx's co-operative society of the future there will presumably be no individual rights which limit the freedom of others because production will be based on social co-operation rather than individual appropriation; but the acceptability of this depends upon the rather dubious assumption that human nature will change with the historically-determined alteration of the economic system. It may be true that some versions of the natural rights thesis are extremely individualistic and entail a legal system that is concerned only with private exchanges of rights between individuals to the detriment of those communal values which might come to the fore under some alternative legal and economic structure, but at least, if implemented effectively, they guarantee a security and protection absent in those regimes which are based on a different social philosophy. The human rights which are so castigated by Marx for being the mere expressions of bourgeois capitalism are asserted against *any* form of unwarranted interference and are therefore necessarily universal. It is only because Marx envisaged a utopia in which limitations on freedom would not be required that he was able to dismiss the claims of human rights as appropriate only for egoistic, capitalist man. But if the coercionless, co-operative society fails to materialise, and the legal system which could, in principle, embody positive expressions of human rights is abolished, there is little prospect that the individual will be protected against the invasions of the state. That Marx himself would be horrified by the behaviour of Communist regimes is no doubt true, but the abolition of those systems of law which can effectively protect individual rights finds ample justification in Marxism.

## 4. Economic and social rights

Since the Second World War there has been an expansion in the concept of human rights; there has been a change from what may be called 'negative rights', that is, rights held against the state which require little in the way of public, collective action beyond the establishment of a legal order guaranteeing liberty and security, towards rights which require more positive political action. These latter are called economic and social rights, welfare rights or rights to well-being. This widened concept of rights was given great political impetus by the United Nations Declaration of Rights of 1948. This declaration consisted of two parts, one concerned with the traditional civil rights and the other with things such as medical care, education, political participation and the now notorious right to 'periodic holidays with pay'. While Marxists have always supported such rights they are not exclusively Marxist and indeed many proponents of these welfare rights reject the Marxist general social philosophy. However, the whole concept of welfare rights has been highly controversial, for both political and philosophical reasons. The political reason stems from the fact that the second category of rights was included in the UN Declaration under pressure from the Soviet Union. Some Western writers argued that the satisfaction of economic rights by Communist governments would distract attention from their abrogation of the more basic rights. The philosophical objection was that economic rights were not properly human rights and that a different moral language was appropriate to the welfare aims of the second part of the Declaration.

The general philosophical objection to welfare rights takes the following form. Rights are in principle derived from the right to freedom and are rights held against others who have correlative obligations not to interfere; they are grounded in the idea that individuals are entitled to dignity, respect and autonomy. This philosophy puts the concept of a right into a different moral context from the duty of benevolence, to which the idea of welfare is said properly to belong. In Hart's theory the morality of rights is about the justifiable limitations on liberty; to have a right against somebody is to be entitled to have a claim *enforced* against that person, who in turn has an obligation to honour the claim. To have a right against the state is to have a strong claim not to be interfered with. But in relation to rights to welfare it is often said that no party can be legitimately coerced to honour them. Who is under an obligation to recognise rights to well-being? Those who think that there are rights to welfare normally think of the state as being responsible for the satisfaction of such claims, but they would also argue that individuals may be in positions in which someone has a right against him derived from considerations of another person's well-being rather than from a contract or an agreement. An example of this might be a patient with blood of a rare group having the right to a transfusion from someone else with blood of the same type (Peffer, 1978, pp. 74–5). The important point is that theorists of welfare rights wish to capture the special obligatoriness of the concept of a right so that coercion is legitimate for meeting claims to well-being.

Maurice Cranston (1967; 1973) has been very critical of the attempt to elevate social and economic rights to the status of human rights proper by the authors of the UN Declaration. Cranston argues that the only genuine *universal* human rights are the traditional negative ones and that the inclusion of economic rights in the Declaration involves a 'category mistake', that is, the error of assigning something to its wrong logical 'box'. In Cranston's view, economic rights belong to the category of ideals, not of universally realisable human rights.

He reaches this conclusion on two grounds. First, there is the 'ought implies can' argument. This holds that for any action to be morally obligatory it must be possible for the agent to perform it. Thus, if a child is in danger of drowning in a pond, a bystander who is able to swim and can easily rescue it, *ought* to do so; but the same cannot be said, say, of a person who is ten miles from the scene of the accident and unable to do anything about it. By the same reasoning it is absurd to suggest that all citizens have economic and social rights since in most countries of the world economic conditions make it impossible to implement them seriously. Things are different, however, in the case of the traditional civil rights since a recognition of them normally requires *inactivity* on the part of government; political officials merely have to desist from interfering with the free movement of individuals, imprisoning them without trial, censoring the press and so on. Thus negative rights are genuine universal rights of man while economic rights are ideals or, at the most, rights that belong to members of particular societies at particular times. Cranston's second argument is that negative rights are more important in a moral sense than economic rights. It is simply more vital to individual autonomy that governments refrain from cruel and arbitrary action, and from measures that destroy liberty, rather than provide 'free' social services or holidays with pay.

There is considerable intellectual weight behind the objections to the assimilation of welfare rights to universal rights. One problem not discussed by Cranston is that even if societies can afford to implement economic rights this may have unanticipated consequences for other rights. If a welfare state guarantees individuals incomes higher than they can earn in the market, then it is bound to attract more immigrants than it otherwise would, and thus lead to highly illiberal immigration laws. Similarly, if the state pays for the education of doctors out of general taxation then this may lead to the demand physically to prevent them from leaving the country in order to earn higher incomes abroad.

Strict libertarians argue that considerations such as these, plus the general fact that the implementation of welfare rights abrogates the rights of others because of the increased state power it entails, tells heavily against the expansion of the traditional rights. They might suggest that people's incomes *ought* to be increased (on grounds of general benevolence) but deny that individuals have a right to this in the strict sense of the term.

Proponents of economic and social rights deny the logical distinction that Cranston makes between the two sorts of rights. They say that even the implementation of negative rights requires some sort of positive government action; this is especially true of the right to life and the right to a fair trial, both of which require a considerable range of publicly provided protective services. Indeed, it may be the case that under certain circumstances governments may not be able to implement the customary civil rights. Thus in some cases the application of Cranston's 'ought implies can' criterion may have curious consequences. If a country is rich enough to provide for welfare rights but finds it difficult to guarantee basic negative rights, do the former then take precedence over the latter?

On the assumption that there is no logical distinction between the two sorts of rights it is argued that just as negative or autonomy rights can be derived from the idea of the moral worth of the person, so can rights to well-being. Thus, the respect that is owed to the dignity of the individual requires some recognition of his economic needs just as it requires the recognition of his freedom. Indeed, it would hardly constitute a recognition of individual dignity to say to a person in poverty that he had no *right* to well-being but merely that others had strong moral duties towards him. While there is considerable force to the argument that the concept of respect for persons requires some recognition of the right to well-being, nevertheless, some of the contents of the UN Declaration cannot possibly be considered as human rights, whatever may be said of them as rights that ought to obtain in particular societies.

# 10

# The Public Interest and Democracy

## 1. The public interest

One of the most pressing practical and theoretical problems of modern politics is that of devising procedures and institutions by which collective interests may be advanced. At one time it was argued that 'democracy' would be adequate for this since it was thought to be, in principle at least, a system in which the 'people', as opposed to an irresponsible minority, ruled. However, theory and experience indicate that there is no *necessary* connection between democratic procedures and the advancement of common interests. Not only is there the problem of the oppression of minorities under a democracy, but also the likelihood that the system encourages the pursuit of sectional and group interests to the ultimate destruction of the public interest. Before this can be considered, however, an understanding of the concepts of public interest and democracy is required.

The concept of the public interest can be interpreted not too inaccurately as a sophisticated version of those 'aggregative' concepts, such as the 'common good' and the 'general will', which are found in traditional political thought. These concepts are now to some extent discredited, mainly because they elevate aggregates such as the 'group', the 'community' and 'society' to a position where they stand for 'higher' values than those of individuals. These metaphysical entities are thought to represent the 'true' or 'real' purposes of individuals and, indeed, many writers have claimed that the influence of these notions has been responsible for the oppression of individuals and minorities by collective organisations in the twentieth century. Advocates of the doctrine of the public interest, however, argue that the concept describes the *shared* interests of a community and that its promotion, so far from oppressing individual interests, actually enables individuals to secure advantages which they could not otherwise enjoy. Statements about the public interest can then be firmly anchored in the methodological individualist's framework.

Nevertheless, the concept is not without its critics. Political theorists of a Logical Positivist frame of mind still maintain that the concept has no 'operational' meaning, that is, there is no such thing as the 'public' which can be said meaningfully to have an 'interest', and that the concept is used emotively to add honorific overtones to policies which are, in reality, merely to the advantage of individual or private group interests. In this view, to say that 'policy $x$ is in the public interest' is logically equivalent to 'I approve of $x$'.[1] This charge has particular force in modern democracies where strategically-placed pressure groups almost invariably attempt to legitimise their sectional claims in terms of the public interest.

It does not follow from this, however, that appeals to the public interest are devoid of meaning. Also, it is important to note that the refutation of the normative aspect of the concept does not depend solely upon a demonstration of its supposed non-existence in an empirical sense. It is logically possible that a proposed policy is in the public interest but that it ought not to be promoted – perhaps because the advantages it has for the 'public' are accompanied by some undesirable consequence. Yet all too often political argument is impoverished by the assertion that the concept is either operationally meaningless, or that its implementation involves highly controversial assumptions about people's 'true' or 'best' interests.

To demonstrate that rational argument about the public interest is possible we have to specify the kinds of phenomena that are being referred to in the use of the concept.

Following Brian Barry we can say that something, for example a policy or a law, is in a person's interest 'if it increases his opportunity to get what he wants – whatever that may be' (1967b, p. 115). Thus 'interests' are means towards the attainment of ends; something is in a person's interests when it enables him to satisfy future wants. Interests are therefore distinct from wants. A person can be mistaken about his interests in that something that he thinks may advance want-satisfaction may turn out under analysis not to do so. Whereas it would be an example of *moralism* to tell a person that his wants are mistaken, as when people are told that they *ought* not to spend their incomes in certain 'undesirable' ways, this is not the case with interests. People hire experts to handle their interests, and this can only mean that by so doing they hope to put themselves in a better position to satisfy their own future wants.

While it is easy to see how a policy may advance an individual's private interests, it is not so clear that a policy can unambiguously be said to advance the public interest without invoking a metaphysical, organic notion of the 'public'. In fact, further analysis shows that this is quite possible, for there are interests which individuals share as *members of the public* which cannot be promoted except through some kind of public decision-making procedure. We saw this in Chapter 3 in the discussion of public goods. A person increases his opportunities to satisfy his wants when certain things are provided publicly because they would not be provided at all, or perhaps underprovided, through a system of purely private transactions.

It should be clear what the word 'public' means. 'Public' is always contrasted with 'private', so that when we say that the public is affected by an act we mean those 'non-assignable' persons who in various situations cannot be defined as private individuals or as members of private groups (Barry, 1965, pp. 190–2). Thus in a rail strike the public consists of those persons adversely affected by the actions of the members of a private group, the railwaymen's union. A public park is so called because it is available to *anyone* indiscriminately. It is obvious, therefore, that the composition of the public will vary from issue to issue, and that individuals will find themselves sometimes as members of the public and at other times as members of groups opposed to the public. The difficulty is that in many policy disputes an individual may find that he has interests both as a member of the public and as a member of an organised group smaller than the public, and it is not always clear whether his *net* interests lie with the policy that affects him as a member of the public or that which affects him as a member of the group. Furthermore, without some sort of formalised constitutional procedure there is normally no incentive for individuals to promote policies that advance their interests as members of the public. In the absence of sanctions it will always be in the interests of an individual to renege on an agreement to pay his share of a publicly-provided benefit since, from his point of view, his not paying can make little or no difference to its supply. For libertarian political economists this is the primary justification for the state, but the reasoning is applicable to any group containing large numbers (Olson, 1965).

The English utilitarians were very much aware of the problems of the public interest and tried to solve them with the conventional utilitarian calculus. Proceeding from an individualistic framework, Bentham argued that the community is a 'fictitious body, composed of the individual persons who are considered as constituting as it were its members. The interest of the community then is, what? – the sum of the interests of the several members who compose it' (Bentham, 1970, p. 12). The utilitarians had a strong sense of the public interest, that is, they assumed that there was a wide range of public policies which were prevented from being implemented by the existence of 'sinister interests', mainly the landlords. Unfortunately, this 'class' was in control of the political system of nineteenth-century Britain and therefore prevented the advancement of the community's interests. An example was the ability of the aristocracy, through its control of the unreformed Parliament, to retain the Corn Laws which prevented the import of foreign wheat until the home supply reached a certain price. Employers and employees, of course, had a common interest in cheap food. The problem for utilitarians, therefore, was to ensure that public and not sinister interests were maximised (their proposed solution will be considered later in this chapter).

The difficulty with all this is the familiar one of deriving a collective judgement from individual preferences. Since there is no objective measuring rod of pleasure, any aggregate result of a utilitarian calculation must, in a logical sense, be quite subjective. Since individual interests are almost certain to be in conflict the definition of the public interest as a 'sum' of interests is incoherent. As we have seen, the public interest is only meaningful in the context of the evaluation of policies which affect individuals in their capacity as members of the public and it cannot be simply computed from their private interests. This makes it logically possible to say that there can be a public interest while at the same time individuals and groups may have an interest in opposing it. Examples of public or common interests that exist in a reasonably stable and integrated community are those that people have in a common system of law, defence against external aggression and the whole range of public goods that was discussed in Chapter 3.

Another example of the failure to analyse carefully the relationship between public and group interests comes from the 'pluralists' and this failure leads them to eliminate mistakenly the public interest from their political vocabulary. The sociological pluralists, or group theorists of politics, are sceptical of the applicability of the public interest to political and social affairs. They argue that it has no use in empirical work in that there is no such thing as a public interest, beyond the minimal notion of a 'consensus' about fundamental values which every stable society must have, and that in normative political argument it cannot function as a standard for the appraisal of policies. The interesting thing about pluralism is that not only do some of its adherents describe politics as a process of conflict between groups but they also go on to recommend that 'politics' itself, where this means both the voting system in a democracy and the negotiation and bargaining that takes place between organised groups at the stage of policy-formation, ought to be valued as a decision-making process. As long as the decisions made in a community reflect the relative strength and importance of groups then stability, freedom and efficiency are likely to be better promoted by a regime characterised by 'politics' than, say, a liberal market economy or a full-blooded socialist system. In this argument there can be no public interest, only group interests: the crucial point that an individual may evaluate a policy from his position as a member of the public and as a member of a group is lost.

It is easy, however, to show that the persistent pursuit of group interests through the political process leads to a reduction of freedom and efficiency and a failure to promote genuine shared interests, so that each individual member of the community is worse off than he would have been without 'politics'. As Mancur Olson puts it:

> It does not follow that the results of pressure group activity would be harmless, much less desirable, even if the balance of power equilibrium resulting from the multiplicity of pressure groups kept any one pressure group from getting out of line. Even if such a pressure group system worked with perfect *fairness* to every group, it would still tend to work inefficiently. (Olson, 1965, p. 124)

It is important to remember that unlimited pressure group activity may produce results that are favourable to the members of a group but which are unfavourable to *society as a whole*, to which, of course, each group member belongs. To illustrate this simple but often misunderstood point we can take the case of protectionism. Now from the point of view of the consumer and society as a whole, it is clear that free trade between nations is the optimal economic policy since citizens gain from the efficiencies brought about by the international division of labour. But from the point of view of any single producer group it would be better if their products were protected by tariffs from foreign competition while all other goods were allowed to come in freely. But of course, for a government to protect merely one group would be bad politics, leaving aside the question of fairness, since it would presumably mean ignoring other groups equally essential for the welfare of the community. Yet to satisfy all the groups by protective measures would make society as a whole, that is to say, the group members taken individually, worse off than they would be under free trade.

There is another area of contemporary importance which involves an application of the public interest yet has received little attention from political theorists. This is the problem of the rapid depletion of scarce resources. While each individual has an interest as a member of the public in the conservation of certain vital resources, he does not have any incentive to contribute to this by his actions as a private citizen, since these can have only a negligible effect on the determination of economic events. The two solutions to this problem are the reformulated classical liberal position that only a wider use of the price mechanism and a redefinition of property rights can bring a movement towards a harmony between individual and public interests; and the interventionist argument that centralised planning by government is required in order to maximise the public interest.

Classical liberals argue that the price system automatically conserves resources since as a good becomes more scarce its price will rise; this naturally 'rations' its use and also stimulates the search for new supplies or close substitutes. All this may seem obvious enough but what is interesting is the incorporation of a theory of property rights into the argument. It is argued that the price mechanism will not generate the public interest if property rights are inadequately defined. If a system of property rights does not include the right to exclude people from the use of a resource then wasteful consumption will become endemic and a rational allocation of resources will not emerge, the community as a whole being worse off.

Three types of rights are delineated: communal, state and private.[2] A communal right to use a resource exists when any person in the community is entitled to use some resource without restriction. This resource might be a common piece of land, the produce of which is available to all indiscriminately. This will, under certain conditions, lead to overuse and what is called the 'tragedy of the commons'. Since communal rights do not exclude anyone from the use of the resource we can expect the rapid depletion of the game and stock of common lands, so making everybody worse off in the long run. Only if rights to restrict the use of property develop will this be prevented. A developed property rights system may give the state, through its officials, the right to exclude, or this may accrue to individuals through a system of private ownership.

The classic example of how the 'tragedy of the commons' was averted by the development of property rights is that of Indian tribes whose members habitually hunted animals only for their immediate needs; the existence of communal rights to the stock did not therefore bring about its depletion (Demsetz, 1967, pp. 350–3). However, the advent of the fur trade meant that there was a much greater use of the stock: had the system of communal rights remained, no individual would have had any incentive to economise and the animal resources would have been quickly depleted. Fortunately, a system of property rights developed which included the right to exclude so that stocks could be conserved despite the change in their use brought about by the fur trade.

Present-day economic liberals have applied this concept of property rights to a number of areas such as pollution, the preservation of fisheries, and the continuing struggle to prevent 'desertification' in Africa (Burton, 1978, pp. 84–8). Not surprisingly they stress the advantages of a system of private property rights over a state system. The argument is that individuals have a greater incentive to be informed about economic conditions than the officials of the state and that the market is a better restraint on the squandering of resources than is the political system (which is what the public officials are accountable to). There is also the not inconsiderable point that economic liberals claim that state action is an inherent threat to liberty.

While this approach still retains a concept of the public interest, and shows how a public interest may exist even when groups and individuals appear to be in conflict with it, it is a somewhat limited conception. The idea seems to be that people have a common interest only in relation to rules and that the potential conflict between an individual's private and public interests can be resolved if institutions are designed which give individuals an incentive to promote their shared interests. What is excluded is the idea that governments ought to be permitted to promote the public interest where this exceeds their traditional function of enforcing general rules. This follows from the psychological premises of economic liberals; they assume that the officials of the state, if not bound by strict rules, will maximise their own interests rather than those of the public.

Other writers, however, take a less gloomy view of government and argue that under classical liberalism many policies which are in the public interest would not get promoted at all because the requirements for that system are quite strict (the details of various procedural schemes will be discussed later in this chapter). Many schemes to do with welfare, the environment, the arts and so on, which might be said in some sense to be in the public interest, in that an individual's interests as a member of the public would be advanced if they were implemented, would fail under a system of strictly limited government since they would always find some opposition.[3] In modern societies it is difficult for such shared interests to be organised, compared to private interests, and therefore those who favour a more expansive concept of the public interest maintain that only the state can promote it.

The 'narrow' and 'expanded' versions of the public interest come into conflict over the interpretation and evaluation of democracy. Exponents of the narrow version maintain that democratic institutions tend to promote group interests in the guise of the public interest with the result that those *genuine* shared interests that individuals have can attract little electoral support. They therefore recommend severe restrictions on majority rule to protect individual rights from harmful collective decisions. Their opponents take a more optimistic view of 'political man' and argue that rulers do not necessarily use public office to maximise private interests. Party competition under the majority rule procedure is not only adequate to hold government to account, but is also a means of advancing measures for the public welfare which go beyond the mere enforcement of general rules, property rights and the maintenance of stable economic conditions.

However, a discussion of this issue, which is perhaps the most important in contemporary political theory, must be prefaced by an analysis of democracy itself. This is pursued in the following section and the main themes explored here are returned to in Section 3. In the final section of this chapter we will consider some of the issues in democratic theory which fall outside our main analytical framework.

## 2. Democracy

As is the case with so many words in the political vocabulary, the word 'democracy' has acquired remarkably strong emotive overtones. Its use is often as much designed to provoke a favourable attitude towards a political regime as it is to locate particular features of it. Today political systems that differ widely are almost always described as democratic and the word is used in a bewildering variety of contexts.[4]

Thus we have 'liberal democracy', 'social democracy' and 'totalitarian democracy'; the word is also used in non-political contexts, as when people speak of 'industrial democracy'. It would appear from this that the word has little descriptive content and is merely an honorific label attached to those forms of political and economic organisation of which the utterer approves and wishes his listener similarly to approve. But this was not always so. In the nineteenth century democracy had a fairly precise meaning; it described regimes that today would be called liberal democracies and opposition to such political systems was conventional rather than exceptional. However, not since the fascist and nazi tyrannies of the 1930s have political writers (or leaders) openly declared their hostility to democracy in principle.

As the above examples indicate, it is customary to give propositions containing the word democracy some descriptive content by adding an adjective to indicate what *type* of democracy is being discussed. Liberal democracy might then mean a political system in which individual rights are given special constitutional protection against majorities, and social democracy would describe a political system in which, in addition to conventional liberal political rights, there exists a considerable measure of collective action to create social and economic equality. While this approach has some obvious advantages in the way of clarity in political argument it secures these at the cost of assuming away some of the traditional problems that occur with the use of the word democracy. In fact, the word need hardly be used at all: all that a person wanted to express about political systems could be encompassed in words such as 'liberal' or 'socialist'.

There is a case for subjecting 'democracy' itself to further analysis beyond delineating the main features of political systems that happen to call themselves democratic. The fact that the word has been appropriated by thinkers who represent widely different ideologies is no reason for denying that the word has meaning or significance. In fact, some of the more eccentric users of the word reveal inconsistencies and contradictions which the political theorist has a professional duty to expose: analysis of this kind is not dependent upon there being a peculiar 'essence' of democracy, knowledge of which can be discerned by the philosopher. The first step in such an analysis is to dispel the illusion that the term democracy always stands for that which is good or virtuous about a political system. If democracy is used to describe the 'good society' then there will indeed be as many types of democracy as there are visions of utopia and the word will lose all descriptive meaning. However, once we can recognise the legitimacy of saying that, for example, 'decision *x* was arrived at democratically but its implementation involves the violation of an individual right', then it will be possible to develop a 'critical' theory of democracy. Such a theory includes both an analysis of certain descriptive features of democratic regimes and an appraisal of those features from a more general normative standpoint.

Another way of saying the same thing is to distinguish between democracy as a certain kind of procedure, to be contrasted with monarchy and various forms of oligarchy and élite rule; and democracy as a particular form of society, characterised by such things as extensive popular participation and social and economic equality. While some of the latter features may be relevant to a critical theory of democracy (they will be discussed in a later section of this chaper) too great a concentration on them may distract the attention of the political theorist away from some important analytical problems. It is surely legitimate to describe some regimes as democratic which do not have these attributes, however desirable in an ethical sense they may be. The remainder of this section will thus be concerned with the problems of procedural democracy.

When we speak of procedures we mean simply those rules of a social practice which determine the legitimacy of courses of action; we distinguish these from the results or outcomes of such actions (see Chapter 6 for the discussion of this in connection with justice). Democratic procedures are special sorts of political procedures which are designed to involve the 'people' in decision-making and the making of laws, in the way that monarchical or autocratic procedures are obviously not. Indeed, such an involvement was thought by some political philosophers, notably Rousseau, to solve the problem of political obligation, since individuals would not regard obedience to laws they had imposed upon themselves as restrictive of their liberty.

The origins of the idea of democracy as 'rule by the people' go back to the ancient Greek experience where rule by the *demos* was obviously contrasted with monarchy and aristocracy, but the modern meaning of this phrase is significantly different. In Greek times the *demos* was a section of the population (the poor and numerous) and all types of government were thought of as sectional government. But in modern times purely sectional rule is frowned upon and democracy has come to mean rule by the whole people. In fact, the peculiar virtue of democracy is thought to lie in the fact that it is the only form of government that can, in principle, advance the interests of all the members of a politically organised community. Of course democratic procedures are often used to advance sectional interests and economic theorists of democracy have produced sophisticated arguments to show that under certain conditions this will invariably happen, but the normative arguments for democracy now turn largely upon the idea that it is uniquely concerned with shared values.

Taken literally, the phrase 'rule by the people' presents an impossible ideal for democratic theorists. This is not only because of the commonplace observation that *direct* democracy, a system in which decision-taking and law-making is a function of the whole community unmediated by any form of representation, is impossible to realise in all but the smallest of societies, but also because 'ruling' implies ruling over someone or some group, and if all the people rule, over whom is it that they rule? What is surely meant is that in a democracy legitimacy is a function of laws being a product of a *majority* decision, where access to that decision-making process is not restricted to some particular class or group. This last point implies that democracy entails some commitment to political *equality*; not an absolute equality, since any form of rule necessarily involves some political inequality, but in the sense of no race, class or individual being arbitrarily deprived of the opportunity of participating in the political process. It is of course almost a truism to say that democracies will vary in the extent to which the ideal of equal political participation is approached.

If democracy is defined in terms of majority rule, where the composition of a representative assembly and decisions taken in that assembly are determined by a majority vote, it poses severe problems both at the normative and descriptive levels. Are people really prepared to accept majority rule procedures as legitimate in all cases? Of course they are not and there is no reason why they should. The problem is that in any community characterised by divisions which are of a permanent kind, for example, divisions of race or religion, majority rule procedures simply entrench the position of the dominant race or sect. The example of Northern Ireland demonstrates the poverty of pure majoritarianism. Both Protestant and Catholic communities can appeal to the majority principle: the former has a clear majority in the six counties while the latter would be substantially ahead in an all-Ireland context. However Ireland is politically constituted there will always be a potentially alienated minority. The distressing fact is that in terms of world politics the Irish case is the norm rather than the exception. Majority rule procedures are only acceptable when the *major* interests of particular groups within the community are not at stake. There is also the problem, to be considered below, that the majority principle may not reflect the *public* interest even in a reasonably homogeneous community. Thus for a variety of reasons political theorists are reluctant to define democracy in terms of pure majoritarianism alone (Barry, 1979).

A further problem is that even if a majoritarian voting procedure is consistent with stability and the protection of minority interests, the necessary qualifications for participation in the political process are by no means clear (Dahl, 1979). All democracies impose some conditions for participation, but there is by no means universal agreement on what these should be. There cannot be an unrestricted franchise since no one has recommended that minors or the severely mentally deranged should be allowed to vote, but beyond this opinions vary. Until recently countries which disenfranchised women would not have been denied the title of democracy and theorists of liberal democracy have often exluded some categories of people, or given special weightings to others. John Stuart Mill, who favoured extra votes for the educationally qualified, is a clear example of the latter.[5] It is no answer to say that Mill was therefore not a 'true democrat' because, since all theories of democracy include some qualifications for participation, it is incumbent on Mill's critics to say what these are and why they are better than his. There will always therefore be an element of arbitrariness about electoral qualifications even though most people would agree that for a system to be democractic all sane adults should be entitled, as of right, to participate.

At the descriptive level it is argued persuasively that the majority principle is inadequate for marking off democratic regimes from non-democratic ones. The most casual observations of Western democracies reveal that governments rarely satisfy the majority principle. This is clearly seen in Great Britain whose 'first past the post' electoral system virtually ensures that most governments are minority ones; indeed, the sometimes eccentric (by the strict standards of egalitarian democracy) relationship between votes cast and seats won means that occasionally the major opposition party may have a bigger share of the popular vote than the government.

For these and other reasons some democratic theorists have suggested that majoritarianism is not a decisive feature of democracy and that consequently the fear of the 'tyranny of the majority' has proved to be unfounded. In this view, which is a version of 'pluralism', democracy is characterised by 'minorities rule' in contrast to the minority rule of non-democratic, one-party states (Dahl, 1956; 1971). What is distinctive about pluralist democracy, or 'polyarchy', is the presence of a multiplicity of competing interests and groups in a system in which power is decentralised so that no one interest can dominate.

The system is thought to have considerable normative value precisely because it is *not* majoritarian and because the competitive nature of the process, and the fact that access is open to all, enables it to approach a rather modest standard of political equality. Against this it is often said that it falls a long way short of political equality in that it clearly favours established political groups and militates against the poor and unorganised; and also that the struggle for power between powerful organised groups means that shared interests are not always promoted (see Section 1 of this chapter).

It seems curious that the majority principle, which appears to be one of the defining characteristics of democracy, should, on analysis, turn out to play such a small role in the system, yet it would be unwise to eliminate it entirely. It is honoured, albeit imperfectly, in many Western democratic systems and, superficially at least, it seems to meet some of the requirements of political equality. Where collective decisions have to be taken it seems more reasonable to go for a quantitative judgement than for a qualitative one, since any departure from the former implies that certain people are especially qualified to make such judgements. It is this that marks off a democracy from a meritocracy. While it is true that in areas where collective decisions have to be taken some theorists dispute that majority rule procedures will maximise the public interest, the main disagreement amongst political theorists is the range over which majority decisions should be decisive. As we have noted already, when a community is divided along ethnic or religious lines, a genuine democracy will include procedures that maximise the interests of all rather than numerical majorities, and even in relatively homogeneous communities democracy is thought to be consistent with the constitutional protection of individual rights.

It could be said that this account is descriptive of liberal democracy only, and that other ideals are worthy of the title. There is some truth in this, but it should also be noted that its properties may, as a matter of fact, meet the more general standards of 'democracy', such as political equality and participation, better than any existing alternative. It is doubtful if one-party democracies or people's democracies can ever reach these standards, even though such regimes, it is said, are legitimised by 'popular enthusiasm'. This is because the absence of genuine choice between political alternatives removes the possibility of there being even the minimum of control over government by the people.

The prevailing problem in traditional democratic theory is that of reconciling the aim of 'government by the people' with the obvious fact that government itself is a minority activity. However much the development of democracy may take account of representation, of competition between groups and accountability of governments through periodic elections, there have always been social theorists who have argued that democracy of *any* type is impossible because of the inevitability of *élite rule*. Those who take this view are not making the trivial observation that the exercise of government must be in the hands of a minority – even Rousseau was insistent that democratic *government* was impossible (although the making of general laws was not) – but the potentially more damaging point that élite rule is necessarily *irresponsible*, in that élites are not accountable to the people and that genuine choice between alternatives is impossible. In this general view, democracy is not the name of a specific form of government, since all governments are in principle the same, but is a 'political formula', or 'myth', designed to deceive the masses into thinking that they can have some influence over government.

The élitist thesis is generally associated with the Italian writers, Pareto (the mathematical economist whose ideas we have already discussed in relationship to the role of the state) and Mosca, whose sociological theories were formulated earlier this century.[6] While the conclusions each writer drew about the possibility of democracy were not markedly dissimilar, their foundations were rather different and worth a brief discussion.

Pareto's demonstration of the inevitability of élite rule was based on the psychological premise of the fundamental inequality of men; while his argument looks historical it was profoundly ahistorical in that he interpreted the whole of human history in terms of the 'circulation of élites'. Elite leadership was a function of the predominance of certain pyschological attributes, which he called 'residues'. The most important of these were those of 'courage' and 'cunning' and a ruling élite would be composed of individuals who possessed one of these properties: put metaphorically, élites would consist of either 'lions' or 'foxes'. The circulation of élites occurred through changes in these residues. The egalitarian premise of democracy was fallacious because individuals would display the qualities necessary for ruling to a vastly unequal degree. In fact, outside purely economic relationships, Pareto thought that individual behaviour was fundamentally irrational, so that responsible self-government was an impossibility. Elites would only change through changes in 'residues' and democratic procedures could in no way affect this.

Mosca's élitism was more historical and sociological than Pareto's. The dominance of élites, and the consequent rigid division of society into two strata, were explicable in terms of social developments rather than deduced *a priori* from a small number of slender propositions about human nature. In comparison to the masses, who will always be unorganised, élites will be organised and, if not exactly cohesive, will present a unity which will guarantee their survival irrespective of democratic electoral processes. The qualities that sustain an élite will vary from one historical period to another, but in modern industrial society wealth, knowledge and bureaucratic skills predominate. In fact, the élite consists of two layers, the higher stratum of leaders who control the machinery of the state and a second stratum of trained administrators and technicians – although the latter body must not be relegated to secondary importance, as it is essential to the survival of the state. While Mosca was more favourably disposed than Pareto to representative democracy, and even hinted at the possibility of competition operating so as to restrain rulers, his general conclusion – that the democratic ideal functions largely as a myth – was not dissimilar from that of his compatriot.

It was J. S. Schumpeter (1954) who managed to construct a theory of democracy that was compatible with a certain kind of élitism. What made some of the traditional theories of democracy so vulnerable to the élitist criticisms was that they set impossibly high standards. They assumed that democracy required that government should reflect the 'will of the people', so that the outputs of the democratic machine simply represented the desires of the electorate.[7] Schumpeter easily showed that such a picture was highly unrealistic; it assumed that there is an homogeneous people's will when in fact, all large societies are characterised by a multiplicity of conflicting wills; it depended upon a high level of rationality when Schumpeter argued that in public affairs people's behaviour is likely to be irrational (in matters affecting their private interests Schumpeter maintained that people have a very much greater incentive to behave rationally); and it took no account of political leadership, the fact that all government involves action taken independently of the 'people's will'.

Despite this profound scepticism Schumpeter still thought that the word democracy had descriptive content and that a democratic system had much to recommend it. In effect, he turned traditional democratic theory upside down and argued that a democratic system was not characterised by translation of the people's will into government action but by competing parties offering alternative programmes to the electorate; the voters having little direct influence over the content of such programmes. The people were in fact limited to choosing a government, and what marked off democratic from non-democratic regimes was nothing so pretentious as 'government by the people' but the fact that, in the former, political competition existed and provided some minimal degree of accountability. It also necessitated some basic freedoms since a competitive party democracy required the freedom to form associations and propagate ideas. In a celebrated phrase Schumpeter defined democracy as 'that institutional arrangement for arriving at political decisions in which individuals acquire the power to decide by means of a competitive struggle for the people's vote' (1954, p. 229). Indeed, Schumpeter was one of the first democratic theorists to draw a direct analogy between political and market behaviour.

In Schumpeter's rather meagre account of democracy, participation is strictly limited and the influence that voters have over government policy is minimal; also, a system with a severely restricted franchise would count as democratic as long as competition determines the party that is to govern. His was a purely procedural account of democracy; it is no more than a method for producing a government and is compatible with almost *any* kind of society. Schumpeter did however, believe that under certain conditions it is likely to be a benign form of government, or at least less malign than the known alternatives. These conditions include a relatively homogeneous and 'open society', a professionalised and experienced bureaucracy, and recognised restraints on 'politics'. This last point is most important and Schumpeter insisted that if too many economic and social activities become subject to democratic politics the system will come under great strain. This would follow from Schumpeter's belief that the level of rationality achieved in political activity is very much less than that in economic behaviour. This insight has been confirmed in many sociological studies of voting behaviour which have revealed evidence of ignorance on the part of the electorate which would have alarmed the 'classical' theorists of democracy.

Those who share Schumpeter's contention that democracy is to be interpreted as a 'method' of government stress that its connection with liberty is instrumental rather than conceptual. While we have just noted that party competition requires some liberties if it is to work at all, this does not mean that the outcomes of democracy may not be illiberal in a general sense. In fact, liberal individualists insist that *all* forms of government should be restricted by general rules and that protection of freedom cannot be guaranteed by putting government into the 'right hands' but by carefully limiting the range of collective action.

## 3. Procedural democracy and the public interest

In the preceding section we were concerned in a very general way with the major characteristics of procedural democracy. In recent years there has been a growing body of knowledge on the workings of this system much of which casts doubt upon whether it is possible for democracy to work in the way that the early enthusiasts for the ideal intended. Of most importance is whether it can produce the public interest or those values which individuals share as members of the community. Of course, many people think that democracy should do more than this (see the next section of this chapter) but one important justification for democracy is that it is a desirable form of government precisely because it is concerned with general rather than sectional interests.

The first systematic attempt to demonstrate that democratic procedures would generate the public interest was made by the utilitarians, Jeremy Bentham and James Mill. As we have seen, the utilitarians mistakenly thought that the public interest could be summed up from private interests, but if their argument is re-interpreted to mean that the public interest represents those interests which individuals have as members of the community (in fact, there is some evidence that Bentham on some occasions took this view) then it is possible to see if their constitutional proposals will lead to the maximisation of community interests.

James Mill's *Essay on Government* (1955), first published in 1820, was the simplest utilitarian demonstration of the case for democracy. In methodology the *Essay* resembles contemporary economic theories of democracy in that Mill attempted to 'prove' the case for democratic government by reasoning deductively from some simple axioms of human nature which are assumed to be universally true. In no way did his case depend on experience or empirical knowledge of the various forms of government.

Mill took an extremely gloomy view of human nature. He assumed that man is motivated purely by self-interest, by the desire to maximise pleasure and minimise pain. Labour is a painful activity and therefore Mill believed that each person will seek naturally to appropriate the product of another man's labour. While men need government to enforce contracts and provide the general conditions for economic activity, Mill assumed that government, unless prevented, will become a 'sinister' interest which seeks to exploit the people. Mill, somewhat implausibly, took it for granted that capitalists and workers had a common interest in opposition to the land-owning class which controlled government at the time he was writing.

According to Mill 'checks and balances', or the separation of powers, could never restrain the actions of government since one part of government would naturally seek to accumulate all power in its own hands. He was firmly wedded to the necessity of the 'sovereign power' idea and maintained that, on *a priori* grounds, the only way for the people to be governed in their interests was for the people to govern themselves. Since 'direct democracy' was impossible in a modern state, he designed a system of representative democracy in which government itself could never emerge as a sinister interest. This was to be achieved by universal suffrage (in fact, Mill restricted the vote to men over forty, but this inconsistency can be ignored for our purposes), the mandating of representatives, provisions for their recall, and annual parliaments. All these devices were for the purpose of making the governing class exactly reflect the interests of the people. Under these conditions majority voting and the secret ballot would produce the public interest out of the purely self-interested actions of individuals.

Criticisms of James Mill have normally centred on his methodology, his conception of man and his complete lack of interest in democracy as anything more than a method of government. However, it may be more useful to comment on the internal logic of his system. It is clear that there is no reason why the majority procedure should generate utility and critics, including Macauley and Mill's son, John Stuart Mill, eloquently expressed a fear of majority tyranny. James Mill's only fear was the political power of the aristocracy and he assumed a harmony between the middle and working classes. He failed completely to anticipate the rise of party and class politics under democratic rules. He was aware that the working class might vote against their long-term interests but, somewhat inconsistently, argued that education would prevent this. He seemed unaware of the possibility of coalitions of private interests dominating under democracy, and his own belief in the necessity of a concentration of power at the centre further increased the possibility of the system producing undesirable and unintended consequences.

Problems of this type have exercised the minds of contemporary economic theorists of democracy who follow Mill's methodology but dispute his optimistic conclusions. Their main concern has been to suggest certain institutional arrangements which will ensure the maximisation of genuine public interests in a democracy. It is true however, that most of these theorists interpret the public interest in a particularly narrow way, and their critics maintain that under simple majority rule a greater range of shared values may be promoted. But before we discuss this some mention must be made of a specific logical problem that has perplexed economists and political theorists for the past twenty years. This is the problem, associated with the work of Kenneth Arrow in the field of welfare economics, that under certain conditions, constitutional procedures for the making of collective decisions, of which majority rule is one type, produce inconsistent outcomes.[8] The argument here is not about the moral problems of majority rule, or the likelihood or not of it maximising shared interests, but about the impossibility of any collective decision-making procedure reproducing the same logical features as an individual decision.

Arrow argued that for a collective choice procedure to be rational it has to exhibit the same properties as an individual's rational choice. The most important of these is transitivity; this means that if an individual prefers $x$ to $y$, and $y$ to $z$, then he must prefer $x$ to $z$. An individual's set of preferences will then exhibit an *ordering*. Now if we impose some fairly mild conditions on a collective choice procedure (such as majority rule) it can be shown that a collective ordering of preferences cannot be derived from all the possible individual orderings where there are more than two preferences. The conditions imposed are collective rationality (a social choice must exhibit the same logic as an individual's choice); the 'Pareto principle' (if alternative $x$ is preferred to alternative $y$ by every single individual then the social ordering ranks $x$ over $y$); the 'independence of irrelevant alternatives' (the social choice must not be affected by alternatives not within the feasible set); and 'non-dictatorship' (there is no one individual whose preferences always take precedence over the preferences of other individuals).

The 'impossibility' of democracy can now easily be shown. Imagine three individuals $x$, $y$ and $z$, whose preferences are transitively ordered between three alternatives $A$, $B$ and $C$ in the following way. Person $x$ prefers $A$ to $B$ and $B$ to $C$; $Y$ prefers $B$ to $C$ and $C$ to $A$; and $z$ prefers $C$ to $A$ and $A$ to $B$. Now in a series of pair-wise comparisons a majority prefers $A$ to $B$, a majority prefers $B$ to $C$ and a majority prefers $C$ to $A$. Thus while individual preferences are transitive the collective choice procedure of majority rule produces not a transitive decision but merely 'cyclical majorities'. The disheartening thing for the democrat is that for a transitive result to occur it will have to be imposed by a 'dictator'. This entails a breach of one of Arrow's undemanding conditions.

The following example should illustrate the significance of the problem. Imagine that the distribution of support for the party leaders in the United Kingdom took the following form: Mr Callaghan (42 per cent); Mrs Thatcher (36 per cent); Mr Steel (22 per cent). Further, imagine that the supporters of the leaders ranked their preferences in the following ways: Callaghan supporters preferred Steel to Thatcher, Thatcher supporters preferred Callaghan to Steel, and Steel supporters preferred Thatcher to Callaghan. Using $C$, $T$ and $S$ to represent the party leaders the situation can be represented as follows:

|  | C (42%) | T (36%) | S (22%) |
|---|---|---|---|
| 1st preference | C | T | S |
| 2nd preference | S | C | T |
| 3rd preference | T | S | C |

Now in a series of three votes we get the following results:

(a) $T$ beats $C$ (36 per cent + 22 per cent beats 42 per cent);
(b) $S$ beats $T$ (42 per cent + 22 per cent beats 36 per cent).

Now if $T$ beats $C$ and $S$ beats $T$ for the outcome to be transitive $S$ must beat $C$. But this is not so because the figures show that

(c) $C$ beats $S$ (42 per cent + 36 per cent beats 22 per cent).

Where choosers can rank alternatives there is always the possibility that the democratic process will produce intransitive results. If the system does generate 'cyclical majorities' of the above type, with no clear winner, then a result can only be obtained by relaxing one of Arrow's conditions.

On the whole, political theorists have not been unduly perturbed by Arrow's results. The conventional answer is that where democratic systems involve a straight choice between two alternatives, as in orthodox two-party systems, no 'paradox of voting' occurs, although there is no guarantee that the public interest will emerge from this, or that the 'tyranny of the majority' will be avoided.

In a two-party democracy the 'Arrow problem' is said to be avoided if the preference orderings of individuals are limited to those that are 'single-peaked' (Arrow's work showed that for a social decision procedure to be valid it must be able to handle *all* possible individual preference orderings). Single-peaked preference orderings are those that exhibit a consistency or pattern (which can be represented on a graph) so that, in political terms, a left-wing person will consistently rank policies from left to right (or right to left for a right-wing person). The 'moderate' will consistently rank policies falling to the right and left of his preferred policy, those further to the right and left being the least preferred. It is also assumed that political parties are fully informed about voters' preferences.

In our above example, the orderings would be single-peaked if Steel supporters switched their second and third preferences so that they prefered Callaghan to Thatcher. In this case Callaghan (42 per cent + 22 per cent) beats Thatcher (36 percent) and Callaghan also beats Steel (22 per cent). Callaghan is therefore the winner. It is quite possible that voters' preferences will be single-peaked on separate issues but the paradox is almost certain to occur in a democracy because voting takes place on *amalgamations* of issues (party platforms). Nevertheless, political theorists have often argued that party competition in a democracy does produce determinate outcomes.

In a famous example, Anthony Downs, in *An Economic Theory of Democracy* (1957), assumed that voters' preferences are single-peaked and represented opinion in a uniform spread on a left-to-right continuum with 'extremists' at both ends and 'moderates' in the middle. In a straight fight the party whose platform nearest approaches the preference-ordering of the 'median' voter (the voter exactly in the middle of the continuum) will win. Competition for votes between the two parties will therefore lead to their convergence around the middle. Under these conditions there is a kind of 'invisible hand' in democratic politics which produces a correspondence between government policy and the opinions of the electorate. Of course, there is no guarantee that government policy will represent the 'public interest'; whether it does or not will depend on the opinions of the median voter, and, in the absence of constitutional restraint, a majority will in principle be able to oppress a minority. However, where there is a stable left-to-right continuum, defe·  .rs of competitive party democracy argue that it works tolerably well in producing at least 'moderation'. Where a community is deepiy divided (as, for example, Northern Ireland is) it is quite obvious that unrestricted party competition of this kind will simply produce policies that reflect the interests of the dominant sect.

The radical economic theorists of democracy have, however, seriously questioned the claim that competitive party democracy always works to the public's advantage even in the more favourable political systems of, say, Great Britain or the United States of America. In the real world of democracy there are a number of reasons why this may not be so (reasons which are in fact explored in Downs's book). There is the technical point as to whether the world is single-peaked or not. In fact, what empirical evidence there is suggests that voters do not order their preferences in a consistent manner. If they do not, then there is no one platform which will beat all other platforms and a range of winning majorities will be possible (Wittman, 1973). Thus the winning platform will not necessarily represent the preferences of the median voter. It will be impossible to predict how the winning majority will be constructed and the suggested virtue of a two-party system – that it encourages a convergence around the centre – will be lost. The absence of single-peakedness means that the outcome of a democratic election will be quite arbitrary. It has been suggested that the only way that the opinions of the median voter could be reflected in the outcome of a democractic vote would be for each issue to be voted on *one at a time*, on the assumption that preferences were single-peaked over each issue (see Frohlich and Oppenheimer, 1978, pp. 124–5).

Of equal significance is the fact that parties will not be fully informed about voters' preferences and will have to rely on organised groups to transmit this information. In the process preferences will be distorted, and perhaps moulded to suit the interests of the group. Strategically-placed interest groups can press upon government policies which may not be to the advantage of the community at large. Lastly, in most working democracies it is not necessary for a party even to secure a majority of votes to gain office so that it becomes much easier for party strategists to put together winning coalitions.

It is perhaps the differences between competition in politics and competition in economic matters that are of direct interest to economic theorists of democracy. They assume that, in the absence of externalities, enlightened self-interest in an economic market will lead to a social optimum, but in a political market certain key factors are absent, most noticeably a budget constraint (Brittan, 1975).

The political market consists of parties (entrepreneurs) and voters (consumers). To get elected, political entrepreneurs will put together programmes that appeal to voters as members of private groups rather than as members of the public. There is no incentive for entrepreneurs to offer policies that maximise the public interest because the benefits of these are likely to be spread thinly throughout the population at large, and are long-term in their effect, while those that favour private groups are tangible and immediate in their impact. It is in the public interest that no private groups be privileged by the tax system yet it is in the interests of, for example, mortgagees that their tax relief should continue and that measures should be taken to protect the mortgage rate from the upward movements of all other interest rates. It is not in the public interest that unprofitable industries be subsidised from general taxation, yet it clearly is in the interests of employers and employees in these industries to be so favoured. It is not in the public interest that public expenditure on services should be significantly increased above the level at which individuals would be prepared to pay for them voluntarily, but party competition for votes inevitably tends to push up public expenditure because there are more votes to be gained from such a policy than are to be gained from a policy of restraint. This is because the benefits of the latter, although they accrue to the public, are indirect. The absence of a budget constraint means that, whereas excessive individual expenditure is automatically curtailed in an economic market, government can pursue its vote-buying policies by running a budget deficit, which may be financed by inflation since taxation to pay for excessive government services is a vote loser. But once again policies of 'no inflation' and balanced budgets are public goods for which there is no incentive for the individual elector in the competitive political process to vote. Of course, there is a constraint somewhere since governments cannot pursue inflationary policies for very long without the collapse of the currency; and a return to economic prudence will be brought about by international factors. Financial prudence will be dictated by international monetary institutions and these will lay down strict conditions for their support of the currency. This ultimate restraint is, however, long term and indicates, in effect, the failure of democratic political institutions to generate those policies that are in the interests of the public.

It might be thought that voter rationality, as discussed by traditional democratic theorists, would operate so as to prevent such unintended consequences of the vote-maximising process, but it is obvious that, in the economist's sense of rationality, the opposite is the case. No one individual or group can have any incentive to promote the public interest in a democracy since he (it) cannot be sure that others will do likewise. It is for this reason that democratic governments are peculiarly prone to the pains brought about by the scramble over distributive shares between powerfully organised groups. Schumpeter and others have stressed the fact that people cannot be expected to be as rational in the public world as they are in their private affairs where the costs of various courses of action are more clearly evident. In fact, economic theorists of democracy have had great difficulty in explaining why people vote at all given the vanishingly small value of the vote in most constituencies!

This is in essence the economic theory of democracy. It is thought to have a special application to Great Britain because the British political system imposes virtually no constitutional restraint on government, and has a 'first past the post' electoral system. This latter point means that normally parties do not have to secure the support of even a majority of electors in eaoh constituency in order to win and therefore have a great incentive to produce policies that directly favour determinate groups rather than the public at large. The absence of a written constitution means that the elected government, which rarely has the support of a majority of the voters, is unlimited in political authority. Two related points have been stressed in this context: first, the abandonment of the former conventional rule that governments ought to balance their budgets; and secondly, the removal of traditional restraints, such as the gold standard, on the government's exercise of its monopoly of the supply of money (Buchanan, 1978; Rowley, 1979, pp. 17–18). It is argued that the operation of all these factors has threatened freedom in Britain and will ultimately destroy democracy itself. Economic theorists of democracy maintain that competitive party democracy works effectively only when the behaviour of political actors is subject to strict rules. In this they are following the insight of Schumpeter, who argued that democratic stability was only possible when the range of social and economic affairs subjected to political resolution was narrowly circumscribed.

Radical individualist's are doubtful if any kind of collective decision-making procedure can be made consistent with liberty, even conventional liberal democracy operating under ideal conditions. They maintain that attention should not be directed towards designing some procedure by which individual preferences can be translated into collective choices, but towards designing institutions which protect individual voluntary exchanges. In effect, the 'Arrow problem' is sidestepped by severely reducing the range of collective choices. This seems to be the approach of James Buchanan and Gordon Tullock in their important work *The Calculus of Consent* (1962).

The authors argue that under majority rule public expenditures will always be higher than the sums individuals would pay if they were to finance the activities by voluntary exchanges. This means that people have costs imposed on them which make them all worse off in the long term. They postulate that if there is agreement on an initial distribution of property in a community then each individual's interests would be advanced under a system which required unanimous agreement (in practical terms this would have to be a unanimity of representatives) for any collective expenditures. Buchanan and Tullock do not eliminate the public interest entirely – individuals do have interests as members of the community – but they reduce it to those issues where unanimous agreement can be secured. This means that many shared interests would not be promoted because a minority whose private interests exceeded their interests as members of the public could always veto such proposals. However, under majority rule individuals will have costs imposed on them in that they will be forced to pay for activities they do not want undertaken.

Unanimity does not mean that virtually nothing will ever get done. In fact, it will encourage bargaining and 'log-rolling' between political actors. A representative who wishes to secure the collective delivery of a good or service that affects only his constituency will have to attract the support of other representatives by agreeing to support their projects. This process allows for various 'intense preferences' to be expressed. Under orthodox democracy a relatively apathetic majority may stand in the way of a proposal for which a minority may have strong preferences, but under unanimity, vote-trading allows these preferences to be expressed without others having costs imposed on them. The trouble is that a strict application of the unanimity rule makes the cost of bargaining high: small minorities will almost certainly set very high prices for their agreement and the authors therefore are prepared to modify unanimity in order to reduce bargaining costs. For most proposals they favour a weighted majority somewhere between straight majority rule (which imposes 'external' costs on the minority) and unanimity (which involves such high bargaining costs that many desirable projects would not be undertaken).

Although Buchanan and Tullock's extremely individualistic solution to the problems posed by democratic decision-making has found favour only in the specialised world of public choice theory, the basic logic of their argument can be discerned in all those procedural theories of democracy that are more concerned with the placing of limitations on the exercise of collective choice than with finding ways of implementing the people's will. They are part of a long tradition of political thought that, starting from pessimistic psychological premises, naturally assumes that those entrusted with political power will use it for their own advantage. The problem therefore is to place obstacles in the way of the exercise of political power. One reason why this approach has not been fashionable, despite the clear evidence that unrestricted political power almost always produces undesirable consequences, is that while limiting power protects individual rights it also places a veto in the hands of those already in a privileged position. The price of security against majority oppression is the preservation of economic inequality which becomes the cause of permanent resentment. It is true that Buchanan and Tullock's highly theoretical argument assumes the problem away by postulating an agreement on the distribution of property, but in reality the problems are likely to be formidable.[9]

A further objection to the various models of limited government is that in them the public interest – where that means something more than agreement on rules, referring instead to positive policies which advance the well-being of the community – will be neglected (Barry, 1965, ch. xv). In a reasonably homogeneous community, wide and amorphous interests may be better advanced by majority-rule democracy than by the bargaining process that occurs under the Buchanan – Tullock type of system, as long as there is no single party domination. However, majority-rule democracy requires considerably more coercion because of the fact that it will rarely be in a person's private interests to act voluntarily for the public benefit. To say that governments ought to promote a wide range of public interests requires a change in the psychological assumptions that underlie the economic theory of democracy. Buchanan and Tullock and others, carry over the apparatus of microeconomic theory into the political realm; they maintain that it is wrong to assume that because politicians and bureaucrats are not involved in private economic relationships they do not have the same motivations as market transactors. It cannot be assumed that they will maximise the 'public interest' merely because they are in public office.[10] The problem is that the acceptance of these assumptions involves the limitation of the public interest to the enforcement of general rules and the provision of the traditional public goods, while their replacement by a more optimistic view of 'political man' involves the risk that not only will individual rights be threatened by majorities but also that coalitions of private group interests may well damage those public interests that even the radical individualists accept.

226  *Values*

## 4. The radical critique of liberal democracy

A large part of contemporary democratic theory is not much concerned with the rather complex reasoning used to explain the relationship between individual values and social choice that characterises the theory of procedural democracy. In fact, Marxists are fundamentally opposed to the individualism that constitutes the methodology of this approach. The main objection is that democracy should not be viewed merely as a device for maximising individual utilities but is a way of life or conception of the good society in which communal values of friendship and co-operation take precedence over individualism. The radical critique is sometimes conducted within the procedural framework in that contemporary liberal democracies are criticised precisely because, for mainly economic reasons, they fail to fulfil traditional democratic ideals of political equality, freedom and governmental accountability, but normally it centres on a wholesale rejection of the traditional liberal's concept of political man as narrow and demeaning.

Not all objections to the utility-maximising approach are Marxist, or even collectivist, in inspiration. Some writers regard a democratic system as an ethical system of rights and duties which cannot be measured for success in terms of its satisfaction of individual desires. Even Rawls, who in many ways writes in the individualist tradition, rejects the idea that even an ideally-working competitive party democracy is sufficient to generate just legislation. He does not suggest that this might emerge from improved institutions alone but maintains that legislators must be imbued with a 'sense of justice' (1972, pp. 359–62). Others critics of the utility-maximising approach object in principle to the application of the methodology of microeconomics to the political sphere and argue that a democratic society generates those values of co-operation and fraternity that are said to be absent from the self-interested world of economic markets.

The democratic society that is said to generate these values is of course, distinguished from existing democratic political systems. The neo-Marxist political theorist, C. B. Macpherson (1966; 1973; 1977), has written at great length on these differences.

Macpherson claims that there are two elements in Western democratic theory. One is the familiar one of utility maximisation (a liberal democratic political system is the essential complement of a free economy) and the other is concerned with the maximisation of *powers*. This latter element, which Macpherson traces from J. S. Mill's modification of orthodox utilitarianism, is an ethical concept which interprets man as a *doer* and a *creator* rather than as merely a consumer. A truly democratic society will promote these powers of creativity and social co-operation rather than maximise aggregate satisfactions. The utility-maximising model of democracy is ethically deficient because the exchange process conducted within the capitalist economic system entails a transfer of powers (in the ethical sense). Because access to the market is unequal and the worker has to sell his labour power to capitalist owners, his powers of creativity and free choice are thereby reduced. Macpherson concedes that existing liberal democracies have conserved civil and political liberties more effectively than existing socialist regimes but argues that there is no inherent reason why a system of socialist ownership may not develop in such a way as to end the transfer of powers that takes place under capitalism while maintaining liberty. He argues that welfare state institutions, which tend to some extent to make goods and services available on the grounds of need rather than contribution to the social product, do not fundamentally alter the characteristics of liberal-democratic society.

Macpherson also denies that liberal societies, merely because they grant universal suffrage, choice between political parties and civil liberties, are exclusively entitled to the use of the word 'democracy'. He claims that there are other, equally valid variants (1966, ch. 1). Communist countries might qualify if they, for example, granted full intra-party democracy and opened up their closed bureaucratic systems. Third World countries, which have no experience of Western individualism, to the extent that their governments are legitimised by mass enthusiasm, also fulfil the ideals of some historical theories of democracy.

The difficulty with Macpherson's argument is that he evaluates existing liberal democracy by reference to some 'ideal version' of democracy, rather than by comparing it directly to existing alternatives. It is not all that difficult to show that Western capitalist countries, with their considerable economic inequalities, remote governments, bureaucracies and absence of real opportunities for ordinary citizens to influence policy-making, do not meet the high standards of political equality and participation set by some traditional democratic theorists, but it is more important to make realistic comparisons between these countries and their socialist and Communist opposites in terms of more modest objectives, such as personal freedoms, civil rights, relief of suffering and general standards of living. It is difficult to conceive of any economic system which will not involve a 'transfer of powers' and a reduction of freedom, in Macpherson's sense, as long as there is scarcity and the consequent need for the division of labour and some form of ownership of resources (be it public or private). A more feasible reform programme for liberal democracies would be to work for a wider dispersal of private property and the removal of monopoly and other forms of privilege.

However, radical critics of liberal democracy have persistently turned towards collectivist solutions to the problems of modern democracy. Whereas individualists have suggested that some of the problems associated with collective choice can be coped with by reducing its extent, socialists have recommended that they are best solved by actually extending such choice and changing the way it operates. This is what lies behind the demand for more 'participation': it is said that the threats to equality and political liberty entailed by the existence of 'big government' and bureaucracy can be removed by decentralising government to smaller units, such as the region and locality, rather than by trying to dispense with government in certain areas. It is to be noted that individualists and socialists are often attacking the same problems but the former's solution is to reduce the area of social life occupied by government, whatever form government should take.

The advocates of participation[11] claim that political equality is denied in competitive party democracies since the activity of the citizen is limited merely to choosing his political leaders on periodic occasions. This is especially damaging in contemporary industrial societies since the ever widening range of government activities means that changes occur which seriously affect individuals and communities and yet these individuals and communities have very little control over government under conventional democratic rules.

Theorists of participatory democracy therefore recommend that politics should be a *continuing* activity and not just confined to elections at regular intervals. It is assumed that if decision-making is decentralised away from the bureaucratic state into smaller communities this will enable individuals and groups to produce laws and policies directly related to their needs and interests. Participatory devices would also involve considerable use of referenda and other means of establishing close consultations between government and the people.

An important inspiration for this approach is the democratic philosophy of Rousseau, whose ideas are especially appropriate for small, closely-knit communities. While Rousseau felt that democratic government in an *executive* sense was an ideal highly unlikely to be realised in most societies, he thought that the people could be directly involved in the making of general laws. The legislative process would be characterised by discussion and debate in order to determine what laws are in the general interest. Rousseau's ideas can, however, be interpreted in a procedural sense because he thought that under certain conditions majority rule will produce beneficial outcomes for individuals as members of the community. This will be so if individuals are imbued with a sense of public spirit and are approximately equal: if these conditions hold, citizens acting self-interestedly will produce the public interest (or General Will). Like some contemporary public interest theorists Rousseau was very much aware of the likelihood that large and unequal groups will become sources of loyalty apart from the community at large.

Contemporary theories of participation, like Rousseau's, depend to a large extent on man's nature being 'moralised' by the process of democratic consultation and social interaction. Those selfish motivations which might lead to anti-social outcomes may be harnessed for the public good under the right conditions. John Stuart Mill, unlike his father, also viewed the democratic process as an 'educative' one: it was not just a machine for generating satisfactions but was an activity which helped to form a more desirable human character.

The difficulty with such doctrines is that if the necessary conditions cannot be satisfied and if human nature refuses to be 'moralised', there is no protection for the individual who finds himself at odds with collective decisions (although this particular criticism cannot be directed at John Stuart Mill). While it is true that collective decisions of small communities are likely to be less oppressive than those of centralised state bureaucracies this is not necessarily so. If individuals are allowed to move freely from community to community, that will itself afford some protection – but modern states are not likely to allow these decentralised political entities the independence of action that is required for a *variety* of institutions to emerge.

It is remarkable that most theories of participation do not consider decentralising decisions down to the level of the individual, so that fewer decisions are taken politically or collectively. The general argument in favour of this is that political action, where that involves debate, consultation and continuous participation, is just too costly for most people to indulge in. Most people cannot be expected to expend the time and energy which are required for rational participation, and this means that participatory politics will be dominated by small numbers of people for whom the opportunity costs of political activity are low. In fact, it was a commonplace argument of nineteenth-century critics of democracy that even mild democratisation proposals would lead to power being exercised by 'wire-pullers' and adroit political operators. The problem is compounded by the fact that most participatory theorists of democracy show little interest in the traditional protection of individual liberties, such as the separation of powers and the rule of law. In fact, if collective wills were really allowed to determine *all* political decisions this might result in illiberal policies which would be at variance with the personal values of the participatory theorists.[12]

As in so many other areas in political philosophy the differences between the various democratic theories can be explained to some extent in terms of different conceptions of human nature. Those with a more optimistic view of political man, or who at least believe that man has a *potentiality* for spontaneous virtuous action, are eager to dispense with traditional restraints in the belief that a better society will emerge from positive political action, while the more pessimistic 'liberals' base their arguments for limited government and restraints on politics largely on what they regard as unalterable features of the human condition. If most people are 'maximisers' then institutions will have to be designed so as to prevent one individual's maximisation harming others, and liberals regard maximisation in politics as being potentially more harmful than in economics.

# Notes

## Chapter 1

1. It is now the orthodox view in the philosophy of science that no amount of confirmation can establish a scientific hypothesis. The correct procedure does not involve the constant verification of empirical generalisations but consists of rigorous attempts to refute or falsify hypotheses. See Popper (1957) for the application of this view to social science.
2. For the view of economics as a positive science which uses very similar methods to those used in natural science, see Friedman (1953). F. A. Hayek (1967) has a rather different understanding of economics. While not denying that in principle all the sciences share a common methodology he nevertheless maintains that the 'complexity' of social phenomena means that predictions can never be as detailed as those found in, say, physics.
3. It must be stressed that this is no more than a convenient label for a common approach to social and political matters. Not only would many people object to the word 'liberal' in the label but also the word 'rationalist'. This is because 'rationalist' is used to describe the political theorist who believes in the reconstruction of the social world according to abstract rational principles. However, the word rationalist can still be used to describe a theorist who both stresses the importance of the evolution of rules and practices and takes a critical reflective attitude towards them.
4. There is an enormous literature on Marx and Marxism but little agreement amongst scholars as to the meaning of the doctrine. A meticulously researched subject is the question of whether there is a real difference between the early philosophical and metaphysical exposition of Communism and the later sociological, economic and historical version. Some critics suggest that there is while others maintain that Marx's thought exhibits a structural unity. For good introductory books see G. Lichtheim (1961), S. Avineri (1968), D. McLellan (1973) and M. Evans (1975).
5. This is what Marxists mean by the 'unity of theory and practice'.

## Chapter 2

1. While Bentham and Austin were legal positivists there is a close connection between the command theory and the normative doctrine of utilitarianism (see Chapter 5).
2. The clause that guarantees equal representation for the states in the Senate.
3. Liberal-rationalists constantly stress that rules are needed because of the unalterable fact of man's ignorance. Since each person can only have a limited knowledge of the world about him, rules are required to set standards of behaviour so as to make social life predictable for individuals. It follows from this that it is impossible to *design* a set of laws which anticipate all possible cases. It is for this reason that some liberal-rationalists argue that certainty in the law is more likely to come from the gradual evolution of a common law system than one based on statute.

## Chapter 3

1. An extreme organic and authoritarian version can be found in B. Bosanquet (1899). This book was severely attacked by L. T. Hobhouse (1918) in *The Metaphysical Theory of the State*. However, Hobhouse belonged to the same intellectual tradition.
2. This was because he thought that all social order was the product of sovereign power.
3. Market socialism specifically does not require a large role for collective action. In this doctrine socialism is more about equality and the elimination of market *power*, than about extending the role of the state.
4. For a lucid explanation of the Pareto principle, see A. J. Culyer (1973, pp. 6–15). It should be noted that the Pareto principle could operate as an efficiency criterion for a socialist society. If a collectivist planner was informed of the tastes of all individuals, and of the costs of producing desired goods, he could (logically) satisfy the efficiency criterion without a market and private ownership; of course, many liberal economists maintain that this is impossible in practice.
5. The classic example of an 'attenuation of property rights' is the policy of rent control, which has been adopted by almost all liberal democracies in the mistaken belief that it will ease the housing problem.

## Chapter 4

1. Although it could be argued that this is unfair to Machiavelli, in that he is really a political theorist of *republican* government and that this encompasses politics, legitimacy and the rule of law.
2. An example of this might be Franco's Spain.
3. Brian Barry's *Power and Political Theory* (1976) contains a number of important articles and an extensive bibliography.

4. In modern social theory the theorists of élite rule, notably Pareto and Mosca, might be said to be postulating certain very general propositions about power. There will be some discussion of their ideas in relation to democracy in Chapter 10.

## Chapter 5

1. It is of course true that Titmuss believed in the *state* delivery of welfare services. Presumably, his followers would say that compulsion will always be necessary here as long as the capitalist system inculcates 'selfish' values.

## Chapter 6

1. The bulk of this section is taken from Chapter 7 of N. Barry, *Hayek's Social and Economic Philosophy* (London: Macmillan, 1979).
2. It should be noted that Rawls had been communicating his ideas in article form since the early 1950s.
3. For a valuable discussion of this distinction, see K. J. Arrow (1973, p. 247). It is worth noting that most objections to the type of approach adopted by Rawls centre on its supposed vacuousness rather than its conflict with the 'productivity' principle.
4. Of course, most adherents of this chilly doctrine do not deny that people have *moral* obligations to the needy.

## Chapter 7

1. This line of reasoning is developed by Rees (1971, p. 22).
2. Even Tawney believed this, see *Equality*, p. 46.
3. This does not, of course, prove that the extra money is spent more effectively.
4. There are numerous articles on this subject, especially recommended are Judith Jarvis Thomson (1973), Robert Simon (1974) and Paul Taylor (1973).

## Chapter 8

1. Sir Isaiah Berlin implied this in his *Two Concepts of Liberty*, first published in 1958, but amended his argument in the Introduction to his *Four Essays on Liberty* (1969).
2. For a criticism of Hayek's conception of liberty (which is not unlike that of Locke) along these lines see R. Hamowy (1961).
3. All references are from *Four Essays on Liberty*.
4. This appears under the title, 'Morals and the Criminal Law' in Lord Devlin's collection of essays, *The Enforcement of Morals* (1965).

## Chapter 9

1. Recent important introductory books on rights include D. D. Raphael (1967), M. Cranston (1973) and E. Kamenka and Alice Erh-Soon Tay (1978).
2. Thomas Szasz (1961) is a vigorous advocate of the idea that there is no such thing as genuine 'mental illness' which justifies the forcible detention of individuals in institutions.
3. Curiously, this judgement on natural rights is common to utilitarians and Marxists.


## Chapter 10

1. Among the most vigorous opponents of the idea that the public interest has any cognitive meaning is F. Sorauf (1973).
2. See H. Demsetz (1967, p. 54). Much of my analysis is taken from this article and A. Alchian and H. Demsetz (1973). See also Steven S. Cheung (1978).
3. See Brian Barry (1965, pp. 234–6). Barry argues for a much wider concept of the public interest than that favoured by the 'property rights' theorists.
4. There is an enormous number of books on democracy. The following are recommended: G. Sartori (1965), Jack Lively (1975) and Barry Holden (1974).
5. Mill was also an early advocate of proportional representation. For a comprehensive survey of Mill's ideas on democracy see J. H. Burns (1957).
6. For an introduction to the social theories of Pareto and Mosca see James H. Meisel (1965). Mention should also be made of R. Michels who, after studying the practice of social democratic parties, concluded that what he called the 'iron law of oligarchy' prevented the fulfilment of their democratic aspirations.
7. Schumpeter's account of what he called 'classical democracy' was something of a ragbag of utilitarian theories and 'popular' notions. For a criticism see J. P. Plamenatz (1973).
8. Kenneth Arrow (1963). Arrow has also presented his theory in a number of articles, see especially (1967a) and (1967b). Of course the 'paradox of voting' discussed by Arrow has a long history.
9. Buchanan (1975, ch. 1 and 2) discusses the problem of the distribution of property in a contractual model.
10. While bureaucrats obviously cannot maximise profits as entrepreneurs are assumed to do, their behaviour has been interpreted in terms of similar psychological assumptions by political economists. Bureaucrats are said to maximise the size of their bureaux, or some other phenomena which cannot be measured in monetary terms. See William A. Niskanen (1973) and Tullock (1976).
11. For a comprehensive coverage of the varieties of participatory theory see G. Parry (1972) and Carole Pateman (1970); for a critical review of the subject, see J. R. Lucas (1976).
12. These values seem to include egalitarian economic policies, a strong commitment to personal freedoms, especially in such matters as sex and

drugs, and a permissive attitude towards crime and punishment. It is almost certainly the case that greater involvement of the people in decision-making would produce repressive laws in relation to personal liberties and crime and punishment.

# Bibliography

Aiken, H. D. (1948) *Hume's Moral and Political Philosophy* (New York: Hafner).

Alchian, A. A. and Demsetz, H. (1973) 'The property rights paradigm', *Journal of Economic History*, xxxiii.

Arendt, H. (1961) 'What is authority?', in *Between Past and Future* (London: Faber and Faber).

Arrow, K. J. (1963) *Social Choice and Individual Values*, 2nd ed. (New York: Wiley).

Arrow, K. J. (1967a) 'Values and collective decision-making', in P. Laslett and W. C. Runciman (eds), *Philosophy, Politics and Society*, Third Series (Oxford: Blackwell).

Arrow, K. J. (1967b) 'Public and private values', in S. Hook (ed.), *Human Values and Economic Policy* (New York University Press).

Arrow, K. J. (1973) 'Some ordinalist–utilitarian notes on Rawls's theory of justice', *The Journal of Philosophy*, Lxx

Austin, J. (1954) *The Province of Jurisprudence Determined*, edited by H. L. A. Hart (London: Weidenfeld and Nicolson).

Avineri, S. (1968) *The Social and Political Thought of Karl Marx* (Cambridge University Press).

Ayer, A. J. (1956) *The Revolution in Philosophy* (London: Macmillan).

Bachrach, P. and Baratz, M. (1962) 'The two faces of power', *American Political Science Review*, 56.

Barry, B. (1965) *Political Argument* (London: Routledge and Kegan Paul).

Barry, B. (1967a) 'Justice and the common good', in A. Quinton (ed.), *Political Philosophy* (London: Oxford University Press).

Barry, B. (1967b) 'The public interest', in A. Quinton (ed.), *Political Philosophy* (London: Oxford University Press).

Barry, B. (1973) *The Liberal Theory of Justice* (Oxford: The Clarendon Press).

Barry, B. (1976) 'Power: an economic analysis', in B. Barry (ed.), *Power and Political Theory* (London: Wiley).

Barry, B. (1979) 'Is democracy special?', in P. Laslett and J. Fishkin (eds), *Philosophy, Politics and Society*, Fifth Series (Oxford: Blackwell).

Barry, N. (1979) *Hayek's Social and Economic Philosophy* (London: Macmillan).

Bastiat, F. (1964) *Selected Essays on Political Economy*, edited by George B. Huzzar (New Jersey: Van Nostrand).

Baumol, W. J. (1965) *Welfare Economics and the Theory of the State*, 2nd ed. (London: Bell).

Benn, S. I. (1967) 'Freedom and persuasion', *Australasian Journal of Philosophy*, 45.

Benn, S. I. and Weinstein, W. L. (1971) 'Being free to act, and being a free man', *Mind*, 80.

Bentham, J. (1843) 'Anarchical fallacies' in *Works*, edited by J. Bowring.

Bentham, J. (1948) *A Fragment on Government and An Introduction to the Principles of Morals and Legislation*, edited by W. Harrison (Oxford: Blackwell).

Bentham, J. (1970) *Introduction to the Principles of Morals and Legislation*, edited by J. Burns and H. L. A. Hart (London: Athlone Press).

Bentham, J. (1970) *Of Laws in General* (London: Athlone Press).

Berlin, Sir I. (1955–6), 'Equality', *Proceedings of the Aristotelian Society*, LVI.

Berlin, Sir I. (1969) *Four Essays on Liberty* (London: Oxford University Press).

Berman, H. (1963) *Justice in the USSR* (Harvard University Press).

Bosanquet, B. (1899) *The Philosophical Theory of the State* (London: Macmillan).

Bottomore, T. B. (ed.) (1963) *Karl Marx: Early Writings* (London: Watts).

Brittan, S. (1973) *Capitalism and the Permissive Society* (London: Macmillan).

Brittan, S. (1975) 'The economic contradictions of democracy', *British Journal of Political Science*, 5.

Buchanan, J. (1965) *The Inconsistencies of the National Health Service*, (London: Institute of Economic Affairs).

Buchanan, J. (1975) *The Limits of Liberty* (University of Chicago Press).

Buchanan, J. (1978) *The Consequences of Mr Keynes* (London: Institute of Economic Affairs).

Buchanan, J. and Tullock, G. (1962) *The Calculus of Consent* (Ann Arbor: University of Michigan Press).

Burns, J. (1957) 'J. S. Mill and democracy, 1829–61', *Political Studies*, 5.

Burton, J. (1978) 'Externalities, property rights and public policy', epilogue in S. Cheung, *The Myth of Social Cost* (London: Institute of Economic Affairs).

Cheung, S. (1978) *The Myth of Social Cost* (London: Institute of Economic Affairs).

Chomsky, N. (1959) 'Review of B. F. Skinner, *Verbal Behaviour*', *Language*, 35.

Coase, R. (1960) 'The problem of social cost', *Journal of Law and Economics*, 1.

Cooper, M. and Culyer, A. (1968), *The Price of Blood* (London: Institute of Economic Affairs).

Cranston, M. (1953) *Freedom: A New Analysis* (London: Longman).

Cranston, M. (1967) 'Human rights, real and supposed' and 'Human rights: a reply to Professor Raphael', in D. D. Raphael (ed.), *Political Theory and the Rights of Man* (London: Macmillan).

Cranston, M. (1973) *What are Human Rights?* (London: The Bodley Head).

Crosland, C. A. R. (1962) *The Conservative Enemy*, (London: Cape).

Culyer, A. (1973) *The Economics of Social Policy* (London: Martin Robertson).
Dahl, R. A. (1956) *A Preface to Democratic Theory* (University of Chicago Press).
Dahl, R. A. (1958) 'A critique of the ruling elite model', *American Political Science Review*, 52.
Dahl, R. A. (1971) *Polyarchy* (Yale University Press).
Dahl, R. A. (1979) 'Procedural democracy', in P. Laslett and J Fishkin (eds), *Philosophy, Politics and Society*, Fifth Series (Oxford: Blackwell).
Demsetz, H. (1967) 'Toward a theory of property rights', *American Economic Review*, 57 (Supplement).
Devlin, P. (1965) *The Enforcement of Morals* (London: Oxford University Press).
Downs, A. (1957) *An Economic Theory of Democracy* (New York: Harper and Row).
Dworkin, R. (1977) *Taking Rights Seriously* (London: Duckworth).
Edgeworth, Y. (1897) 'The pure theory of progressive taxation', *Economic Journal*, vii.
Engels, F. (1968a) 'The origins of the family, private property and the state', in *Marx and Engels: Selected Works* (London: Lawrence and Wishart).
Engels, F. (1968b) 'Socialism: Utopian and Scientific', in *Marx and Engels: Selected Works* (London: Lawrence and Wishart).
Evans, M. (1975) *Karl Marx* (London: Allen and Unwin).
Feinberg, J. (1973) *Social Philosophy* (New Jersey: Prentice – Hall).
Flathman, R. (1976) *The Practice of Rights* (Cambridge University Press).
Foley, D. K. (1978) 'State expenditure from a Marxist point of view', *Journal of Public Economics*, 9.
Frankena, W. (1962) 'The concept of social justice', in R. Brandt (ed.), *Social Justice* (New Jersey: Prentice – Hall).
Friedman, M. (1953) 'The methodology of positive economics', in *Essays in Positive Economics* (University of Chicago Press).
Friedman, M. (1962) *Capitalism and Freedom* (University of Chicago Press).
Friedman, M. (1967) 'Value judgements in economics', in S. Hook (ed.), *Human Values and Economic Policy* (New York University Press).
Friedrich, C. J. (1973) 'Authority, reason and discretion', in R. Flathman (ed.), *Concepts in Social and Political Philosophy* (New York: Macmillan).
Frohlich, N. and Oppenheimer, J. (1978) *Modern Political Economy* (New Jersey: Prentice – Hall).
Furniss, N. (1978) 'The political implications of the Public Choice – Property Rights school', *American Political Science Review*, 72.
Gluckman, M. (1965) *Politics, Law and Ritual in Tribal Society* (Oxford: Blackwell).
Golding, M. (1975) *Philosophy of Law* (New Jersey: Prentice – Hall).
Green, T. H. (1941) *Lectures on the Principles of Political Obligation*, edited by A. D. Lindsay (London: Longman).
Hamowy, R. (1961) 'Hayek's concept of freedom', *New Individualist Review*.
Hare, R. M. (1963) *Freedom and Reason* (Oxford: The Clarendon Press).
Harris, R. and Seldon, A. (1979) *Over-ruled on Welfare* (London: Institute of Economic Affairs).

Hart, H. L. A. (1958) 'Positivism and the separation of law and morals', *Harvard Law Review*, lxxi.

Hart, H. L. A. (1961) *The Concept of Law* (Oxford: The Clarendon Press).

Hart, H. L. A. (1963) *Law, Liberty and Morality* (London: Oxford University Press).

Hart, H.L. A. (1967) 'Are there any natural rights', in A. Quinton (ed.), *Political Philosophy* (London: Oxford University Press).

Hayek, F. A. von (1944) *The Road to Serfdom* (London: Routledge and Kegan Paul).

Hayek, F. A. von (1952) *The Counter-Revolution of Science* (Glencoe: The Free Press).

Hayek, F. A. von (1960) *The Constitution of Liberty* (London: Routledge and Kegan Paul).

Hayek, F. A. von (1967) *Studies in Philosophy, Politics and Economics* (London: Routledge and Kegan Paul).

Hayek, F. A. von (1973) *Law, Legislation and Liberty*, vol. 1, *Rules and Order* (London: Routledge and Kegan Paul).

Hayek, F. A. von (1976) *Law, Legislation and Liberty*, vol. 2, *The Mirage of Social Justice* (London: Routledge and Kegan Paul).

Hegel, G. W. F. (1942) *The Philosophy of Right*, trans. T. M. Knox (Oxford: The Clarendon Press).

Hobbes, T. (1968) *Leviathan*, edited by C. B. Macpherson (Harmondsworth: Penguin).

Hobhouse, L. T. (1918) *The Metaphysical Theory of the State* (London: Allen and Unwin).

Hohfeld, W. (1919) *Fundamental Legal Conceptions* (Yale University Press).

Holden, B. (1974) *The Nature of Democracy* (London: Nelson).

Holmes, O. W. (1897) 'The path of law', *Harvard Law Review*, 10.

Husami, Z. (1978), 'Marx on distributive justice', *Philosophy and Public Affairs*, 8.

James, M. H. (1973), 'Bentham on the individuation of laws', in James, M. H. (ed.), *Bentham and Legal Theory* (Northern Ireland Legal Quarterly).

Kamenka, E. (1969) *Marxism and Ethics* (London: Macmillan).

Kamenka, E. and Erh-Soon Tay, A. (eds) (1978) *Human Rights* (London: Arnold).

Kay, J. and King, M. (1978) *The British Tax System* (London: Oxford University Press).

Kinsey, R. (1978) 'Marxism and the law', *British Journal of Law and Society*, 8.

Krader, L. (1968) *Formation of the State* (New Jersey: Prentice – Hall).

Lichtheim, G. (1961) *Marxism* (London: Routledge and Kegan Paul).

Lively, J. (1975) *Democracy* (Oxford: Blackwell).

Lloyd, D. (1972) *Introduction to Jurisprudence* (London: Stevens).

Locke, J. (1960) *Two Treatises of Government*, edited by P. Laslett (Cambridge University Press).

Lucas, J. R. (1966) *The Principles of Politics* (Oxford: The Clarendon Press).

Lucas, J. R. (1971) 'Against equality', in *Justice and Equality*, edited by Hugo A. Bedau (New Jersey: Prentice – Hall).

Lucas, J. R. (1972) 'Justice', *Philosophy*, 47.

Lucas, J. R. (1976) *Democracy and Participation* (Harmondsworth: Penguin).
Lukes, S. (1972) *Individualism* (Oxford: Blackwell).
Lukes, S. (1974) *Power: A Radical View* (London: Macmillan).
Lyons, D. (1965) *Forms and Limits of Utilitarianism* (London: Oxford University Press).
Mabbott, J. D. (1956), 'Interpretations of Mill's "Utilitarianism" ', *Philosophical Quarterly*, vi.
MacCallum G. (1972) 'Negative and positive liberty', in P. Laslett, W. C. Runciman and Q. Skinner (eds), *Philosophy, Politics and Society*, 4th series (Oxford: Blackwell).
Macpherson, C. B. (1966) *The Real World of Democracy* (Oxford: The Clarendon Press).
Macpherson, C. B. (1973), *Democratic Theory: Essays in Retrieval*, (Oxford: The Clarendon Press).
Macpherson, C. B. (1977) *The Life and Times of Liberal Democracy* (London: Oxford University Press).
Marcuse, H. (1964) *One-dimensional Man* (Boston: Beacon Press).
Marcuse, H. (1967) 'Repressive tolerance', in R. Wolff, Barrington Moore, *A Critique of Pure Tolerance* (Boston: Beacon Press).
Marcuse, H. (1969) *An Essay on Liberation* (Boston: Beacon Press).
Marx, K. (1971) *Early Texts*, edited by D. McLellan (Oxford: Blackwell).
Marx, K. (1977) *Selected Writings*, edited by D. McLellan (London: Oxford University Press).
Maynard, A. K. (1975) *Experiment with Choice in Education* (London: Institute of Economic Affairs).
McLellan, D. (1973) *Karl Marx: His Life and Thought* (London: Macmillan).
Meisel, J. (ed.) (1965) *Pareto and Mosca* (New Jersey: Prentice – Hall).
Melden, A. I. (1977) *Rights and Persons* (Oxford: Blackwell).
Meyer, A. V. (1962) *Leninism* (New York: Praeger).
Mill, James (1955) *An Essay on Government*, edited by C. V. Shields (New York: The Liberal Arts Press).
Mill, John Stuart (1944), *Utilitarianism, Liberty and Representative Government*, edited by A. D. Lindsay (London: Everyman).
Mill, John Stuart (1974) *On Liberty*, edited by Gertrude Himmelfarb (Harmondsworth: Penguin).
Miller, D. (1976) *Social Justice* (Oxford: The Clarendon Press).
Mills, C. Wright (1959) *The Power Elite* (New York: Galaxy).
Moore, G. E. (1903) *Principia Ethica* (Cambridge University Press).
Niskanen, W. A. (1973) *Bureaucracy: Servant or Master?* (London: Institute of Economic Affairs).
Nozick, R. (1974), *Anarchy, State and Utopia* (Oxford: Blackwell).
O'Connor, D. (1967) *Aquinas and Natural Law* (London: Macmillan).
Okun, A. (1975) *Equality and Efficiency* (Washington DC: The Brookings Institution).
Olson, M. (1965) *The Logic of Collective Action* (Harvard University Press).
Parent, W. (1974) 'Some recent work on the concept of liberty', *American Philosophical Quarterly*, 11.
Parry, G. (ed.) (1972) *Participation and Politics* (Manchester University Press).

Partridge, P. H. (1963) 'Some notes on the concept of power', *Political Studies*, 11.

Pateman, C. (1970) *Participation and Democratic Theory* (Cambridge University Press).

Peffer, R. (1978) 'A defence of rights to well-being', *Philosophy and Public Affairs*, 8.

Peters, R. (1967) 'Authority', in A. Quinton (ed.), *Political Philosophy* (London: Oxford University Press).

Pigou, A. (1920) *The Economics of Welfare* (London: Macmillan).

Plamenatz, J. (1973) *Democracy and Illusion* (London: Longman).

Polsby, N. (1963) *Community Power and Political Theory* (Yale University Press).

Popper, Sir K. (1957) *The Poverty of Historicism* (London: Routledge and Kegan Paul).

Popper, Sir K. (1962) *The Open Society and Its Enemies*, 4th edition, vol I, *Plato*; vol II, *Hegel and Marx* (London: Routledge and Kegan Paul).

Popper, Sir K. (1976) *Unended Quest* (London: Fontana/Collins).

Raphael, D. D. (1967) 'Human rights, old and new', in D. D. Raphael (ed.), *Political Theory and the Rights of Man* (London: Macmillan).

Rawls, J. (1972) *A Theory of Justice* (London: Oxford University Press).

Raz, J. (1970) *The Concept of a Legal System* (Oxford: The Clarendon Press).

Raz, J. (1977) 'The rule of law and its virtue', *Law Quarterly Review*, 93.

Rees, J. (1971) *Equality* (London: Macmillan).

Robinson, R. (1964) *An Atheist's Values* (Oxford: The Clarendon Press).

Rothbard, M. (1970) *Power and Market* (California: Institute for Humane Studies).

Rothbard, M. (1973) *For a New Liberty* (New York: Macmillan).

Rothbard, M. (1977) 'Robert Nozick and the immaculate conception of the state', *Journal of Libertarian Studies*, 1.

Rousseau, J-J (1913) *The Social Contract and Discourses*, edited by G. D. H. Cole (London: Dent).

Rowley, C. K. (1979) 'Liberalism and collective choice', *National Westminster Bank Review*.

Russell, B. (1938) *Power: A New Social Analysis* (London: Allen and Unwin).

Sartori, G. (1965) *Democratic Theory* (New York: R. Praeger).

Sartorius, R. (1971) 'Hart's concept of law', in R. Summers, *More Essays in Legal Philosophy* (Oxford: Blackwell).

Scarman, L. (1974) *English Law: The New Dimension* (London: Stevens).

Schubert, G. (1959) *Quantitative Analysis of Judicial Behaviour* (Glencoe: The Free Press).

Schumpeter, J. S. (1954) *Capitalism, Socialism and Democracy*, 4th edition (London: Allen and Unwin).

Simon, R. (1974) 'Preferential hiring', *Philosophy and Public Affairs*, 3.

Skinner, B. (1972) *Beyond Freedom and Dignity* (London: Cape).

Smart, J. J. C. and Williams, B. (1973) *Utilitarianism: For and Against* (Cambridge University Press).

Sorauf, F. (1973) 'The conceptual muddle', in R. Flathman (ed.), *Concepts in Social and Political Philosophy* (New York: Macmillan).

Stephen, J. F. (1967) *Liberty, Equality, Fraternity*, edited by R. J. Whyte (Cambridge University Press).

Szasz, T. (1961) *The Myth of Mental Illness* (New York: Dell).

Tawney, R. H. (1969) *Equality*, fifth edition (London: Allen and Unwin).

Taylor, P. (1973) 'Reverse discrimination and compensatory justice', *Analysis*, 33.

Thomson, J. (1973) 'Preferential hiring', *Philosophy and Public Affairs*, 2.

Titmuss, R. (1970) *The Gift Relationship* (London: Allen and Unwin).

Tucker, R. (1970) *The Marxian Revolutionary Idea* (London: Allen and Unwin).

Tullock, G. (1976) *The Vote Motive* (London: Institute of Economic Affairs).

Twining, W. and Miers, D. (1976) *How to Do Things with Rules* (London: Weidenfeld and Nicolson).

Wasserstrom, R. (1971) 'Rights, human rights and racial discrimination', in James Rachels (ed.), *Moral Problems* (New York: Harper and Row).

Weber, M. (1947) *Theory of Social and Economic Organisation*, translated by A. M. Henderson and T. Parsons (Glencoe: The Free Press).

Weldon, T. D. (1953) *The Vocabulary of Politics* (Harmondsworth: Penguin).

Weldon, T. D. (1956) 'Political principles', in P. Laslett (ed.), *Philosophy, Politics and Society*, First Series (Oxford: Blackwell).

Williams, B. (1963) 'The ideal of equality', in P. Laslett and W. C. Runciman, *Philosophy, Politics and Society*, Second Series (Oxford: Blackwell).

Wilson, J. (1966) *Equality* (London: Hutchinson).

Winch, P. (1958) *The Idea of a Social Science* (London: Routledge and Kegan Paul).

Winch, P. (1967), 'Authority', in A. Quinton (ed.), *Political Philosophy* (London: Oxford University Press).

Wittman, D. (1973) 'Parties as utility maximizers'. *American Political Science Review*, 67.

Young, M. (1961) *The Rise of the Meritocracy* (Harmondsworth: Penguin).

# Author Index

# Subject Index